What Readers acros
Are Saying about

MW01064503

"Your book and I have been constant companions since I purchased it. What a treasure trove of information!! Your book was worth every penny I paid for it and more. Thank you!"
M.M.

"I sure like the way you put this together. It is just as if you are right here talking me through it."
Brenda Bjornberg – Malad City, ID

"You clearly put a practical perspective on how to proceed."
D.W. – Arlington, VA

"Thank you very much for the wonderful piece of work. It is a comprehensive manual for both experienced and inexperienced factors."
Brian Jovanovic – San Diego, CA

"Easy to read, full of clear examples."
B.M., Phoenix – AZ

"I would just like to thank you for taking the time to answer some of my questions concerning the factoring business. It's nice to actually speak to someone who has been doing the business and hear some of your experiences. Your information has been helpful."
D.F. – San Jose, CA

"I wanted to let you know that your book has definitely helped me in building a business plan, and I have found it to be an invaluable resource!"
M.T. – Woburn MA

"It contains information that is otherwise hard to come by."
M.B.

"I greatly appreciated the comments from someone who has been there."
T.F. – Sturbridge, MA

"Just a short line to let you know how much I enjoyed your book. It has been extremely helpful in my start up plans. I have followed your advice and feel even better prepared now. It is an invaluable tool for beginners or veterans."
J.U. – Turlock, CA

"First book on the subject that actually got into the detailed mechanics of delivering factoring services. Very granular -- especially liked the flow chart encapsulation of the processes."
P.A. – Washington, D.C.

"Thank you for all of the assistance you offered. There have been a number of people who have offered advice, but no one has offered themselves and their personal experience like yourself."
S.N. – Lighthouse Point, FL

"You have obviously filled a needed gap. I'm sure many people are as grateful as I."
W.F. – Germantown, MD

"Your book simplified and explained so many items that must be known by factoring brokers and small funding sources. It was the one item that took us from thinking about it to doing it. When I was looking for a book on the subject, I was directed to this book and told that many recommend it. 'If there is only one book that you buy, this is the best one,' she told us. It has given us the tools we needed to become a small factor. "
Jay Karp – Olney, MD

"My background is in lending, banking and financial planning. The book is well written for someone with little to no understanding of the subject."
Kelley Tetzlaff – Mesa, AZ

"Thanks, Jeff. I wish I would have purchased the book sooner."
Sedro Wooley, WA

Factoring Small Receivables

How to Make Money
in Little Deals
the Big Guys Brush Off

Jeff Callender

Sixth Edition

DASH POINT PUBLISHING

Federal Way, Washington

Factoring Small Receivables
How to Make Money in Little Deals
the Big Guys Brush Off
by Jeff Callender

Published by:
Dash Point Publishing, Inc.
6104 Browns Point Blvd. NE
Tacoma, WA 98422-1324 U.S.A.

Web Sites: www.DashPointPublishing.com
             www.SmallFactor.com
             www.Factoring-Small-Receivables.com
Email: info@SmallFactor.com

ISBN, print ed.	1-889095-01-X
ISBN, eBook ed.	1-889095-02-8
First Edition:	April, 1995
Second Edition:	August, 1995
Third Edition:	May, 1996
Fourth Edition:	
First Printing	March, 1998
Second Printing	March, 1999
Third Printing, Revised	March, 2001
Electronic Edition	March, 2001
Fifth Edition	January, 2002
Electronic Edition	January, 2002
Sixth Edition	May, 2003
Second Printing	December, 2003
Electronic Edition	May, 2003

Several names of people and companies are used as samples in this book. Any similarity between these samples and names of actual people and companies is unintended and purely coincidental.

While the author has made every reasonable attempt to obtain accurate information, occasional errors are inevitable because information, particularly relating to web site addresses, links, and data, is subject to change. The author and publisher hereby disclaim any liability for problems due to errors, omissions, or changed information in this publication.

Printed in the United States of America.

Library of Congress Control Number: 2003092214

Dedication

This book is dedicated to my parents,
who have always been there.
Always.

Also by Jeff Callender

Books and eBooks
The Small Factor Series includes:
1. *Factoring Fundamentals*
   How You Can Make Large Returns in Small Receivables
   ©2003

2. *Factoring Small Receivables*
   How to Make Money in Little Deals the Big Guys Brush Off
   ©1995, 1996, 1998, 2001, 2002, 2003 (6th edition)

3. *Factoring Case Studies*
   Learn and Profit from Experienced Small Factors
   ©2003

4. *Unlocking the Cash in Your Company*
   How to Get Unlimited Funds without a Loan
   ©2003

Growing Your Company without Debt:
How Today's Small Business Can Get Cash by Tomorrow
(Booklet, eBooklet, & Audio)   ©1996, 1998, 2002

Software/Forms
Record Keeping Templates   ©2002, 2003
APR & Income Calculators   ©2002
Factor Consultation Form   ©2003

Internet Resources
www.Factor-Tips.com Web site and free e-zine
www.SmallFactor.com Web Site
www.DashPointPublishing.com Web Site
www.DashPointFinancial.com Web Site
www.Factoring-Small-Receivables.com Web Site

Contents

Index of Charts

Index of Documents

About the Author

Jeff Callender grew up in Riverside, California, and graduated from Whittier College near Los Angeles. He received his Master of Divinity from Pacific School of Religion in Berkeley, California, in 1978. He then served as a Presbyterian pastor in three congregations in Washington state until 1993.

Jeff has been involved in factoring since 1994. At that time he became a Certified Factoring Specialist through the International Factoring Institute of Orlando, Florida. He then started his company (now Dash Point Financial Services, Inc.) and soon began factoring small receivables.

He writes a regular column on small receivables for *The American Cash Flow Journal*®, a national publication of the American Cash Flow Association. He is a regular speaker at the ACFA's annual Cash Flow conventions. He funds a modest number of factoring clients and provides numerous resources and consulting services for people interested in becoming small factors. For more information, go to his web sites at www.SmallFactor.com and www.DashPointFinancial.com. Further information about this book can be found at www.Factoring-Small-Receivables.com. To order his resource materials, go to www.DashPointPublishing.com.

Jeff is married and the father of a grown son and daughter.

Acknowledgements

I owe a debt of gratitude to the following individuals for their contributions to this edition. Their suggestions and improvements have made this work what it is.

Robert Branscomb for his professional insights regarding key person insurance and liability insurance.

Kari and Kevin Clark of Premier Funding in Lebanon, Oregon, for their contribution to the chapter "Bookkeeping with QuickBooks®."

Gaye Hanson for her encouragement at the right time.

Stewart Martin, Attorney and Counselor at Law, for the chapter in which the legal structures of co-factoring are discussed.

Ernie Zerenner for his contribution to the chapter "Break-Even Analysis."

The section "Factoring Software Evaluation Questions" is reprinted with permission of **Bert Goldberg** from literature published by **Distinctive Solutions**.

Information about FactorSoft is copyrighted and provided courtesy of **Bayside Business Solutions**. FactorSoft is a trademark of Bayside Business Solutions, Inc. All other trademarks, registered trademarks, service marks, product and company names are the property of their respective owners. Copyright 2000-2001 Bayside Business Solutions, Inc. All rights reserved.

Cover picture by Arthur S. Aubry/Getty Images

Important Notice

Preface

This is the second book in *The Small Factor Series,* which opens the door to the remarkable and lucrative investment of factoring small business receivables.

The first title, *Factoring Fundamentals: How You Can Make Large Returns in Small Receivables,* introduces the reader to the basic concepts of factoring. *Fundamentals* describes what factoring is, how it works, businesses which can benefit, the remarkable returns possible, risks involved, and how to minimize those risks. It helps the reader define the meaning of "success," whether factoring is an appropriate move for his or her circumstances, and closes with a look at four small factors who enter the field from very diverse backgrounds, with quite different purposes.

Factoring Small Receivables is the "nuts and bolts" hands-on manual for running a small factoring operation. It includes first-hand lessons from the factoring industry, identifies where to find operating capital, provides marketing strategies, and describes numerous common mistakes small factors all too often make. In these pages you'll find discussions on due diligence, credit reports, reviews of factoring software, a chapter on record keeping, another about bookkeeping, a sample factoring transaction from start to finish with an accompanying flowchart, and a multitude of online and offline resources available for small factors.

While *Factoring Small Receivables* is the second book in sequence of The Small Factor Series, it was actually the first written, with the first edition published in 1995. The current edition has been rewritten to take its natural place in the Series, and provides updates and new material, as each edition has before it.

The purpose of the third book, *Factoring Case Studies: Learn and Profit from Experienced Small Factors,* is to illustrate the many principles and instructions provided in the first two books. While *Fundamentals* and *Small Receivables* are filled with chapters of instruction, training, and how-to information, *Case Studies* demonstrates how these actually work in real situations with real people. The 21 case studies are written by eight small factors from across the country, and provide unique and powerful lessons in running a factoring operation.

The fourth book, *Unlocking the Cash in Your Company: How to Get Unlimited Funds without a Loan,* is written for potential factoring clients – owners of small businesses who can utilize factoring to benefit their business. This book compares factoring to more traditional financing, explains who is eligible, suggests features and services to look for in a factor, and discusses how to find a factor. *Unlocking the Cash* also describes the application process, due diligence procedures to expect, what to tell customers, normal factoring procedures, and faulty assumptions people make about factoring. It encourages the reader to visualize specific enhancements and advantages factoring can provide his or her business.

While *Unlocking the Cash* is primarily written for prospective clients, its point of view provides further insight for those who wish to participate as small factors or broker consultants. The book also serves as a marketing tool to prospective clients for factors and brokers seeking new business.

I present this book – and this series – for your benefit, as well as the benefit of the countless number of small business owners whose companies, and all the individuals whose lives they impact, can be improved by your factoring service.

Jeff Callender

Part 1

The Basics

20 – Factoring Small Receivables

1
Introduction

For Whom This Manual Is Written

This manual is for two types of people: the factoring professional who would like to increase business by acting both as a factor as well as a broker, and the individual who would like to learn to factor small receivables as a supplement to other income and/or investments.

There is a large amount of business right in your back yard with clients whose receivables are too small for big factors to find profitable. This creates a perfect niche and a big market for the little guy: you and me.

The next chapter is for those new to factoring. You'll find a general description of factoring, what businesses it can help, and how it can help them. While the factoring industry is sophisticated and competitive, there is at present a huge market for factoring small receivables. Small factors who are aggressive, prudent and knowledgeable can make a good income. This manual is intended to help the beginning factor get his or her business under way and further develop those who have already started.

This book has one theme: you can have a successful business by factoring small, local clients that larger factors won't accept. The pages that follow show how.

My Story

In the early 1990's I had been a Presbyterian parish pastor for 14 years and served three different congregations in Washington state. I was in my early 40's and realized parish ministry was not what I wanted to do with the rest of my working life. At the end of 1992, I left the security of a monthly paycheck and a familiar, significant role in the community to look for something I was missing: time with my family, a different way of helping people, a chance to work for myself at home, and a means of providing better income.

After nearly a year of working for myself, I received a letter inviting me to a free seminar that described something called "factoring" – a term which was completely new to me. I went, heard an interesting, smooth presentation and decided to enter the industry. The organization's introductory tape said you needed three things to succeed: a genuine liking of people, a desire to help them, and being in a transition in life. These described me perfectly and I was more than ready to get started.

I attended training in January of 1994 and began working the business part-time. In August I went full-time and continued this way for the next five years. Over that time I experienced great success, but also some significant factoring losses. I came to appreciate the risks that lie in the underbrush, along side the treasures that await small factors.

I then owned a sign shop franchise for a year and factored my own receivables, which showed me personally how factoring helps small businesses when used correctly. Later I worked for a year as an account manager in the operations division for a large factor. There I learned first-hand how the "big guys" manage accounts, which further refined my factoring procedures.

Now I am factoring my own clients again. My time is an enjoyable blend of factoring, consulting with/teaching small factors, writing, and speaking. The book you are reading is the culmination of all these experiences.

How This Manual
Came to Be Written

Back in the mid 1990's, about a year after working part-time and then full-time as a broker, I had spent a LOT of money on advertising and running the business and still had nothing to show for it. I ran across an ad on the Internet – a far cry from what it is today! – that caught my eye. It was a "Factoring

Manual" entitled *Accounts Receivable Factoring Manual* (©1993) and written by Joseph Casano of Gulf Coast Factoring in Pass Christian, Mississippi, who had worked as a small factor for five years.

I was amused that the only mention of brokering (compared to my training manual's exhaustive tome) was one paragraph that said, in effect, you can get nice finder's fees from large factors by referring bigger deals you can't fund yourself. End of brokering education. The rest of the manual provided the basics of what you need to know to factor small deals. I found it very helpful for it gave me the courage to dabble in this on my own.

Factoring a few small deals quickly showed me that brokers experiencing the same problems I did can nevertheless be successful as small factors. So can people who are interested in entering the factoring business to supplement regular, investment, or retirement income if they are willing to learn and will do what it takes to make the business work. What it takes is some guts, bucks, common sense and a healthy dose of caution.

The first two editions of this manual were written specifically for trained factoring brokers. The second edition added a section on choosing a bank and another about how much money is needed to factor. New chapters included "Co-Factoring" and "Factoring Software." Also added were more form samples and an index to charts.

By the time the second edition was circulating, I discovered many readers had no training or background in factoring. The third edition began with a new chapter, "What Is Factoring?" with introductory information for this wider audience, plus guidelines for planning your business in a chapter called "Charting Your Course." It also added the chapter "Marketing: How to Find Clients," another chapter "Common Mistakes," and updates to the chapter "Factoring Software."

The fourth edition added a means of calculating your company's profitability with the new chapter "Break-Even Analysis," which included numerous diagrams to explain the step-by-step process. Another new chapter, "Due Diligence" (greatly expanded from a section in earlier editions), provided a discussion of how to limit your risk when considering new clients. The chapter "Factoring Software" was updated, as were several forms in the chapter "A Sample Factoring Transaction." With the additional information, the order of a few chapters was changed for more logical flow. Finally, a Glossary was added.

The revised fourth edition (and first eBook edition) provided updates to the chapter on factoring software, as well as updated verbiage throughout the book bringing it into the new millennium.

The fifth edition added three new chapters entitled "Credit Reports," "Preventive Maintenance," and "Factoring Resources." It also added information to the chapters "Marketing" and "Common Mistakes," and further updated the "Factoring Software" chapter. This edition also integrated numerous web links throughout the book to sites beneficial to small factors, which are links in the eBook version.

The creation of Dash Point Publishing, Inc. accompanied the fifth edition and with it the publishing company's web site, www.DashPointPublishing.com, where the author's materials can be purchased online. Also, www.SmallFactor.com matured as a significant portal site for small factors. Finally, with the fifth edition the author launched a twice monthly e-zine called *FactorTips* (www.Factor-Tips.com).

What's New in This Edition

The present sixth edition has divided the book into four Sections and an Appendix, a format similar to the other books in *The Small Factor Series*. This edition provides a great deal of new material, as well as many updates throughout the book which include the following.

- Three new chapters have been added:
  - "UCCs" provides an explanation of the Uniform Commercial Code and its role for securing your factoring funds. This chapter highlights changes made in the so-called "Revised Article 9" and how these impact your factoring business. Additionally, this

chapter includes numerous firms which exist to make your UCC searches and filings much easier.

- "Factoring and the USA Patriot Act" introduces the reader to impact this new legislation (related to the federal government's Homeland Security program) and its impact on the factoring industry.

- "Bookkeeping with QuickBooks®" shows how to set up and use this software in your factoring business.

- The chapter "Money, Money, Money" adds:

  - New information regarding the use of self-directed IRAs and Self-Employed 401(k) Plans as potential sources of capital.

  - Three factor funding sources – companies who are in business to provide capital to factors – are listed for the first time.

- The chapter "Common Mistakes" has added yet another new mistake to avoid.

- The chapter "Reducing Your Risk" has expanded information on setting credit limits and time limits, a new discussion on establishing reserves, plus information on credit insurance which is presented for the first time.

- The chapters "Due Diligence," "Credit Reports," and "Factoring Resources" each have added new information and eliminated material that has become outdated.

- Updates to the "Factoring Software" chapter are provided, including the addition of a fourth software product, BluBeagle™, and an analysis of which software best fits the circumstances of particular factors' needs.

- The chapter "Record Keeping" has been reorganized and expanded. New forms and documents have been added, while several existing forms have been revised.

- Two articles from the e-zine *FactorTips* are included in the Appendix.

These changes have made the 6th edition over 430 pages in length, well over a hundred pages more than the previous edition. Despite these significant additions and improvements, the retail price of the book has been reduced by $20.

You will find within this manual the nuts and bolts of factoring small receivables and some practical wisdom that has helped my business. Let's roll up our sleeves and get started.

2
What Is Factoring?

Factoring Defined

The Latin word "factare" means "to make" or "to do." Obviously the word "factory," the place where products are made, comes from this Latin root. Likewise, "factor" comes from the same word, so a factor is someone who "makes it happen" – who "gets it done." As we'll see below, this has been true for some time.

Factoring, by definition, is the purchase of accounts receivable at a discount – for less than their face value – for immediate cash. When a business sells a product or service to a customer, that business provides an invoice stating the products or services sold and the amount the customer has agreed to pay. It is an IOU from the customer to the business. Sometimes these invoices are paid immediately. Sometimes they are paid over the course of 15, 30, 60, or 90 days or even more. Quite often, larger customers take longer to pay. An unpaid receivable or invoice has value. Factors are businesses who pay cash now for the right to receive the future payments on a client's invoices to their customers. Customers are often called "debtors" in factoring parlance.

Because so many customers wait weeks or even months to pay their bills, a cash flow problem can arise for the companies to whom they owe money. Instead of having to wait for payment on a product or service that has already been delivered, a business can factor – sell – its receivables for cash at a discount off the face amount of the invoice. This almost instant cash offers a number of benefits to cash-starved companies: they can meet payroll, fund marketing efforts, have working capital, pay taxes, or meet many other needs. This cash can provide the means for a manufacturer to replenish inventory and to make more products to sell without having to wait for earlier sales to be paid.

A typical business that extends credit will have ten to twenty percent of its annual sales tied up in accounts receivable at any given time. Just think for a moment about how much money is tied up in 60 days' worth of receivables, and then think about what a business could do with that cash if it were on hand. You can't pay the power bill or this week's payroll with a customer's invoice; but you can *sell* that invoice for the cash to meet those obligations.

Factoring is not a "loan" – it is the sale of an asset. A loan places a debt on a balance sheet, and it costs interest. By contrast, factoring puts money in the bank without creating an obligation to pay it back. Thus having more cash on hand and fewer receivables strengthens one's balance sheet. Loans are largely dependent on the borrower's financial soundness. With factoring, it is the soundness of the client's customer that matters most – a real plus for new businesses without an established track record.

Because factors do not lend money but rather buy invoices, they look at prospective clients differently than a bank. A bank makes a loan with the assumption that the business to whom the loan is made will be stable enough to repay. Factors look to the stability of the *customers* of the business clients, because the *customers* will be paying the factor – not the client. Thus the focus is different: and because the focus is more on the customer than the client, factors often welcome clients that banks turn away. In fact, bank referrals provide factors some of their best leads.

So factoring is not only an excellent means for expanding a business, it may provide the only means when traditional loans aren't available.

The History of Factoring

Today, the most common form of factoring fits conveniently in your wallet – the credit card. A consumer makes a purchase from a merchant, who in turn sells this "receivable" to the credit card company at a discount. The credit card company, acting just like a factor, receives its money by charging the merchant a 1% to 6% fee for receipt of immediate cash, and also accepts the responsibility for collection of the debt. While we may not call this factoring, it is, in essence, what factoring is all about – selling accounts receivable at a discount for immediate cash.

Aside from credit cards, the practice of factoring is widely unknown in our country. But it has been around for more than a thousand years: the Romans issued promissory notes at a discount.

Do you know how the Pilgrims financed their trip to America? Since the Pilgrims did not have enough capital for their journey, they negotiated an agreement with a London businessman named Thomas Weston. An iron merchant, Weston advanced money for repayment at a future date, using as collateral the Pilgrims' accounts receivable for the raw materials the colonists shipped to London. However, he probably bought the receivables at a great discount because of the high risk involved with transporting and receiving the raw materials from America.

Factoring as it is now practiced in the United States began in the garment industry in the 19th Century and has grown steadily and expanded to other industries. Up until the 1980's, factoring was limited to mostly large corporations involving very large dollar amounts. That decade brought a change in the factoring industry. With the savings and loan crisis during those years, banks became much more cautious about lending money, especially to businesses. Since then, standard practice for banks is to require at least two or three years' of financials from a business before they will even consider a loan request. Consequently, newer businesses or those who don't meet a bank's often rigid requirements need an alternative source of financing for their business. More and more therefore are turning to factors.

How Factoring Works

An Example

Let's say a business has a $10,000 invoice. It could be for $100, $1,000, $100,000 or $1,000,000...the principle is the same. This invoice is billed to a good customer who will take 30 days to pay. Rather than waiting that length of time, the business factors the invoice and receives a 75% advance, or $7,500, in cash the next day from the factor through a bank wire, direct deposit, or check. The invoice is mailed and 30 days later, the customer pays the factor the full amount of the invoice, $10,000. With that $10,000, the factor reimburses himself the $7,500 advanced, keeps his fee of 5%, or $500, and pays back the balance, $2,000, to the client.

In essence, this is what happens with just about all factoring transactions. A business pays, in this example, $500 to have $7,500 tomorrow, and gets the other $2,000 in a month. Meanwhile, what has the $7,500 in hand enabled the business owner to do? He can buy inventory to make more sales, have cash on hand to take advantage of discounts, provide working capital to pay bills, meet payroll, pay taxes, or whatever the business might need. The company has accessed instant cash for an otherwise non-performing asset: receivables. No debt is generated, the fee is paid after the cash advance is received, and the cash has enabled the company to increase profits with greater sales volume. Further, the fee has more than paid for itself.

You're probably beginning to see how a business can grow from factoring receivables.

Recourse and Non-recourse Factoring

As all business owners know, any time credit is extended to a customer there's a chance that customer, for a variety of reasons, will not pay the bill. What happens when a factor buys an invoice which the customer doesn't pay? The answer depends on whether a recourse or non-recourse factoring agreement is in place, and the reason for nonpayment.

When the factor and the client establish their financial relationship as one with **recourse**, the factor determines how long he will wait to be paid by the client's customers – usually a period of 60, 90, or 120 days. If the customer does not pay in that length of time for whatever reason, the factor has "recourse" to the client to recoup whatever amount is owed the factor. In essence, the client "buys back" the invoice previously sold (usually through a deduction from new invoice advances or rebates due the client) to cover the factor's unpaid advance, expenses and fee.

In **non-recourse** factoring, the factor does not have a claim against the client if the customer cannot pay. In such arrangements, the factor is assuming the risk of nonpayment (essentially offering credit insurance to the client) which provides an added bonus to the client along with the other advantages of factoring. Non-recourse factoring, according to the language of most factoring agreements, is in effect when the customer is *unable* to pay; that is, if the customer goes bankrupt, goes out of business, or otherwise can't pay the bill. However, if there is a dispute and a customer *won't* pay, the factor *will* have recourse. The client is expected to do what is necessary to satisfy the customer so the invoice is paid.

Most larger factors that purchase invoices totaling $100,000 or more per month will usually offer both recourse and non-recourse factoring, but some provide strictly non-recourse funding. This is of benefit to the client; but keep in mind, non-recourse factors must be even more careful about which customers they will factor as they are at greater risk of losing money. Thus, they may be more selective about the clients and customers they will accept.

Smaller factors who deal in sums less than $100,000 per month will often be strictly recourse factors. Recourse factors may be especially careful and limit their selection of clients to those who are financially stable and/or who have a large number of customers or very stable customers which tends to limit risk. If an invoice isn't paid and goes to recourse, the client must be able to make good on the loss or the recourse factor will lose money.

When a business owner decides to factor, he should factor only those customers whom he is absolutely certain will pay in a dependable manner. A common mistake with clients new to factoring is to want to factor poor-paying or non-paying customers. However, this is one of the worst things that can be done. Why?

1) Factors' discount rates (fees) are based on the length of time a customer takes to pay. The longer an invoice is unpaid, the higher the fee. The fee for an invoice that is unpaid after 90 days will be far higher than that for an invoice paid within 30 days.

2) When recourse occurs, the client has to reimburse the factor for the amount advanced plus his fee; thus, factoring non-paying customers can harm a client's cash flow more than help it. If a client has poor paying customers, a collection agency is the best resource, not a factor.

3) A bank makes money on interest as a loan is repaid. A factor makes money on fees generated as the client makes money. The more a client's business grows and he factors his invoices, the more the factor makes. Hence a client and factor are business allies. If a non-paying customer harms a business, this will in turn harm a recourse factor because the client's cash position is weakened. A non-recourse factor is simply out the money. In any case, everyone's better off to factor good paying customers who pay from about 15 days to 60 days (30 to 45 is best) and pay dependably.

Types of Businesses
Which Benefit from Factoring

What types of businesses can benefit from factoring? The list is virtually as long as the index to the Yellow Pages. Let's review the kinds of companies who can benefit from factoring and the kinds of customers they need to have.

Any company, whether starting out, experiencing a growth phase, or mature in years, needs good cash flow. If a company's cash flow is good and always has enough to pay its bills, meet payroll and taxes, and can expand to its desired size unaided, factoring isn't necessary. However, if improved cash flow is needed, factoring can be one of the best ways to get it.

A company considering factoring will need to have at least one customer whose invoices can be factored. Young companies several months to a few years old, as long as they have good receivables, are often good candidates. Their customers need to be other businesses, or government agencies such as school districts, city, county, state or federal branches whose receivables are assignable. The receivables should be with dependable, good-paying customers who simply take longer to pay.

Customers who are very large corporations often make their suppliers wait 60 or more days to pay as part of the terms for doing business with them. These customers are usually good to factor. Companies that sell strictly to consumers won't factor those receivables; however, if a company invoices both the general public as well as businesses or government, the latter can be factored.

The best customers to factor are credit worthy, solid firms who regularly take approximately two weeks to two months to pay. Accounts which fall outside of this window may not be cost effective to factor.

The Cost of Factoring

A moment ago we spoke of a 75% advance rate and a 5% discount fee. These percentages will vary a great deal depending on several things.

The first consideration in establishing a factoring rate is to assess the stability of the customer – the business that will pay the invoice. The more stable and dependable the customer is, generally, the better the rate a factor can offer. If the customers are government agencies, Fortune 500 companies and/or businesses with a high credit rating, the factor's risk of not getting paid is considerably less. If a client sells only to "Mom & Pop" companies who operate on a shoestring, to companies with a history of not paying their bills in a timely manner (or at all), or to those who are in financial trouble, the factor is more likely to charge higher rates, give lower advances or both, or turn down the customer or client outright.

Another consideration in determining rates is in assessing the stability of the client's business, especially for recourse factors. Are company or personal assets sufficient to cover bad invoices? How long has the company been in business, how well does the owner know her business, and how well does she manage her company? How many bad debts has she had? How long do her customers typically take to pay?

Further, the volume of receivables to factor monthly, the length of time one wishes to factor and the size of the individual invoices to factor all play a part in determining rates. Generally, the larger the volume factored each month – spread among credit worthy customers in balanced concentrations, with a stable payment history and reasonably-sized individual invoices – the better the rates will be.

Why? Lower risk and lower administrative cost to the factor. If a business "spot" factors (factors once or an occasional invoice here and there), it will take as much time to set up the account, perform the due diligence, and manage the account as it does if one factors a steady stream of invoices, week in and week out, over a span of several months or years. The factor won't make as much in fees from spot factoring and thus may charge more. Some factors require clients to factor a certain volume of invoices for a certain period of time. Rates are then calculated on this basis. These arrangements are often called "contracts" or "long-term contracts."

The size of invoices also can make a difference. Suppose Business X wants to factor $30,000 a month. This total is made up of 3 invoices of $10,000 each between 3 different customers. Business Y also wants to factor $30,000 a month but his invoices are for $100 each between 300 different customers. It doesn't take a rocket scientist to realize that the time involved for the factor to process the invoices for Business Y will be much longer, and thus more expensive, than those for Business X.

Obviously, a business owner wants a factor who will agree not only to rates he can handle, but one who will take on the size and kind of customers he has. Therefore, it's almost impossible to say what a factor will charge in fees and provide in advances. Each client must be considered unique, with rate and advance calculations based on each situation. However, there are some general standards that are common across the industry.

Unless a business is in the medical or construction industry, factoring advances for clients with stable customers will typically fall in the 70 to 90% range. If customers have tenuous credit histories, the advances may drop to between 40 to 60%. If customers are exceptionally strong or the client has been factoring for some time, advances may enter the 85% or even 90%. It's rare for them to go much higher than that. Overall, 70% to 80% is a good rule of thumb for most receivables.

The discount, or factoring fee, will depend on how long the invoice takes to pay; consequently, rates can be all over the playing field. Some factor's fees are based on the first 30 days the invoice is out. Then they increase the rates every 15 days thereafter. For example, a factor might charge 5% for the first 30 days and an extra 2% for each 15 days after that. If an invoice is out for 31 to 45 days the discount becomes 7%. If it's out 46 to 60 days, it's 9%; and, if it takes 61 to 75 days to pay, it becomes 11% and so on. This helps illustrate why companies don't want to factor invoices that are too old or aged as they can become quite expensive. On the other hand, they also wouldn't want to factor an invoice that will only be out a few days: the fee wouldn't usually be cost-effective for such a short wait.

Calculating the discount can be done with a variety of combinations. Some factors base it starting with the first 30 days, some on the first 15, some on the first 10. Some increment the times thereafter every 30 days, some every 15, some every 10, some every 7, some every single day, with various percentage rates for each of these. Each factor has his or her own way of calculating discounts; some are very flexible and will work with the client to reach an agreeable rate while others are fairly strict about rates and offer fees based on charts with a "take it or leave it" basis. Both the factor and client have overhead expenses and desired profit margins, so negotiating fees must be done with respect for the needs of both parties.

It's not uncommon for many business owners, and especially accountants, to find factoring rates compared to standard loans to be rather shocking. "After all," they reason, "if I borrowed money from a bank at 5% a month, that works out to an Annual Percentage Rate of 60%! That's outrageous!" There are several answers to such a reaction, and each must be considered carefully.

First, if a business can get a bank loan, they are usually better off to do so. But if one is unable to get a loan, the interest rate at which loans are made becomes moot. Moreover, remember that factoring is not a loan; it's the purchase of accounts receivable. A business is not borrowing money at an interest rate: it is selling an asset for cash and receiving a service. Factoring is generally comparable to 2% net 10 rates many businesses routinely offer customers (2% discount if paid in 10 days). Thus, comparing factoring rates to interest on bank loans is the proverbial comparison of apples to oranges.

It is helpful if a business owner selling his receivables considers the expense of factoring to be an integral part of running the business rather than interest on a loan. Just as a business can't exist without office or shop space, lights, phone, and employees, businesses also can't exist without adequate cash flow. Business owners don't think twice about paying rent, utilities, phone bills and payroll; if factoring is what it takes to get cash flow under control, they should consider the cost of factoring as part of the normal costs of running their business. In time, some will not need to factor and dispense with it; others choose to factor over the long term and make it a standard way of doing business.

Calculating Profits

How can you calculate whether factoring will improve one's bottom line? Below is a simplified Income Statement to determine if factoring will help.

Chart 1: Sample Income StatementXYZ Manufacturing Company				
	Before Factoring		With Factoring	
Gross Revenues	100,000		200,000	
Cost of Goods Sold	60,000	60%	120,000	60%
Gross Profits	40,000	40%	80,000	40%
Less:				
Variable Expenses	15,000	15%	30,000	15%
Fixed Expenses	20,000	20%	20,000	10%
Overhead	35,000	35%	50,000	25%
Cost of Factoring	0		5,000	
Total Expenses	35,000	35%	55,000	28%
Net Profit	5,000	5%	25,000	13%

Study this statement (the Cost of Factoring is based on $100,000 worth of invoices at 5%). Then insert a real company's figures, and see if factoring can significantly improve the bottom line. In order to estimate what Gross Revenues might be with factoring, ask: "How much could this company make if it had an unlimited supply of cash on hand?" Perhaps it could double revenues as XYZ has in the example; perhaps they would be less, perhaps more. At any rate, run the numbers and see if factoring makes sense. If it does, you might ask: "Can this business afford *not* to factor?"

Other Services Factors Offer

Factors can quickly run credit checks on prospective customers, saving the potential disaster of unknowingly accepting a customer who might never pay. Most small business owners don't have the know-how or inclination to check customers' credit reports themselves, but jump at the idea of a factor doing it for them.

Many factors take over a business' billing responsibilities or even management of all their accounts receivable. This enables the owner of a small business to concentrate on growth, and saves a larger company the expense of such a department. Factors commonly verify invoices before making advances, which provides a built-in means of quality control and speeds up customer payments. Because factors normally report payment histories to credit agencies (and receive a lower rate on their cost of credit reports for doing so), customers often pay factors more quickly than vendors.

Many businesses offer discount terms to companies to pay quickly. If a business offers 2% net 10, or a 2% discount if a customer pays in 10 days, it's already discounting for quicker cash. Factoring can make such discounts unnecessary and cost about the same, while offering many more benefits.

Especially for smaller and younger companies, factors can be a source of business leads, networking connections, and vendor sources. As an interested third party, often with years of business experience, the factor can make observations and suggestions to enhance the daily operations of a business, trim costs, and increase income.

As you can see, factors provide a great deal more than simply improved cash flow. They bring services and expertise from which nearly any business, and certainly a young and growing business, can benefit.

3

What I've Learned about the Factoring Industry

The First Lessons

Costs. If you intend to factor as a supplement to your regular income and want to have only one or two clients at a time, your start up costs will be minimal – especially if you already have the office equipment mentioned below. However, if you plan to make factoring your full-time business, your first consideration is start-up costs.

Whether or not you go through formal training (which is definitely helpful), there are expenses. If you plan to have more than one or two clients, you'll function best with a computer, copy machine, fax machine, and printer. Fortunately All-in-1 machines (copier, printer, fax, and scanner) are now reasonably priced and worth the investment. It's best to have a dedicated a telephone line or at least a separate number with a unique ring. Then there's office space if you don't work at home, office furniture, business license, office supplies and the like. You should carefully think through what you really need and keep overhead to a minimum. My rule of thumb: don't buy something until you experience the need for it at least twice; never buy ahead of time what you only *think* you will need.

Another expense you must also keep in mind is marketing. There are many ways to market your service and an entire chapter is dedicated to this (see "Marketing: How to Find Clients"). If you are factoring part-time and want just one or two clients, marketing may be easy: you very likely know a few small business owners who can benefit from your service. However if you plan to factor more than lightly, you should allocate a healthy amount of your operating budget for marketing efforts, especially to start.

Realistically it will take some time and money to launch your factoring service. If it will be your full-time work, you need to look at several aspects of the business you might not have considered. Book 1 in this series, *Factoring Fundamentals: How You Can Make Large Returns in Small Receivables* is written to help those contemplating becoming a small factor. It looks at the subject from several standpoints – financial, time availability, tolerance for risk, family considerations, and more. Several questions are posed to help the reader "look" before "leaping" and decide if this is a wise move for his or her circumstances – *before* a dime is invested in small receivables.

If your factoring business will be full-time, be sure you have enough socked away – both to live on and with which to run your business – to carry you for at least two years. It also helps enormously to have a spouse with an income to help in the short run. I would not have made it if this were not true in my case. Several other training grads with whom I stayed in touch said the same thing; they couldn't have stayed in business when their companies were young without the income from their spouse's job. If you don't have this security for at least a year or more (not to mention your spouse's and/or other family members' support), you'll have a tough row to hoe as a full-time factor.

It may take anywhere from six months to two years to really get your factoring business off the ground and profitable. Like anything worthwhile, expect there to be moments of discouragement and even a few times when you feel like throwing in the towel. You must know your tolerance for such dips in the road, and determine ahead of time that when they come you will hang in there.

Start Gradually. I started with the impression that if I worked full-time, making $100,000 a year is not only possible but fairly easy in this business. My experience has been that it is possible after you have been at it a while; but starting full-time is anything but easy, especially the first year. Therefore start gradually.

When I was just starting as a factoring broker, the success stories of other newcomers making numerous deals their first month or two left me feeling like a failure and more discouraged than hopeful. I had worked extremely hard for several months and had nothing to show for it. It took close to a year before things clicked. For me, that started when I began factoring small, local deals in addition to operating as a broker. After working in the business part-time for six months and then full-time for another six months, I had made less than $300 brokering (all of which came in about the ninth month – not exactly what I expected). Two classmates made zero the first year. However, after factoring small local deals for about three months, I had grossed $3,000 with far less effort than I spent brokering; and it steadily improved from there.

If you have a related business and/or financial background, experience in a specific factorable industry, and excellent contacts, you will have a far easier task than if you don't. Who you know is at least as important as what you know in this business.

The Stigma of Factoring. Unfortunately you will find that some people familiar with factoring view it negatively and factoring does not have the stellar image we might wish. A bank manager once told me his colleagues consider factors to be "the used car salesmen of the financial world." Isn't that inspiring?

Regrettably, the people who often could be good sources of leads – accountants, bankers, attorneys – are the ones with negative opinions about factors. Not all such professionals are against factoring, but several either look down their noses at it or just don't mention it to clients who would benefit. And most frustrating, many such "money-people" just don't fully understand factoring.

There is a need to re-educate people who think factoring is only a last-gasp effort to save a sinking ship. Most of the businesses who factor today do it because they are growing, not because they are dying. This needs to be impressed on everyone you talk to, both the uninformed as well as the misinformed.

Full/Part Time. If you wish to factor only a small, limited number of clients as a means of supplemental investment or retirement income, factoring small receivables can be quite rewarding. As discussed in *Factoring Fundamentals,* part-time factoring can be a great move for investors with a regular job, retirees, and those wanting to create another income stream as an add-on to their current business.

In my case, after attempting to do the business part-time I had more success working it full-time. I found most business people you need to contact work regular business hours, and you usually can't prospect successfully on evenings and weekends. It's hard enough doing that during regular working hours. I used various marketing methods that could be done at odd times; and while the response was fairly good, I eventually had to talk with these people during normal working hours.

You can get started while you do something else, but be aware that factoring takes time, energy and focus. Unless you keep your client load intentionally small, it can be tough to split a busy factoring business with another demanding job.

Why Big Factors
Don't Want Small Deals

One of the first lessons brokers learn is that factors have minimums. That is, most say, "I don't want deals that are less than $10,000 or $25,000 or $100,000 per month." This very important fact not only tells you where you can and can't take clients as a broker; it creates your niche as a small factor.

Some factors say they have "no" minimums or "low" minimums, often putting $5,000 or $10,000 as the lowest they'll accept. However, when presented with bona fide prospects with monthly volumes under $10,000 they usually turn them away because they will not make enough with such clients (see Chart 2 below). Why then do they claim to accept such deals when in fact they reject those that come along? To attract more business, particularly if someone "on the border" appears to be ready to grow rapidly. If other factors know you really will accept such small clients they turn away, these factors can be a source of referrals.

Many of the deals you'll find, especially at a local level when you start, are small. When you're new at this game, these are the ones that are best because your inexperience will be evident to bigger companies with bigger needs. However, if you find a young, growing company with a struggling business owner, you may form a quick camaraderie with such a person because you're both in a similar situation.

Sadly, larger factors with $20,000 or more minimums put factoring out of the reach of many of these smaller companies. These potential clients could benefit from factoring but can't get it (nor bank loans nor anything else). The reason big factors don't want them is not because they're selfish or mean-spirited; it's simple economics. Big factors, by virtue of the volume they do, must pay staff to find new business, manage the accounts, and run the office. This labor isn't cheap. Each factor's minimum represents what they must make to break even to factor an account. Factoring a client below their minimum causes them to lose money. How?

Suppose a factor takes on an account with $3,000 in invoices per month. If these invoices produce a 5% fee, the factor makes $150. However, out of that $150, staff costs to service the account may be $75. Add to this the factor's cost of money, broker's fee, taxes, overhead, other operating expenses, and they don't make much – if anything. They're better off spending their staff resources on $50,000 to $500,000 accounts that will be worth their time and investment.

Chart 2 is a simplified explanation of factors' expenses, which vary according to their size and overhead costs.

Monthly Expenses	Beginning Factor	Small Factor	Larger Factor
Rent	0	500	2,000
Phone/Utilities	50	500	3,000
Operat'g Expenses, Taxes	250	1,000	15,000
Payroll	700	6,000	30,000
Total	1,000	8,000	50,000
Above expenses = 5% of:	20,000	$160,000	1,000,000

Chart 2: Break Even Points

Monthly invoice volume needed to break even (based on 5% avg. fees)

Typical number of clients:	4	20	50
Avg. monthly volume needed per client	$5,000	$8,000	$20,000

As you can see, each factor has monthly expenses (overhead) which must be covered by their business income (factoring fees collected). In order to make this amount, the factors must have sufficient monthly invoice volume which will produce fee income of at least the size needed to break even. Divide the monthly invoice volume by the number of clients each factor has and you have the average monthly volume each factor needs per client to break even. See the chapter "Break-Even Analysis" for an in-depth look at calculating a break-even point and how this can help you plan for your business needs and growth.

Why You and I
DO Want Small Deals

One reason you don't want to bother brokering small deals is that you probably can't! Bigger factors don't want small deals. Another is simple: your broker fee, if you can find someone who'll accept the deal, is minuscule.

For example, say a factor makes a 5% fee and pays you a 15% brokering commission (i.e. 15% of his fee; 10-15% is standard[1]). On a $1,000 invoice the factor makes $50 then pays you $7.50 plus his overhead. How much have you invested in time, effort, and phone charges to make that $7.50? Too much. If you're going to broker, go after bigger accounts of at least $20,000 or more; it's the only way to make money – as a broker. (See Chart 3)

		Chart 3: Brokering Small Transactions			
Invoice Size	80% Advance	Factor's Fee	Factor's Gross Inc.	15% Brkr's Fee	Factor's Net Inc.
1,000	800	5%	50	7.50	42.50
5,000	4,000	5%	250	37.50	212.50
10,000	8,000	5%	500	75.00	425.00
20,000	16,000	5%	1,000	150.00	850.00
50,000	40,000	5%	2,500	375.00	2,125.00

However, as a small local factor, going after smaller accounts is a different story. Factoring $5,000 worth of invoices generates $250 every month. Once this account and a number of others like it are set up, it becomes more valuable for you. Why? You don't have the staff and overhead to pay that the larger factors do, nor do you pay a broker's fee. This is money going into your pocket, not to employees. The only person you have to pay is you; and starting your factoring business this way is a good way to begin. (See Chart 4.) Further, your risk is limited to the $4,000 advance ($5,000 x 80%). If one such loss occurs you should be able to recover.

---

[1] Factors who pay more than 15% may not be able to offer competitive rates if a client is seriously comparing and shopping for fees.

Chart 4: Factoring Small Transactions					
Invoice Size	80% Advance	Factor's Fee	Factor's Gross Inc.	0% Brkr's Fee	Factor's Net Inc.
1,000	800	5%	50	0	50
5,000	4,000	5%	250	0	250
10,000	8,000	5%	500	0	500
20,000	16,000	5%	1,000	0	1,000
50,000	40,000	5%	2,500	0	2,500

What about using brokers yourself with small deals? It's okay to have a broker bring you a few deals to get started; but after that, you're better off relying on word-of-mouth and your own marketing and networking efforts to obtain new clients with small invoices.

Brokers just don't make enough on very small invoices as you can see in Chart 3 above. Assuming a 5% factoring fee, you will make more factoring a $5,000 invoice ($250) than you will brokering a $20,000 invoice even if you make a 15% brokering commission ($150). A 10% broker commission is common, and that would only equal a $100 commission. Thus you can realistically make 2½ times as much factoring $5,000 as you would brokering $20,000.

One of your greatest advantages as a small factor – and one of the most enjoyable aspects of factoring over brokering – is the fact that you're the boss! If you've brokered deals with larger factors, you have no doubt experienced the frustrations of slow response time, an unwillingness to factor a prospect you find promising, rates or advances the client doesn't find appealing, and the sense that the factor's only in it to make a buck and protect him/herself. Because you're in the trenches with your small client and also making the funding decisions, you can act extremely quickly to set rates, negotiate terms and close a deal you otherwise might lose if it were in the hands of someone else.

Because you don't have the bureaucratic hassles of someone looking over your shoulder, a committee who must make a decision, or a mile of red tape to work around you can fund someone based on as much due diligence as you think you need, or simply a gut feeling. (However, you also live with the consequences!) If snags develop, you rely on your own creativity to overcome them. This can be an exciting part of your business, but one you must treat with great respect, because it can both make and break you as a factor.

Used well, your flexibility can land you many new accounts, earn you good money, and make you a hero in the eyes of clients who otherwise would be turned down – and possibly go out of business. Used poorly, you can be out of business very quickly with some nasty debts that can be difficult to repay.

The other reason you want small clients is quite logical: as they grow, so do you. There is a strong possibility that a client's business will grow because of factoring. An account that starts factoring $2,000 a month can grow to $4,000 in three months, to $10,000 in nine months, to $25,000 in eighteen months, to $40,000 in a couple years. Handled carefully, you will profit handsomely from and with a client like this and grow right along with him. Best of all, because you've gained this client's trust and loyalty, he will stay with or return to you when he is bigger and needs a factor on a regular or occasional basis for those $100,000 to $500,000 invoices.

There are very few large factors who will take on clients with monthly volumes of $3,000 or $4,000. Lucky for you and me!

Small Numbers Add Up

How much money can you make factoring small deals? It depends on how much money you have with which to factor and your rates (more on these in later chapters). It's not hard to calculate...it's simply a matter of small numbers adding up. (The chapter "Break-Even Analysis" helps you calculate this.) If you factor four clients at an average of $5,000 each per month and charge an average fee of 5% on each one, your gross profit is $1,000. Factoring ten clients at $5,000 per month each you'll make $2,500. Double the number of clients to twenty and you make $5,000. Double these twenty clients' average monthly volume to $10,000 and you're making $10,000.

That's not a bad monthly income for a one-person business. Meanwhile, when you run across accounts larger than those you can or want to factor yourself – and you will – co-factor or broker them. Add several hundred if not a few thousand dollars in broker fees to your factoring fees, and you have a very nice income indeed.

Just remember it takes a while to build up to these "small" numbers. Rome wasn't built in a day.

Part 2

Digging Deeper

4
Charting Your Course

Form and Direction

Once you've determined becoming a factor is a good move for you and before you start getting your money on the street, there is one more important preliminary step: determine the form and direction your business will take. While you may not need to go to the effort of a full business plan (not a bad idea though especially if you have some serious funds to invest), you should at least jot down your goals and what you hope to accomplish before you spend a lot of time, money, and energy. Review these goals regularly (at least every quarter or so) and update them as conditions change.

The form and direction your business takes will depend on your life's circumstances and what you wish to do with your factoring service. These, in turn, determine the amount of money you need to earn and the capital you need to have. If you wish to use the money you make factoring as supplemental funds to enhance your present income, the amount needed may be different from what it would be if this is the sole means of support for a growing family.

To prepare a map that will guide you as you develop your factoring business, write down your answers to the questions that follow. Keep handy both your written answers and the copies for future use; and make a note in your tickler file to review and update this information at regular intervals.

The Plan for Your Factoring Business

1. What is the intended use of the income you will make from factoring?

    __ Investment income to build your portfolio and net worth.

    __ Supplement to pension/retirement/present income on which you live.

    __ Primary income from which you will support yourself and family.

2. On a monthly average, how much do you *need* to earn in order to meet the intended use of factoring income in Number 1?

    First year $_____   Yearly Total: $_____

    In 1 year $_____   Yearly Total: $_____

    In 2 years $_____   Yearly Total: $_____

    In 3 years $_____   Yearly Total: $_____

    In 5 years $_____   Yearly Total: $_____

3. On a monthly average, how much do you *want* to earn in order to meet the intended use of factoring income in Number 1?

    First year $_____   Yearly Total: $_____

    In 1 year $_____   Yearly Total: $_____

    In 2 years $_____   Yearly Total: $_____

    In 3 years $_____   Yearly Total: $_____

    In 5 years $_____   Yearly Total: $_____

4. In order to meet the amounts in Numbers 2 and 3, you need a specific amount of capital (factoring funds). Chart 6 (in the chapter "Money") indicates your income if your average gross fee on all your transactions is 5%. Remember you must subtract your cost of money, operating expenses and bad debts from your gross income. How much will you need to fund monthly advances in order to meet your needs and wants in Numbers 2 and 3 above? (Use Chart 6, columns 2, 3, and 6.)

    In 1 year $_____   In 3 years $_____

    In 2 years $_____   In 5 years $_____

5. List below the source and amount of funds you intend to use as working capital (factoring funds):

First year

Source _____   Amount $_____

Source _____   Amount $_____

Source _____   Amount $_____

Source _____   Amount $_____

                                                         Total $_____

Second year

Source _____   Amount $_____

Source _____   Amount $_____

Source _____   Amount $_____

Source _____   Amount $_____

                                                         Total $_____

Third year

Source _____   Amount $_____

Source _____   Amount $_____

Source _____   Amount $_____

Source _____   Amount $_____

                                                         Total $_____

Fourth year

Source _____   Amount $_____

Source _____   Amount $_____

Source _____   Amount $_____

Source _____   Amount $_____

                                                         Total $_____

Fifth year

Source _____   Amount $_____

Source _____   Amount $_____

Source _____   Amount $_____

Source _____   Amount $_____

                                                         Total $_____

6. In order to meet the amounts in Numbers 2 and 3 above, which of the following do you intend to do?

    __ Start small and remain small.

    __ Start small and grow to a certain size.

    __ Start small and grow as large as you can.

7 a. Do you wish to work alone throughout the course of your factoring service, or do you plan to have one or more people work the business with you?

    __ Alone   __ 1 Other   __ More than 1 other

  b. If you plan to have others work with you, how many do you plan to include?

  _____

  c. Approximately when will this person or persons begin?

  _____

  d. What roles will each of you play? _____

  _____

  e. Approximately how many hours per week will this person or persons work and how much will each be paid?

  _____

  _____

8 a. To start, do you plan to work from your home or an outside office?

  _____

  b. Do you intend to keep working from this location or eventually work elsewhere?

  _____

9. List the office equipment you will use to provide your factoring service.

Equipment	Have	Need	*If Needed:* Approx. Cost	When to Obtain
_____	—	—	$_____	_____
_____	—	—	$_____	_____
_____	—	—	$_____	_____
_____	—	—	$_____	_____
_____	—	—	$_____	_____
_____	—	—	$_____	_____
_____	—	—	$_____	_____
_____	—	—	$_____	_____

Total $_____

10. What measurable means (e.g. number of active clients, monthly/yearly volume, monthly/yearly net or gross fees, personal income, etc.) will enable you to say "My factoring service is presently succeeding" at these intervals:

First year _____

_____

_____

In 1 year _____

_____

_____

In 2 years _____

_____

_____

In 3 years _____

_____

_____

In 5 years _____

_____

_____

58 – Factoring Small Receivables

5

Bits of Wisdom for the Small Factor

Why You're in the Factoring Business

Let's get something clear from the beginning: why do you want to be in the factoring business? The quick response for many people is "to make money." Fair enough. But if that's the only answer you have, you're missing the boat and probably will be either less than successful or not have many friends as you amass your wealth from factoring.

The overriding reason to be in the factoring business is to help your clients. If your only purpose is the money you make, your clients will sense this quickly or eventually learn it, and their trust in you will become shrouded. But if you make it clear by everything you say and do that your first and major concern is the success of their company, you will earn devoted and loyal clients, even friends, for years. Many will more than gladly give you referrals and recommendations. My approach with clients is, rather openly, "I'm here, first and foremost, to help with your cash flow and make your business what you want it to be. If I can make a good living this way, then so much the better." You'll need to prove this over and over; and if you do, you will have no trouble finding clients.

This is not to say that you should help clients at the expense of your own financial security; no one expects that. Besides, if you take on an account you shouldn't just because you want to help someone, you may be out of business yourself in no time. The point is this: who's first on your list of priorities? If it's not the client, you will have far fewer.

Factor Small Deals, Broker Big Ones

Because most bigger factors don't want small deals, a niche is created which you, the small local factor, can fill nicely. Filling this niche is the key to growing your factoring business, and leads to the recurrent theme of this manual – and to the motto of the small factor. Repeat it over and over; make it your mind set: "Factor small deals, broker big ones. Factor small deals, broker big ones...."

Factoring small invoices with small local companies is the best way to learn first-hand what factoring involves and requires, and is the logical next step after training to be a broker consultant. By being a factor for small accounts, you'll be a much better broker for big ones. When you've gone through the set-up procedures, done background checks, made verification calls, paid advances, kept the necessary paperwork, called slow paying customers, received customers' payments, paid the rebates and done everything else necessary, you'll know exactly what larger factors need and want, and why. You'll be their favorite broker when you bring them the six- and seven-figure deals with all the i's dotted and t's crossed, because you now think like they do and will be able to help them close larger deals more easily and quickly.

To be a successful small factor, you'll need to set some standards as to

- the maximum size of invoice you will factor
- how much total monthly volume you'll do
- how much monthly volume you'll do with a specific client and/or customer
- how much total money you'll have invested with a specific client and/or customer, and
- at what point you're more comfortable brokering instead of factoring

To a large degree, these selections will depend on 1) how much money you have to factor; 2) the level of risk you can tolerate, i.e. how much money you can afford to lose at a given time; and 3) the time you wish to devote to factoring.

Decide the maximum advance you will give a new client to start, the size of advance you prefer to give when a client or customer is new, and the average monthly amount you wish to factor with a client. If someone wants to start with more than your limit, you may simply broker him. However, if he is able to start small and build up to some larger amount, and it's an account you want to keep rather than broker, find another small factor with whom to co-factor the account. This way, not only will you keep in close contact with a loyal client, you'll make more income by splitting a factoring fee and risk than by getting only a broker's fee.

For example: a client factors $5,000 a month. At 5%, you make $250 as her factor. Her business grows and she wants to factor $10,000 a month. Now you make $500 as the factor. She continues to grow until she wants to factor $20,000 a month. Not wanting that much invested in a single client or not having enough money to factor her now, you could broker the account and make a 15% fee ($150). This is less than you made when she started factoring; however, you could now co-factor her. You and a co-factor would each contribute half the advance payment and you would continue to make $500. (See Chart 5.)

Chart 5: Co-Factoring Small Transactions					
		Half of	5%	0%	Half of
Invoice	80%	80%	Factor's	Broker's	Factor's
Size	Advance	Advance	Fee	Fee	Fee
5,000	4,000	2,000	250	0	125
10,000	8,000	4,000	500	0	250
20,000	16,000	8,000	1,000	0	500

Co-factoring can be a good arrangement for the small factor. It can also be better for the client-factor relationship and trust. Such clients will usually rather stay with you than begin a relationship with a new, unknown factor who might operate differently. Further, the client need not be aware you are co-factoring, as all the paperwork continues to go through your books, and the outside funds you're using are transparent to her.

Clearly, it's beneficial to have other factors you know and trust with whom to co-factor. Keep in touch with other brokers and small factors you meet at conventions, seminars, networking meetings, etc. whom you like, trust, and with whom you want to do business. It can pay handsomely for you both.

Keep It Local

As a general rule when starting out, try to factor businesses in your local area. A "local area" in Montana can be geographically a lot larger than one in New York City; but the point is, deal with people you can meet face-to-face on a regular basis. This will provide an ample number of clients, as well as some built-in safeguards.

You'll Know Your Client Better. When you see where a client works and/or lives, you quickly get a feel for his personality, the kind of business he runs, his strengths and weaknesses as a business person, perhaps his family demands and many other worthwhile facts. You'll see for yourself how (un)sophisticated his bookkeeping is and (un)organized his office space may be. You're more likely to be familiar with his customers and can learn first-hand what his relations with customers are. In a word, you can enter your client's world and see how to best help him, as well as be aware of potential or actual problems that may impact your investment.

Trust. Mutual trust can be built more quickly. As the chapter "Reducing Your Risk" mentions, trust is the name of the factoring game. Your client is trusting you with some very private and very important information, which is the lifeblood of his business: receivables. From his perspective he is trusting you with his money. You can earn his trust more quickly in person when he sees how you operate. You can demonstrate that you sincerely are there to help his business by your attitude and efforts to do what's best for him and also prudent for you. Likewise, you can get a reading of his trustworthiness when you deal personally with a client regularly, tour his facility, see what his office looks like (messy or neat as a pin), meet his employees or spouse, have lunch occasionally, and so on.

Invoice and Money Transfers. When a client is within driving distance, you can easily exchange invoices and Schedules of Accounts, ask questions quickly if you're unclear about something and transfer funds to him personally or even into his bank account directly at no cost. When you factor someone in another state, some of that familiarity disappears. In order to get the money to him quickly you may need to send it next-day express mail or bank wire it. This can cost from $10 to $20 a pop, a sum which is quite a bite out of very small accounts. However, a check mailed to a local address will usually arrive the next day for no more than the cost of a single stamp. If he picks it up it's free.

Better yet, as long as your client load is fairly small, you can make deposits into clients' bank accounts. Simply get a client's bank and account number, make the check out to his business, endorse it on the back saying, "For deposit only, ABC Company, Acct. #0000000," fill in a deposit slip from the bank and deposit it with the teller. Then fax the receipt to the client or copy it and send or hand him the original. Keep the copy for your records. Best of all, some banks will let you make transfers from your account to your client's without a check – you just make an intra-bank transfer if you use the same bank. This can be done with a simple transfer slip, phone call, or internet transaction.

Electronic ACH payments, if your bank provides them and you qualify, is also a means of easy, quick, and inexpensive funds transfers. More on ACH a bit later.

Problems. Should a problem arise (say a customer disputes a charge), you can discuss it immediately and get things cleared up right away. If you want to make a change in your factoring methods or if your client doesn't understand something, you can discuss the matter with a quick, local phone call or work it out over a cup of coffee. I find the ease and informality of doing business locally and in person preferable to limiting my contact to the phone with distant clients. Finally, in a worst case scenario, if your customer or client doesn't pay, you know where the client lives and works and how to find him. If he's disappeared, you'll know that a lot sooner if his office is 2 miles away than if it's 2,000 miles away.

Referrals. People are more likely to do business with people they know, like and trust, than with a stranger. Being in a community where you are known automatically creates a circle of influence by virtue of people you know, and people they know. What's more, when your local clients know you personally and trust you, and you've proven to be an asset to their companies, your name will get around as being someone good with whom to do business. People will call hoping you can help them like you helped their friends; and this will, in turn, benefit your business in every way. This can enable you to trim your advertising budget to a point where you only work from referrals.

In short, keep your factoring clients local when you start. It's much easier and will enable you to be successful more quickly. It will also lead to contacts with bigger clients whom you can broker for nice finder's fees.

If you run across small clients in other areas, see if there's a colleague there who will factor them. They'll appreciate the referral and may return the favor. Alternately, the factor in that area may agree to co-factor with you. Let the local factor make the contacts, do the due diligence, record keeping, etc., while you make a nice co-factoring fee for simply providing half the funds. Just be sure you trust the other factor, are comfortable with his due diligence and method of operating, get regular reports of the account and stay in touch. If you don't do the record keeping and control the cash flow, you have little or no control over the account so you must only work with co-factors you completely trust. To lessen your risk, you may want to co-factor only as the "recording" factor (see the chapter "Co-Factoring").

Choose Your Bank Carefully

Deciding which bank you'll use may not consume much thought; but if you are in an area where you have several banking choices, choose your bank carefully.

First, shop the banks for checking account charges (try to get free checking), minimum balances, understandable and complete monthly statements, and internet banking services. Even more, get to know the branch manager well. Take him out to lunch once you set up your account. Not only can this person be a great source of referrals, he also can be a handy problem solver if there is ever a problem with your account.

Also, be sure the manager understands what you're doing as a factor and will accommodate any special banking needs you have. Many banks will not let you deposit checks made out to your client. Be sure the banker understands why you may need to do this. Even if customers are instructed to make checks out to the factor, some will make checks out to the client anyway and you need to be able to deposit these checks. Therefore, make sure your bank has on file a copy of your contract with each of your clients. The contract must specifically give you power of attorney to endorse and deposit their checks into your account. If a bank won't cooperate with you on this critical matter, find one that will.

Since 9/11 finding a bank that will cooperate in this regard has become much more difficult than it once was. With the Patriot Act banks are especially concerned over the appearance of money laundering activity, and some bankers use this as the reason for not allowing you to deposit checks made out to another party. However, the same bankers who use this excuse usually do not really understand factoring and are more concerned with a superior or bank regulator who is always looking over their shoulder, waiting for them to make a mistake. It is safer and easier for a banker to simply say your request "cannot be done," rather than to really learn about what you're trying to do, or stick his neck out just a little to accommodate this banking need of your business.

If you have had a close banking relationship for many years with a local bank, you *may* find them receptive to this request…but don't count on it. If you find resistance, simply go up the ladder and keep asking to speak with someone further up until you find someone who understands what you're requesting. If and when you finally find that person, their simple say-so is enough to immediately make this service available to you. If you never find such a person, you'll have to try another bank or have customers make all payment checks out to your company (more on this later).

You may want to consider a small community bank over a large national bank for a variety of reasons. Community banks may be more likely to take a personal interest in your business, be more willing to extend you a line of credit with which to factor, and provide financial advice as you grow your business. Further, they may be more likely to refer small clients to you more often than the larger banks. They may or may not be willing to allow you to deposit checks made out to your clients.

One of the biggest considerations in choosing your bank is obvious: convenience. Because you will make frequent runs to the bank for deposits, use a bank that is close to your home or office and is open hours most convenient to your schedule. Some banks have branches located in or beside large grocery stores that are open more hours than regular bank branches.

If your bank provides ACH payments and you qualify, this is a very handy way of making deposits to your clients. Instead of writing a check and depositing it into your client's account, or mailing or sending it by overnight courier, or wiring funds, you simply sit at your computer and make a transfer of funds via the internet in a matter of seconds. This is far faster, cheaper, and easier than all the other methods of transferring funds to your clients and definitely the most convenient way to run this part of your business.

However, because these transfers are made through the Federal Reserve Bank and go directly from your bank to your client's bank, you are electronically withdrawing funds. That means you're transferring *the bank's* money with no float and an immediate transfer of funds, which the bank looks upon as a loan. Therefore in order to qualify for ACH payments, you must apply for the privilege just like you would for a bank loan, with your business financials, tax returns, personal credit report, the whole bit. If you can't qualify for a loan, you won't be approved for ACH. While you may look upon this simply as a substitute for writing a check, the bank doesn't, so be prepared. However, if you can qualify for this service, it is well worth the effort. It will save you many hours of preparing, mailing, or depositing checks. For the author's first experience of applying for ACH payments, see the article from *FactorTips* in the Appendix.

Another bank service to consider is a lockbox. This is a post office box that is owned and managed by the bank or a lockbox company. You direct all your payments to this box number, and the bank retrieves the payments, opens the envelopes, deposits the checks into your account, and provides you with a daily report of payments received. If your bank will not allow you to receive checks made out to your client, this may be an alternative (though many banks still require checks be made out to you or to the bank). Make sure of your bank's policy as to whom the checks must be made to if you want to use a lockbox.

Lockboxes are often used by larger factors as they do the task of an employee for much less than the cost of an employee. A small factor needs to determine if his operation is large enough to justify this expense, which will run around a couple hundred dollars a month, depending on the services needed. For those whose time is tight or who don't want to make a regular trek to the post office and/or bank, lock boxes can be worthwhile. For part-time or very small operations, however, they may be too expensive.

Clearly, spending a few extra hours choosing the financial institution best suited to your needs can save driving, time, and even money in the long run.

Legal Assistance

Small factors frequently need the services of a skilled, competent business attorney. While legal expenses can be steep for any new business, failure to obtain professional legal advice can be far more costly in the long run. To find one in your area, contact the nearest State Bar referral service or ask other business owners who their business attorney is. Contact a few of the lawyers to learn their fields of expertise, with which issues they can and cannot help you, and their rates. You'll need to feel confident that your hard-earned money is being spent on competent, valuable legal advice and assistance, so choose your lawyer carefully. Members of the International Factoring Association (IFA) have access to a list of attorneys who specialize in factoring. See the chapter "Factoring Resources" for more benefits the IFA offers.

Remember that attorneys charge by the hour, and once you have retained yours, the clock starts ticking the minute they pick up the phone, start writing a letter, or begin legal research for you. In addition to hourly fees, attorneys charge for faxes, long distance calls, copies, and every little item they can track. Depending on your area and the demand for the lawyer's services, expect to pay at least $125 to $250 per hour. If your attorney charges $200 an hour, your bill for a 15-minute phone call will be $50…plus long distance charges, if your lawyer calls you long distance. If you have frequent or extensive legal work done, this professional cost can be one of your larger budget expenses.

Start Small and Don't Take on Too Much

The first few months you factor, you are vulnerable to mistakes and losses by virtue of your inexperience. You will learn from every transaction and every client. Common sense says to learn from those smallest in volume. The first account I factored was a one-person carpet cleaning company that factored less than $2,000 a month and submitted around seven invoices per week – each worth from $60 to $80. This client was a big factor's nightmare: a jillion little invoices, piles of paperwork and mailing, lots of verification calls, and a small fee ($2,000 x 5%) of $100 a month. Now subtract the cost of money, stamps, phone calls, etc., not to mention a $20 broker's fee, and you're not being paid much for your efforts. But what experience!

However, I couldn't have asked for a better first client. He had factored with a large factor who nearly put him out of business (never gave him reports, didn't pay several rebates, didn't keep in touch with him, and eventually closed their local office). He was probably nothing but a headache for them and I was surprised they took him on. He needed to factor for both cash flow and structure (his records were literally in a shoe box). But we were a good match. He knew how factoring worked and was patient as I learned the ropes. The dollar amounts weren't critical if either of us made mistakes…which we did. He factored several invoices to start for which he had already received payment from the customer! Clearing that up was a learning experience for both of us.

Working with him gave me confidence to do other deals. Learning with small clients helps you streamline the factoring process and prepares you for the larger accounts as they arise. After a few months of factoring small clients, you are able to take on more and bigger ones because you've gotten some bugs worked out of your system – and you are able to present a more professional appearance.

To begin with, don't take on more clients than you can handle either in terms of dollar totals or paper work. If you take on clients that push your financial limits, having one go bad on you early can knock you out of business in a hurry. You will be learning from the first few clients you factor; and you are most vulnerable at this time to taking on a client and/or customer who is a bad risk. Better to lose small amounts on small accounts.

Further, there is a lot of paper work involved in factoring. This manual provides the record keeping that works for me and which should for you as well. However, no matter how simple a system is, you'll want to customize it to your own needs and preferences. It will take a while to get the hang of what you're doing, work out the kinks and streamline your records. Again, learning the ropes is best done with small accounts and small volumes. Feed yourself in small spoonfuls while you're learning to eat.

So start small, be willing to take clients too small for anyone else at first, and learn as you grow. It's better to goof on a client with $60 invoices than one with invoices of $600, $6,000, or $60,000 – even if you can afford to factor the larger ones.

Don't Get Greedy

One of the first things you will realize when you start factoring is how much more money you can make factoring larger invoices. As we saw in Chart 3, with a 5% rate you will make $50 on a $1,000 invoice, $500 on a $10,000 invoice, and $1,000 on a $20,000 invoice. Those increasing numbers can make a rookie factor greedy. At this point you must be careful.

The second client I took on lived out of state, agreed to excellent rates and wanted to factor significantly more than my first client. Due to my inexperience, I did inadequate due diligence and the account turned ugly. To make a long story short, I spent many long, frustrating hours over several months trying to recoup what at the time was a large portion of my factoring money. Worse, I had to pay interest on money I no longer had, I lost the potential income the funds would have generated and I spent even more money trying to recover these funds. It was a sobering experience that could have killed my factoring business almost as soon as it was born.

The "make your early mistakes with small invoices" rule rings loud and clear here. Yes, you can certainly make more on bigger invoices; but you can also LOSE more – a lot more! Losing a large amount of money can be more than a painful lesson; it can knock you out of the game altogether, especially early in your factoring career. On the other hand, losing small amounts as you learn the ropes is likely to teach you a painful lesson as to whom to factor and whom not to factor, but it will not put you out of business.

Even if you can survive a large loss early, it may take a long time to recover your initial factoring pool of funds. Doing so can only be done by obtaining more funds while you're still paying for what you lost. However, now you have less to work with and will therefore make less in fees. You can make a lot of money factoring, but a single big mistake can take it all away in one fell swoop.

The lessons are obvious: be careful whom you factor and don't get greedy – ever! Factor small amounts to start with and build up the numbers gradually. You may take a chance once or twice, and profit; but taking a big chance once too often will sting you. A person who worked for a large national factoring company for some time told me that many small factors start off well and do fine for about 4 or 5 years, but then take a big hit and go out of business. Even experienced, successful factors suffer serious losses, and it can happen to rookies even more easily.

So run your business accordingly; spread your money around in small enough piles that if you lose any one or even two of them, the rest will keep you going and you will hardly feel a ripple. It's the old "don't put all your eggs in one basket" adage. That saying's been around a long time because the wisdom therein is true – especially for factors.

6

Money
Money
Money

The Cardinal Rule of Money

This brings us to the Cardinal Rule of Money. This Rule is the same whether you're factoring, gambling or playing the stock market. Each has a certain kinship with the other: risk. The Cardinal Rule of Money is, **"Don't risk more than you can afford to lose."** Don't bet the farm. Don't ante up everything you have. When going into a casino, you must decide your limit, how much you're going to play with, the most you're going to play in a given hand and the total amount you can stand to lose. Do this even before you walk in the door. Then stick to your limits...and have fun!

When you factor an account, you are taking a calculated gamble that runs something like this. Assume an 80% advance and 5% fee: on a $100 invoice, you are betting $80 that the invoice will be paid and you'll make $5. On a $1,000 invoice, you're betting $800 that you'll make $50; on a $10,000 invoice it's $8,000 and $500, and so on. Viewed this way, you may think the risk isn't worth the return, which may be true. However, with good due diligence, analysis of the businesses involved and enough transactions, you can make the odds of losing as small as possible. While risking $80 to make $5 may not sound like a good proposition, when you make enough $50's and $500's and $5,000's on deals that you know are as safe as possible, you spread your risk well and make fees that add up.

Another parallel is an auction. The only way to come out ahead in an auction is to decide before the bidding begins the maximum amount you will bid for an item. Otherwise, in the excitement of bidding, you can get carried away and end up spending lots more than something is worth. Factoring is the same: in the excitement of making larger and larger fees, you may find yourself with an account that's not worth what you're putting into it in terms of time, hassles or possible losses.

The players who are most successful in the long run are the most patient, careful and methodical – not the highest rollers. While factoring is not for the faint of heart, neither is it for the reckless.

How Much Money You Need to Factor

In an earlier section entitled "Small Numbers Add Up," we spoke of grossing $5,000 or $10,000 by factoring 10 or 20 clients a month. Naturally, it takes some seed money to be able to factor just one client for any amount. Without money to start with, you can only be a broker in the factoring business.

As a factor, you use a pool of funds that is regularly recycled. If you have $20,000 available, you could factor five clients monthly for $4,000 each (assuming their customers pay every 30 days). If you have $100,000, you could factor ten clients for $10,000 each or some other combination. However, in reality, it's not quite that clean. You'll have some accounts pay in 15 days, others in 60. The juggling act you continually play as a factor is keeping your money on the street every day possible so that it's working for you, while taking care to not run out of funds when a client comes to you to factor another set of invoices. If your pool runs dry, you'll either need to obtain more funds, co-factor a transaction or (heaven forbid) turn your client down. Hence it behooves you to know approximately when an invoice will be paid, when new invoices will be coming in and how much you will have available at a given time. Good software will help enormously here (see the chapter entitled "Factoring Software").

How much money you have to factor will determine how much you make before overhead expenses. Determine how much your money costs you (from loans and other sources) and use

Chart 6 to estimate your factoring income. Remember, the numbers assume all your money is on the street and doesn't include bad debt losses.

Chart 6: Amounts Needed to Factor

Amt of Invcs	Amt in Advncs 80%	Amt in Advncs 70%	5% Avg Factor Fees	0% Cost of Money	Income Before Overhd	Annlzd ROI w/ 80% adv	Annlzd ROI w/ 70% adv
10,000	8,000	7,000	500	0	500	75%	86%
25,000	20,000	17,500	1,250	0	1,250	75%	86%
50,000	40,000	35,000	2,500	0	2,500	75%	86%
100,000	80,000	70,000	5,000	0	5,000	75%	86%
250,000	200,000	175,000	12,500	0	12,500	75%	86%
500,000	400,000	350,000	25,000	0	25,000	75%	86%

(=12% APR)

Amt of Invcs	Amt in Advncs 80%	Amt in Advncs 70%	5% Avg Factor Fees	1% Cost of Money	Income Before Overhd	Annlzd ROI w/ 80% adv	Annlzd ROI w/ 70% adv
10,000	8,000	7,000	500	70	430	65%	74%
25,000	20,000	17,500	1,250	175	1,075	65%	74%
50,000	40,000	35,000	2,500	350	2,150	65%	74%
100,000	80,000	70,000	5,000	700	4,300	65%	74%
250,000	200,000	175,000	12,500	1,750	10,750	65%	74%
500,000	400,000	350,000	25,000	3,500	21,500	65%	74%

(=18% APR)

Amt of Invcs	Amt in Advncs 80%	Amt in Advncs 70%	5% Avg Factor Fees	1.50% Cost of Money	Income Before Overhd	Annlzd ROI w/ 80% adv	Annlzd ROI w/ 70% adv
10,000	8,000	7,000	500	105	395	59%	68%
25,000	20,000	17,500	1,250	263	988	59%	68%
50,000	40,000	35,000	2,500	525	1,975	59%	68%
100,000	80,000	70,000	5,000	1,050	3,950	59%	68%
250,000	200,000	175,000	12,500	2,625	9,875	59%	68%
500,000	400,000	350,000	25,000	5,250	19,750	59%	68%

How Much You'll Make

However you accumulate your factoring pool of funds, you can calculate how much you will earn, broadly speaking, by multiplying the total amount you have on the street by the average fee you charge, then subtracting the cost of your money and overhead. In other words, say you have $40,000 with which to factor and you keep these funds in regular circulation. With an 80% advance, you can factor $50,000 worth of invoices ($50,000 x 80% = $40,000). Multiply $50,000 times 5% (average fee you receive) and you'll make $2,500 gross. Subtract from this the cost of your money (say, an average of 12% APR or 1% per month on the amount you advance) and what you have left, after overhead expenses, is your profit. Given this scenario, with $40,000 on the street – which costs you $400 monthly (1% of $40,000), you'd make $2,100 ($2,500 – $400) monthly, minus overhead. This assumes the money is always on the street, turns regularly, and is not lost to bad debt.

Obviously, you are not going to get rich overnight factoring with numbers like this if this is your full time job. Remember, you're only learning how to swim in the shallow end of the pool – you don't begin by taking on the English Channel on day one. However, if you are working with $40,000 of your own investment money as a part time investor/factor, $2,500 is a great monthly return on $40,000.

Be patient as your factoring clientele and transaction amounts increase, and don't try to grow too fast. Just like a baby, allow yourself a good year to learn how to walk in this business.

The key strategies are to:

1. Have as large a pool of money available to you as you can; the more you have, the more you can make (yet realize that the more clients you factor, the more record keeping you'll have...and eventually that will mean employees).

2. Keep as much of your money on the street as you can. If you're paying to use someone else's funds, you're losing

money if you don't keep it in circulation; if it's your own money, you don't make as much.

3. Pay back loans/lines of credit you're not using as soon as you know you don't or won't need the cash. Don't pay for money you're not using to make money.

4. If possible, use money you don't pay to use (your own or from interest-free sources).

5. Keep your overhead as low as possible.

6. Don't factor accounts that take too long to pay (they tie up your money and may never pay).

7. Be careful which clients and customers you take on, and don't get lazy with your due diligence. One hit not only can wipe out principal and profits, but it can take months from which to recover.

How Much to Charge

This is your call, depending on how much you want to make and what the market will bear. One small factor charges 7 to 10% for the first 30 days and goes up from there, which is a tidy profit. Another charges a flat 9% for the first 90 days. Since around 2% to 5% for 30 days is fairly normal for larger invoices, these may not be out of line. However, realize that those numbers can sound astronomical to potential clients – 10% translates to 120% APR in their minds – and could scare them off.

You will get more business if your charges are in the 5% range; the question is, can you make enough with rates like that? It's up to you. You may or may not want to adjust your rates and advances according to the stability of your clients and their customers; but remember, we're dealing with small potatoes and you may talk your way out of a deal if your rates sound too high. I've found a straight forward approach to work well: "My advances usually start at 75% to 80% may go up slightly after that. Typical rates average around 5% every 30 days, and 1.67% for each additional 10 days, up to 90 days. At 90 days, recourse kicks in. If conditions warrant, the rates may be slightly higher or lower, but that doesn't happen very often."

If you have been trained in using a business calculator you can dig back into your training manual and relearn how to arrive at rates. Personally I find that tiresome. Simple, round rates don't make anybody's head hurt, including mine. As long as you make enough to help clients, run your own business, and get ahead, that's what it's all about. Plus your clients will look upon you as a people person interested in helping them, rather than a number cruncher who makes decisions hunched over a calculator. In their position, which kind of person would you rather deal with?

Where to Get the Money You Need

Your original pool of funds can originate from several sources.

Your Own Resources. These may be the easiest or the most difficult to obtain, depending on how much you have or are willing to use. Your own resources can include savings, inheritances, insurance policies, retirement plans, IRA's, stocks, bonds, mutual funds, the sale of property, valuables, a business, or whatever you may have available. Just remember the Cardinal Rule of Money: Don't play with more than you can afford to lose.

There are two schools of thought on whose money is best to use, your own or OPM (Other People's Money). The advantages of using someone else's resources are:

1. You can make money even if you don't have any of your own, and/or

2. You can build up profits without risking your own money.

The disadvantages of using someone else's are:

1. It's harder to get

2. You have to pay it back (whether you make money on it or lose it), and

3. You probably have to pay it back with interest.

My personal feeling is that it's better to use as much of your own money as possible, but use only money you can afford to lose. If you've got $50,000 or $100,000 available, you can turn quicker profits with that than if you have to pay interest back from the profits you make factoring. Further, if you take a hit, you won't have to pay interest on money you no longer have. If you have $10,000 and want to have a pool of $100,000, use your own $10,000 and get the rest from the sources below. Over time, pay them back to the point where you're using as much of your own money as you can: you'll then make more because the cost of your money is less.

A good strategy for using your own money is this: assuming your company is incorporated, lend your business your own money at 12% interest APR. Write a promissory note with the terms of the loan, just as you would for any private lender (see below). Every month, your company pays interest on the borrowed funds. You can either pull this interest out of the company for your own needs, saving the payroll headaches of salary payments; or if you can afford to, leave the interest in the business so you have more factoring funds available building up over time. Check with your accountant or attorney for the most advantageous way to do this.

Relatives/Friends. After using your own resources, these may be the next best source of funds, as long as you're on good terms and these people trust your judgment. You can offer relatives and friends a far better return on their money than they can get at banks with savings accounts or CD's. However, they need to realize that investing in you poses a greater risk and if you go out of business their money is gone. Be up front about that, but also instill in them the confidence that this will not happen.

What kind of arrangements can you make with relatives and friends? That's up to you. What may be most beneficial to you is to draw up a promissory note (see below), in which they loan you a specified amount of money for a specified length of time (for example, $10,000 for one year) or with some other specified date of maturity. You will pay them a certain interest percentage – 12%, 15%, 18% – you decide what you can handle based on your factoring rates (or figure your factoring rates based on how much the money costs you) but keep it as close to 12% as you can. These rates must be attractive to them and still be profitable for you. You can make payments monthly, quarterly, or roll it over and pay the total interest when the note matures. The terms of the loan will dictate its payback.

Have your note or loan put in writing even with a relative, and stipulate a definite maturity date. The payment schedule, interest rate, and amortization schedule should also be printed and included. All this documentation protects you by proving this money is being loaned to your corporation, not given to you personally. This makes it clear that this is NOT a personal arrangement on which you might be taxed. Also, make it clear the persons giving you the loan are not "investors," as Securities laws don't permit you to take on "investors" unless you meet rather stringent requirements. The penalties for noncompliance can be severe. It's a good idea to have a few months' gap at the end of the note before arrangements for another loan, again to keep the loans from looking like an investment. Give regular monthly printed reports of how much interest they have made (see the sample Lender Report below). This reminds them not only that they are helping your business and you appreciate it, but that they're making money with you.

Lender Report

from
ABC Financial Services
to
John Q. Lender

Amount of Note: $10,000
Interest: 12% APR

Pmt #	APR Interest	Monthly Payments Amt.	Date Payment Due	Date Payment Sent	Amt. Paid to Date
1	12%	$100.00	6/1	6/1	$100.00
2	12%	$100.00	7/1	7/1	$100.00
3	12%	$100.00	8/1	8/1	$100.00
4	12%	$100.00	9/1	9/1	$100.00
5	12%	$100.00	10/1	10/1	$100.00
6	12%	$100.00	11/1		
7	12%	$100.00	12/1		
8	12%	$100.00	1/1		
9	12%	$100.00	2/1		
10	12%	$100.00	3/1		
11	12%	$100.00	4/1		
12	12%	$100.00	5/1		
Totals		$1,200.00			$500.00

You may also find people who prefer to supply funds for specific transactions, clients, or customers. This works much like co-factoring and potentially offers a higher rate of return to your lender. Just be sure you keep careful track of which lender has funds with which client, schedule, or invoice/s; and pay them in a manner agreeable to both of you.

Self-Directed IRAs. Utilizing funds in self-directed IRAs from Equity Trust Company (previously Mid-Ohio Securities) or PENSCO Trust Company can be a great way to obtain working capital from others and provide them with high yielding tax-deferred income. Here's how it works.

Your lender establishes a new IRA with one of these companies with either newly invested IRA funds and/or by transferring money from an existing IRA. The holding company then becomes the custodian of these funds; they do not make recommendations as to where to invest the money; they simply do as directed by the IRA owner. Hence the term "self-directed" IRA.

The owner of the IRA instructs Equity or PENSCO where to invest the funds, who then sends a check as directed. The company receiving the funds makes interest payments to the custodian on behalf of the IRA holder.

How do you get started? First, when you have a lender who wants to place IRA funds in your company, contact either Equity (www.trustetc.com) or PENSCO (www.PENSCO.com) and let them know you own a factoring company and have a private lender with IRA funds. Your lender wishes to invest this IRA with your firm through their company. You will need to fill out paperwork which indicates yours is a legitimate factoring business that meets their criteria to be a recipient of IRA funds.

Meanwhile your lender contacts Equity or PENSCO and fills out forms as well. These documents will include a transfer form, by which funds from an existing IRA fund are transferred to Equity or PENSCO, who then becomes the manager of the fund. The lender can transfer all or just a portion of another IRA when creating the new IRA. The lender also fills out a Direction of Investment form, which indicates the amount and where the individual wishes to place the IRA – in this case, with your company.

You then provide a promissory note or whatever documents you use to securitize the funds and give this to the custodial company. Once all the paperwork is in place (expect it to take about a month when setting this up for the first time) and the custodian has received funds from the investor, the management company sends you a check. And there's your working capital.

You then make interest payments to the management company on behalf of your lender according to the terms of your Promissory Note. These checks are made out, as an example, to "PENSCO Trust Company DBA (IRA holder's name)." You do not send interest payments to the lender, but to the custodial company. They place these payments in an interest-bearing account on behalf of the IRA holder, who can then further direct the use of these funds.

The custodial companies charge fees which are comparable to each other, though calculated somewhat differently. The fee rates depend on the size of the investment and include charges for various management services. About $10,000 is a reasonable minimum amount for one of these investments, as the fees for sums less than this will take too much of the interest you'll pay.

The benefit of this arrangement is that you pay the same interest you would to lenders providing traditional (yet taxed) funds, while your lender receives the interest tax-deferred in her self-directed IRA. She is not taxed on the interest until her IRA is cashed in, probably many years in the future.

Potential lenders probably have IRA funds in relatively low-yield investments. Placing just a portion of these IRA funds in your factoring company at 12% APR (or whatever you pay) is certainly more attractive than low single-digit yields investors are accustomed to receiving – and it's tax-deferred, to boot.

With specific restrictions, you can invest your own IRA funds in your company by using a self-directed IRA managed by either of these two trust companies. The main constraint is this: to invest your IRA in your company, you must be a minority (no more than 49%) owner of your business, and the other owner(s) cannot be close relatives (spouse, parents, children, siblings). These restrictions are dictated by federal law, and either Equity or PENSCO can give more details.

Self-Employed 401(k) Plan. If you want to retain majority or 100% ownership of your company and still utilize your own IRA funds, an alternative is to establish a Self-Employed 401 (k) plan.

Small business owners with no employees or only a spouse as an employee can establish a Self-Employed 401(k) plan and take a loan from that plan. Individuals can borrow up to the lesser of $50,000 or 50% of the balance in their Self-Employed 401(k). If you need access to capital and want to tap into your retirement accounts, establishing a Self-Employed 401(k) plan allows you to borrow from your retirement funds.

The loan from your Self-Employed 401(k) is not treated as a withdrawal. As such is not subject to tax nor the 10% penalty for early withdrawal as long as you repay the loan on time. There is no limit on the amount of money that you can transfer to a Self-Employed 401(k) plan. The transfer can be from a 401(k) you had with a previous employer, from a qualified plan that you currently have in your business, or from your existing IRAs. Once you have money in your Self-Employed 401(k) you can request a loan. A Self-Employed 401(k) loan can be used for any purpose.

Repayment of your loan balance is subject to government guidelines, but generally you have five years to repay the loan. The interest rate on the loan is usually close to the prime rate. Your loan payments and interest payments go into your 401(k) account, so in essence you pay the loan back to yourself. Expect to pay a small administrative fee to process your Self-Employed 401(k) plan loan. Also, you may be subject to mutual fund contingent deferred sales charges or other sales charges when you transfer money into and out of your Self-Employed 401(k) plan.

The Self-Employed 401(k) is for small business owners only. You must be the only employee in your business, or if you have employees all of them must be co-owners in the business or spouses of the owners.

This information is from Lamaute Capital, Inc., an investment brokerage firm in Alexandria, Virginia, specializing in retirement investments. For more information go to their web site at www.investsafe.com, and in particular the page www.investsafe.com/financing4.html.

Investors. Generally, these are best to keep within your circle of friends and relatives. Be careful about advertising for funds, as you can get in hot water with Securities and Exchange laws if you solicit funds for investment. To be safe, refer to anyone who provides you money as a "lender" rather than an "investor." Consult with your lawyer about using someone else's money in your pool of factoring funds to avoid problems with the SEC –

both when you start taking on lenders, and when the number of lenders you have becomes more than a few.

Banks/Institutions. Banks, credit unions, and lending institutions are becoming more creative in ways they loan money, but they're still extremely careful and prove impossible for many small business people to use as a source of funds. Trying to get a bank loan for factoring funds can teach you volumes about the frustrations your clients experience (see the *FactorTips* article "ACH and a Story about Bankers" in the Appendix) when attempting to do the very same thing: trying to get money to start or grow their business. It is likely why they turn to you in the first place.

Banks require at least two or three years' business financials. If your factoring company is new you're probably out of luck getting a business loan or line of credit. Most banks don't want to loan to factoring companies anyway. (Why? See the first two paragraphs of the chapter "Reducing Your Risk.")

Your best bet may be to get a bank or mortgage company financing through a personal line of credit that is based on your regular job (if you still have it), your spouse's job, and/or the equity you have in your home or other property. If you have a fair amount of equity in your home, this may be the best source of fairly large amounts of factoring money, as long as you don't mind having a second mortgage. If your business is the least bit successful, and you haven't taken any bad hits, factoring will easily pay this as you go. However, if you have a major loss, you could lose your home.

Credit Cards. If you have good credit, you probably get frequent invitations in the mail to accept new credit cards, often with no yearly fee and a substantially lower interest rate for the first three or six months. If you decide to use credit cards to pay for receivables you'll buy – and let me be blunt…it's not a good idea – you must make an unbreakable agreement with yourself that funds you obtain this way will be used only for factoring, and not for paying your regular business (or personal) bills.

The reason is simple: credit cards are easy to obtain for those who can qualify for them, but the finance charges can eat you alive if you're not making money from the credit they provide.

Put differently: if you're paying 18% (not unusual) for credit card money, and you use it to pay a $200 phone bill, that bill actually costs you $200 plus the finance charge every month. Worse, it's not generating income to help you pay the debt.

However, if you use credit card money with which to factor, that 18% works out to 1.5% monthly; if you're charging 5% monthly factoring fees, you're still coming out 3.5% ahead (or 42% APR – not a bad investment from any angle). However, keep in mind that most credit cards charge an "advance fee" of 3%, so in reality the cost of cash is: 3% (first month) + interest rate. What's more credit card interest compounds on unpaid balances making it even more expensive than other traditional loans.

The danger of losing advances made from cash borrowed with credit cards makes this type of financing very risky and I discourage you from using it. If you have good credit, credit cards are easy to get but they pose great personal liability. Bad debt losses with credit card-borrowed money can be horribly expensive, possibly taking years to repay. If you don't repay it your good credit rating will be ruined. In general, credit cards are not the way you should finance your factoring company. Remember the Cardinal Rule of Money.

Factor Funding Sources. Companies who fund factors do exist, though they are not interested in funding quite small factors or those who work the business part-time. The three companies listed below have increasingly larger minimums, and you need to be serious about the factoring business to qualify.

Capitol Resource Funding is a factor as well as a lender to factors, so they understand the business very well. This means you don't need to spend hours educating them about what you do, and you certainly don't need to convince them of the value of factoring, as may be the case with other sources of funds. Their mission is not only to fund factors but to provide support services. They offer credit training, operational training, software support, sales training, audit services, and workout assistance.

CRF has two funding programs factors will find helpful. First is their Refactoring Program, which provides up to 100% funding and facilities from $100,000 to $500,000. This program is "hands on" for CRF at the client level. CRF obtains a full credit file on the client and conducts their own due diligence. They specify servicing parameters that are subsequently done by the factor, such as verification procedures, collection procedures, and so on. CRF looks more at the client than the factoring company for repayment (although both this and the Refactoring Program are with recourse to the factor).

A discount fee is charged the factor on the invoices funded. The factor earns the spread between the amount charged to the client and the amount he pays CRF. For example, CRF may charge 1% per 15 days to the factor. Therefore, if the factor charges 2% for 15 days to the client, and the invoice pays in 40 days, CRF earns 3% of the invoice amount and the Factor earns 3% (6% factor fee charged to the client for 40 days, less the 3% charged by CRF to factor).

Their second offering is called the Interfactoring Program, which is a lending program providing up to 85% funding. Here, credit lines from $500,000 to $10 million are available. Factors using this program receive funds which provide a portion of their advances to clients. For example, Capitol Resource Funding might provide 80% of your 80% advance to a client, or 64% of the invoice. Thus for $10,000 worth of invoices you buy, you could borrow $6,400 of the $8,000 you advance. This means you need some cash of your own, but are able to purchase far more receivables than you could without CRF. The factor is required to maintain equity and/or sub-debt in his company, is subject to CRF field audits, and a light review of the clients he is funding.

The larger your line and the more money you utilize, the lower the interest rate you pay. Costs are based on an annual interest rate plus a facility fee on the line of credit. Pricing depends on the track record of the factor and amount of equity/sub-debt. The minimum line of credit offered is usually $1 million (although usage may start significantly less than that). CRF's net pricing is more than a bank, but their flexibility should allow their factor clients to fund more transactions, therefore making this a more profitable method of funding operations.

In short, under the Interfactoring Program, CRF lends to the factor based on the factor's financial and operational conditions. This is available to factors who have a track record, experienced management, operating procedures, and profits. The Refactoring Program is for the small, less established factor, and CRF micromanages more of the process. Their desire is for a Refactoring client to develop and graduate into the Interfactoring Program.

Here is a brief outline of their process.

1. Initial Procedure

   To explore a funding program and obtain a proposal, submit the following:

   - A completed funding application
   - Most recent financial statement
   - Last two year-end fiscal financial statements
   - Articles of Incorporation
   - Sample copy of contract or purchase order

2. Acceptance

   Once you have the proposal of terms, the next things include:

   - A signed acceptance of the proposal
   - Due diligence fee
   - Copy of invoices to be funded
   - Other financial information as required.

3. Due Diligence and Funding

   Upon receipt of the above, the following occur:

   - Balance of financial information is compiled and analyzed
   - Contract assignments are prepared and executed
   - Credit, lien, and judgment searches are conducted
   - Invoices are verified
   - Transaction documents are executed
   - Funds are distributed

Factors who are ready to work at the upper end of small receivables or higher will find CRF to be an excellent resource. Visit their web site at www.crf.com or call 888-273-2424.

Finance Company Services, a division of **Textron Financial**, works with a diversified group of finance companies including asset-based lenders, factors, distressed asset purchasers, specialty and captive lenders, rent-to-own chains, payday lenders, and leasing companies. Their commitments typically range from $2 million to $20 million, with syndication capability for larger facilities. With a $9 billion balance sheet, Finance Company Services has the infrastructure and resources to meet the ongoing capital requirements of their clients.

Additional services include out-sourced due diligence, best practices operational reviews, policy and procedure manual drafting, backroom support, and other incubations services. They also offer a variety of specialized market lending, asset management, and insurance products and services.

Their toll-free number is 866-832-3863; their web site is www.textronfinancial.com.

Foothill Financial Services Funding is a division of Wells Fargo that provides financing for specialty commercial finance companies. Loan sizes are from $10 million to $50 million, while larger transactions would be syndicated. Foothill funds asset-based lenders, factors, real estate lenders, independent SBA lenders, distressed asset acquisition companies, equipment leasing and finance companies, commercial vehicle finance companies, and emerging asset classes

Foothill provides revolving lines of credit for recourse and non-recourse financing of financial assets. They fund up to 90% of eligible receivables, and advance rates are based upon historic and industry default rates, obligor concentrations, and asset term (which are one to five years). Acceptable collateral include accounts receivables, commercial revolving credit notes, short and intermediate term commercial notes, lease receivables, commercial and residential mortgages, and other financial assets. Interest rates are floating over Prime; closing fees, unused line fees and loan administration fees are applicable.

To learn more, visit their web site at www.foothillcapital.com; click on the Business Finance Division link, and from there click on the Financial Services Funding link. Their national headquarters phone number is 800 868-9292.

Other Factors. When used in conjunction with one or more of the above, other factors' resources can be an excellent way to stretch your factoring funds. Become familiar with other factors who are open to this idea, and make arrangements with them to co-factor clients. If you split expenses and income 50-50, the record keeping is pretty straight forward. You may even find larger factors willing to allow you to appear as the sole factor to your clients, while they supply most or even all the funds for your transactions, and pay you a greater fee for doing the record keeping than if you were only the broker. Using other factors' resources allows you to take on more clients you otherwise would have had to broker, refer to someone else, or turn away.

Be aware, however, that most experienced factors who are interested in "participation" (co-factoring) will require that they be the recording factor – i.e. the one providing the back office work. Understandably, they trust their own procedures more than someone else's.

If you must use other people's money and not your own (or you own credit), it may be best to simply borrow it. If you do, the best arrangement for you is to have an unsecured loan based on a Loan Agreement with each lender, and a Promissory Note for each loan. Promissory Note "A" below is used for loans unattached to specific transactions; Promissory Note "B" is used for loans made for particular factoring Schedules or invoices.

Generally, operate your business as a corporation or LLC, and if possible, do not personally guarantee business obligations including the loan obligation provided in the Lender Agreement. However, if the only way to obtain funds is through a personal guaranty, consider using a form similar to the one below. If possible, include a limitation on the guarantee by time, amount, or otherwise. For example, here is a limitation based on time:

"Limitation. This guaranty shall automatically terminate on the 180th calendar day following the first date shown above, and shall not apply to any loans, notes or arrangements by Lender made after that date, nor to any loans, notes or arrangements which are not in default as of that date. However, it shall not terminate as to any loans, notes or arrangements made by Lender in which there is a default as of the termination date, provided that guarantor has received written notice of default prior to the termination date."

Some guaranty forms don't provide for attorney fees and collection costs; you're better off using a form without these when you're the guarantor. The worst form of guaranty to use when you are the guarantor is that used by larger regional banks for commercial loans. Often two or three pages in length with very fine print, it includes waivers for every possible claim or defense a guarantor might have, lasts forever, and covers all forms of debt or obligation the borrower might have to the lender. You will do well to avoid such an extensive guaranty in any circumstance.

Sample Loan Agreement and Promissory Note documents are on the following pages. These documents will vary in form from state to state; there may be state laws and regulations concerning loans of this type. In every important business transaction – including these – you should consult your attorney and accountant about the proper wording of agreements so your interests are protected, and the accounting and tax results can be understood. Word to the wise: consult these professionals before your transactions are consummated.

Lender Agreement

This agreement, dated _____, 200__, is by and between _____ ("Borrower"), whose address is _____ and _____ ("Lender"), whose address is _____.

Recitals

1. Borrower is engaged in the business of purchasing accounts receivable from various clients at a discount below face value; and

2. Lender desires to loan money to Borrower for the purposes, and upon the terms, as set forth herein.

IN CONSIDERATION OF THE FOREGOING, the parties hereto agree as follows:

1. Sums. Lender agrees to loan to Borrower the initial sum of $ _____. Upon the Agreement of the parties, Lender may loan additional sums to Borrower under the terms and conditions provided herein.

2. Sole use. The amounts loaned by Lender under this Agreement are to be used by Borrower solely to purchase accounts receivable from clients of Borrower.

3. Deposits and rate. The amounts loaned under this Agreement will be deposited by Borrower in its working capital account at _____ Bank until such time as funds are withdrawn to purchase accounts of various clients. Borrower will pay Lender simple interest on amounts advanced under this Agreement at the rate of and on a timely basis according to a Promissory Note for each loan the Lender provides.

4. Terms of repayment. Each loan advanced by Lender shall be evidenced by a signed promissory note from Borrower, providing among other items, the terms of repayment.

5. Not a security, business purpose. The parties agree that Lender is making loans to Borrower for a business purpose, that Borrower will use these funds solely in its factoring business, that this is not a personal, family or consumer transaction by either Lender or Borrower, that it is a business loan arrangement not an investment contract, and that repayment by Borrower is due regardless of the operation or profitability of Borrower's business.

6. *(Optional – use only if Lender requires collateral):* Security interest. Borrower hereby grants Lender a security interest in the following personal property ("collateral"), which security interest shall last so long as there is a balance of more than $_____ (the "Floor") owing by Borrower to Lender. The collateral is (a) Borrower's contract rights with, and (b) accounts receivable which are owed to or factored by, the following clients of Borrower: _____.

Lender agrees there is no security interest in contract rights, receivables or other assets related to any other client of Borrower, or of any other assets or property of Borrower, and (upon request by Borrower) Lender shall so certify in writing. To perfect the security interest, upon request Borrower shall execute and deliver to Seller a form of financing statement which describes the collateral in the same way, and which is appropriate in form under all the circumstances. When the total balance of all loans is below the Floor shown above, upon request Lender shall acknowledge the security interest no longer exists and shall terminate any UCC Financing Statements.

7. Obligation. The obligation of Lender to make future loans may be terminated by Borrower at any time, or by Lender on not less than 120 days notice; but that termination shall not affect the then-outstanding obligations to make payments under Notes to Lender. For all loans and notes, the parties agree that there shall be no penalty or fee for any partial or complete prepayment.

Lender

Dated: _____

By: _____

Print Name: _____

By: _____

Print Name: _____

Borrower

Dated: _____

By: _____

Company Name

By: _____

Print Name: _____

Promissory Note "A"

$ _____   _____
                                (City) (State)

                                _____
                                (Date)
FOR VALUE RECEIVED the undersigned promise(s) to pay to the order of
_____ the principal sum of _____
dollars ($ _____) together with interest thereon from date at the rate of
_____ percent (____%) per annum until maturity, said interest being
payable monthly on the _____ day of each and every month in lawful money
of the United States beginning on the _____ day of _____,
200___, in monthly installments of _____ dollars ($_____),
and continuing thereafter until _____.

The maker and endorser severally waives demand, protest and notice of
maturity, non-payment or protest and all requirements necessary to him/her
liable as maker and endorser and, should litigation be necessary to enforce this
note, the maker and endorser waives trial by jury and consents to the personal
jurisdiction and venue of a court of subject matter jurisdiction located in the
State of _____ and County of _____.

The maker and endorser further agrees to pay all costs of collection, including a
reasonable attorney's fee in case the principal of this note or any payment on
the principal or any interest thereon is not paid at the respective maturity
thereof, or in case it becomes necessary to protect the security hereof, whether
suit be brought or not.

This note is to be construed and enforced according to the laws of the State of
_____; upon default in the payment of interest when due, the whole
sum of principal remaining shall, at the option of the holder, become
immediately due and payable and it shall accrue interest at _____ (____%)
percent, from the date of default.

Default shall include but not be limited to non-payment of any respective
installment within ten (10) days from the due date set out herein after ten (10)
days written notice to the undersigned, or nonpayment on three different
occasions of any installments within five (5) days subsequent to the due date
therefor set out herein.

                        (Your Company Name)_____
                        Corporation

        By: _____
                Its President

        Attest: _____
                Its Secretary

Promissory Note "B"

$_____   _____
                                 (City) (State)

                                 _____
                                 (Date)

FOR VALUE RECEIVED the undersigned promise(s) to pay to the order of
_____the   principal   sum   of
_____ dollars ($ _____) together with
_____ percent (_____ %) of fees earned thereon from purchase of
Accounts Receivable effected by the funds provided for this note, to wit:

_____

_____

_____

   The maker and endorser waives demand, protest and notice of maturity, non-payment or protest and all requirements necessary to hold him/her liable as maker and endorser and, should litigation be necessary to enforce this note, the maker and endorser waives trial by jury and consents to the personal jurisdiction and venue of a court of subject matter jurisdiction located in the State of _____ and County of _____.

The maker and endorser further agrees to pay all costs of collection, including a reasonable attorney's fee in case the principal of this note or any payment on the principal or any interest thereon is not paid at the respective maturity thereof, or in case it becomes necessary to protect the security hereof, whether suit be brought or not.

This note is to be construed and enforced according to the laws of the State of _____; upon default in the payment of interest when due, the whole sum of principal remaining shall, at the option of the holder, become immediately due and payable and it shall accrue interest at _____ (____%) percent, from the date of default.

Default shall include but not be limited to non-payment of any respective installment within ten (10) days from the due date set out herein after ten (10) days written notice to the undersigned, or nonpayment on three different occasions of any installments within five (5) days subsequent to the due date therefor set out herein.

                    (Your Company Name)_____
                    Corporation

          By: _____
                    Its President

      Attest: _____
                    Its Secretary

7
Co-Factoring

As mentioned earlier, co-factoring is a tool that can help inexperienced factors feel comfortable with their first few deals, as well as provide extra resources if under-capitalized. But co-factoring assumes both factors hold each other in absolute trust as to honesty and integrity. Both also need to agree about what each looks for in clients, how to screen them, and how to determine advances, rates, and other considerations.

Factors who want to co-factor with you may want you to be bonded (which is reasonable if you don't know each other), need to understand and have confidence in how you operate, and expect you to keep in close contact. The rewards of such a relationship can be great for both of you. You make higher fees than you would brokering and have the funds to handle more and/or larger accounts than you could with only your own resources. The other factor gains new accounts that would be unavailable otherwise, which are serviced by a knowledgeable person right in the field, at a cost less than in-house staff. A win-win proposition all the way around!

If you supply funds to another factor, you must be absolutely confident in his honesty, integrity, due diligence and professionalism with which he handles clients and customers. It's best to personally know factors to whom you are providing funds. If you don't, at least a background check on them is wise. Use a written agreement in all cases. I strongly recommend you know and trust the other factor quite well before you begin doing business, as the potential for incompetence (if not outright fraud) is quite real, and you must protect yourself. On the other hand, remember that factoring is a risky business no matter how skilled and honest you and other factors may be. You can lose money even when you're both above board and everything looks safe. The Cardinal Rule of Money again applies when you co factor.

Using the most appropriate legal documents for co-factoring, especially with someone you don't know well, is something of a legal quagmire, as you'll see below. Consult your attorney as to what is best for your situation. I appreciate my attorney, Stewart Martin, for his extensive input into the rest of this chapter.

Because co-factoring offers such great potential for two or more beginning, small factors, I asked Mr. Martin to provide a form which could be readily used by two factors in this case – one acting remotely and one acting locally. However, such a business relationship is neither simple nor capable of a single form which would apply in very many circumstances. What follows is his response.

There are several phases in a co-factoring relationship: initial discussion, sharing due diligence forms and methods, drafting an agreement, implementing the new relationship and monitoring for changes that will improve the arrangement. Let's look at each.

The Discussion Phase

When you begin talking with a prospective co-factor, explore the normal business practices you each use. Be sure you both see "eye-to-eye" on most if not all critical issues before you do any business together. First consider the limits that you would place on clients and/or customers. List and discuss the due diligence procedures you each use and the comfort level you both need. Also consider how you obtain your clients, what steps you use to qualify them, and other business operations you each find important. This will let you both understand the similarities, and more importantly, the differences between your present business operations. Some folks are more "loose" than others would be comfortable with, or take less time and effort in qualifying a client or customer. By discussing issues like these in advance, you will know whether you can cooperate and feel comfortable working with each other; and, if you can establish that all-important relationship of trust. Also discuss what risks you are willing to take and not willing to take; and which kinds of business owners you trust and do not trust.

We'll use the term "Funding factor" to describe the person who primarily provides funds and "Local factor" for the person who primarily does the operations and due diligence.

An important aspect for the Local factor is how much cash, on a regular basis, the Funding factor can provide. The Local factor wants to establish long-term consistent relationships with his clients, and to do that, needs a regular source of funds. Both co-factors must understand what will be provided by each: advances, due diligence, bookkeeping etc. The forms to be used for each aspect of the business should be exchanged and approved. You may need to compromise in making one or another choice but just be sure that you each agree to use the same documents for your formal agreements.

The Drafting Phase

As you enter the phase of drafting a written agreement between the Funding and Local factor, you should list all the duties of each person. Here are some sample duties that you might consider:

The Local Factor might be responsible for:

- Performing the due diligence (application form, UCC-1, credit checks, etc.)
- Maintaining regular personal contact with the client
- Record keeping and the reception and disbursement of client/customer funds
- Providing regular reports to the client and co-factor.

The Funding Factor might be responsible for:

- Supplying the Local factor with funds for advances
- Reviewing due diligence and reports
- Making observations, suggestions, and raising questions to best serve the client, customers, and both co-factors.

You should carefully define the standards for acceptable clients and customers. Also define the specific steps that the Local factor will go through in the due diligence process.

Now comes the difficult part: what type of relationship will you have? There are a variety of relationships that might provide the same end result: money from the Funding to the Local factor, and service by the Local factor to assure quality. But each of these different approaches has different legal rights and responsibilities, and they fall into patterns based on the evolution of the law in other areas of business and finance. Consider which one may suit your needs, and which one may suit the needs of your co-factor.

Types of Co-Factoring Relationships

The Lender and Business Factor. In this arrangement, the Funding factor would simply act as a lender and provide either fixed amounts of money with a pre-agreed repayment schedule, or meet the "requirements" of the Local factor. Requirements financing gives the Local factor more of what he or she wants, but can make the Funding factor nervous. Under an unlimited requirements arrangement, the Local factor might notify the Funding factor that by next Tuesday $20,000 needs to be wired to the Local's account. Therefore, most requirements agreements will have a ceiling on the amount that is available in a single request, the total amount that is outstanding, and a minimum number of days notice before any request for funds. You will want to think carefully about who has the right to end the relationship, and how the wind-up will occur, etc. This is essential so that the Local factor will have enough lead time to replace the funds or let his clients know there is a limit on the factoring available.

Normally, there is a loan agreement establishing the arrangement overall, and separate promissory notes for each advance or "loan." To secure each loan, there is usually a blanket security agreement, but I use the word "blanket" with caution. A Local factor normally will not want to have only one lender, and may have arrangements with a bank or other lenders or co-factors. So it is important to segregate the lien interests (security interests) which each lender has. If the Local factor already has a blanket lien with a bank, he may need a subordination agreement between the Funding factor and the bank, providing that the

Funding factor's new lien will have priority over the blanket lien of the bank, at least as to certain collateral. So, in segregating the collateral, consider whether you want to do it by client, or by each Schedule of Accounts which are purchased, or some other method. Refer to the preceding chapter on lending arrangements, and the sample Lender Agreement and Promissory Note "B."

Partnership or Joint Venture Agreements. It is not very likely that either of you will be so comfortable that you are prepared to be partners for all purposes. However, there is a special kind of business form called a "joint venture." A joint venture seems similar to a partnership but is limited in the scope of the business, or is limited in how long it lasts. So you might be joint venturers with a particular client for a period of one year, or for that client indefinitely, or for a group of clients for nine months. These arrangements are very flexible, and you should each discuss what makes the other feel comfortable and might be profitable. Besides, in defining how long the relationship could last, you might consider whether it will automatically renew or if it requires a notice from one party or the other to renew. In any partnership or venture agreement, you will want to carefully spell out the duties of each party: to loan funds or contribute them as capital, to do due diligence, to use forms (it is good to attach these as exhibits), to notify each other on a regular basis, to provide certain reports every so many days, etc. Keep in mind that in a partnership or joint venture, to the extent it exists, each person is personally liable for the entire business operation. And, if the public is misled or thinks the authority of a joint venturer is broader than you have provided in your contract, it may have "apparent authority" which could bind you to an even larger scope of responsibility than you thought. So, it is important to discuss which materials will be given to clients, how advertising, telephone listings, and other details which the public will notice are to be conducted.

Agent for Disclosed Factor. Since your prospect or existing client is already used to factoring, another approach is for the Local factor to act as an agent for the Funding factor. In this situation, the ultimate responsibility and power rests with the Funding factor; and, the local factor is their dutiful agent. By "dutiful" I mean that traditional fiduciary duties of loyalty, care, skill and business opportunity would normally bind the Local factor to the Funding factor. If there is any variation from that general rule, it should be spelled out in the agency agreement between the two factors. For instance, since the agent is already in a factoring business it may mean only certain selected opportunities (over $50,000 or in a certain industry) are given to the Funding factor; the rest can be kept with the Local factor and not shared. This agency relationship should be disclosed, normally, to the client who is being serviced. If it is not disclosed, the Local factor will be personally liable and on the hook in every respect.

A Separate Co-Factor Company. The last approach, the most involved, and yet perhaps most powerful in the long run, is to consider setting up a co-factoring company. We know there is strength in numbers, and the combined financial strength of two or more factors, along with their personal guarantees, might allow not only their spare cash to be used, but to obtain reasonable interest rates on bank or private money which can be leveraged by the individual factoring businesses. I suggest that such a separate company be formed as either a corporation or limited liability company (LLC), and I would imagine the individual factors would be shareholders or members of that company. Obviously rules of governance (who has votes, whether there is a single manager or president in charge), percentage interests of ownership, voting, capital contributions, the ability to be "redeemed" out of the company upon demand, who will receive funds (whether in rotation or pro rata availability) and a number of other matters would need to be discussed and agreed in writing. Such a sophisticated arrangement is beyond the scope of this book, but hopefully some of these points will get you thinking if you believe a long-term permanent company is the answer.

Implementing the New Relationship

Selecting which of these methods of co-factoring is most appropriate is difficult, and very important. You should involve your business attorney early to obtain her suggestions about structure and key points to consider in the negotiations. If you don't have one, by all means run to the nearest State Bar referral service and get an experienced attorney by your side. Co-factoring is too risky to try it "alone."

By the way, there are different types and personalities of attorneys. Not all of them are sharks or those who see everything through the eyes of a jury-trial advocate. Some attorneys are entrepreneurial in nature, or more cooperative. You might consider having your attorney read sections of this book. Although you may have to pay for the time reading, ask if she'll volunteer it as background work in preparing to do her legal work. Remember, you probably know far more about factoring now than your attorney will initially. Having a better understanding of factoring and your business will help your attorney give you better advice and more productive suggestions for how to negotiate a co-factoring arrangement.

Monitoring for Changes

Finally, realize that no new venture (including a co-factor arrangement) starts off perfectly. Remember the Apollo missions to the moon? While they were launched in the general direction that would lead them to a moon orbit, hundreds if not thousands of course corrections were required in order to land successfully. Likewise, in your relationship with a co-factor, you should each monitor the other's behavior, live up to the agreement that you carefully drafted, and fine-tune the procedures as well as the whole arrangement as you go along. Probably every week or two you should call your co-factor on the phone and touch bases on co-factored clients. This way, your relationship will strengthen, the quality of each business will improve, and ultimately the profitability of each co-factor will increase. Co-factoring is a complex arrangement, both legally and logistically, so be sure to go into it with your eyes open.

The more time you spend planning, the less likely you will have risks of upset, misunderstanding or losses.

8

Break-Even Analysis

I was in a new client's office one day and noticed the following quote conspicuously printed in large bold letters on her desk hutch:

**"The secret to financial success
is to spend less than you make
and do it for a long time."**

Simple, profound, and true. Volumes have been written about how to be a successful entrepreneur and they all add up to the above one-sentence maxim. This chapter will enable you to determine how much you need to break even by showing how to calculate numbers which add up to spending less than you make. The discipline which unlocks the secret to financial success – "doing this for a long time" – is up to you.

Definitions

Let's begin by defining terms that will be used frequently in this chapter.

Fixed Costs. Fixed Costs are expenses that do not vary with the volume of your business. That is, Fixed Costs will be exactly or nearly the same on a month-to-month basis, regardless of how much business you do. Examples include rent, salaries that remain the same each month, utilities such as heat and electricity (although heat is usually higher in the winter months), and the cost of money which is not tied to sales.

Variable Costs. Variable Costs are expenses that vary with the volume of business. That is, Variable Costs will change depending on business sales. Examples include broker commissions paid and the cost of money directly related to sales. If your factoring volume with clients from a certain broker is $10,000 one month, $20,000 the next month and $50,000 the third month, commissions you pay that broker will be variable, or different each month.

Break-Even Point. The Break-Even Point is the amount of factoring volume from fees generated which is needed to pay the Fixed and Variable Costs. That is, the level at which a business' total costs equal total revenue is the Break-Even Point. For example, if fees generated from $20,000 per month worth of invoices equal $800, and Fixed Costs plus Variable Costs total $800 per month, $20,000 in monthly factoring volume is your Break Even Point.

	$800	Total Revenue
$500		Fixed Costs
$300		Variable Costs
	− $800	Fixed + Variable Costs
	= $ 0	Break-Even

$20,000 is your Break-Even Point.

Operating Profit. The Operating Profit is the amount of fees generated in excess of Fixed Costs plus Variable Costs...or as the earlier quote put it, "spending less than you make." For example, when your fees equal $1,000 per month, Fixed Costs are $500 and Variable Costs are $300, your Operating Profit equals $200:

	$1,000	Fees
$500		Fixed Costs
$300		Variable Costs
	− $800	Fixed + Variable Costs
	= $200	Operating Profit

The fees you brought in are $200 greater than your costs. You profited by $200.

A Sample Break-Even Analysis

There are four simple steps to creating a Break-Even Analysis.

1. Create and scale a chart that will provide a visual means of identifying your Break-Even Point.
2. Calculate and plot your Fixed Costs on the chart,
3. Calculate and plot your Variable Costs.
4. Plot your factoring Fees on the chart, and where the Fees equal the Costs, you have your Break Even Point.

Let's lay the groundwork for a sample situation, and follow each of these steps in creating a Break-Even Analysis.

Let's suppose you have 10 clients with a monthly volume of $100,000. The business is being run from home, and each month you pay yourself $1,000 in salary. $200 is paid monthly to principle for a line of credit to start the business. Telephone charges are $100 per month, and $200 per month is being paid for a car lease. In addition to these fixed costs, each invoice factored has a broker fee of 15% of the factor's fee and a finance charge of 1% per month for the amount borrowed from the line of credit. On average the invoices are on the street for 30 days, your factor's fee is 5% for the first 30 days plus 1% per week thereafter, and you're giving a 70% advance.

Step 1. Create and Scale a Chart. Create a chart with an x-axis running vertically, joining a y-axis extending horizontally. Your monthly Costs (Fixed and Variable) will be tracked on the x-axis of the chart. The volume range of the total invoices you factor per month will be placed on the y-axis of the chart. For illustration purposes, we will use $6,000 in monthly Costs (x-axis) and $100,000 in month Factoring Volume (y-axis) as the maximum values. See Diagram 1.

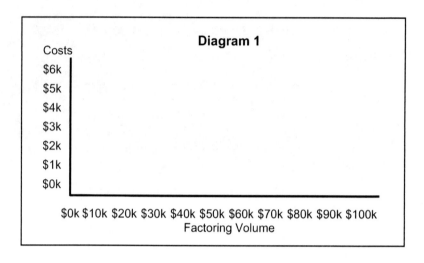

Diagram 1

Step 2. Add Fixed Costs. Total the fixed costs and plot them on the chart as in Diagram 2:

Salary	$1,000
Loan Principle	200
Telephone	100
Car	200
Total Fixed Costs	$1,500

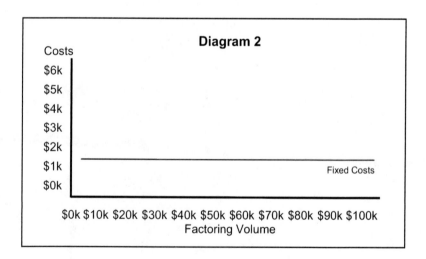

Diagram 2

Step 3. Add Variable Costs. Total the Variable Costs and plot them on the chart, beginning on the line representing the Fixed Costs. Assume $100,000 worth of invoices are being factored with an average factor's fee of 5%. Brokers are paid 15% of factor's fees (=$750) and cost of money is 1% per month (12% APR) of advances on the street (1% of $70,000…which is 70% advances for $100,000 invoice volume… = $700). See Diagram 3.

Broker Commissions	$750
Loan Interest	700
Total Variable Costs	$1,450

Draw a straight line starting at $100,000 on the x-axis (far right), and ending at $1,500 on the y-axis (far left). A straight line is drawn from this point back to the fixed costs at zero volume.

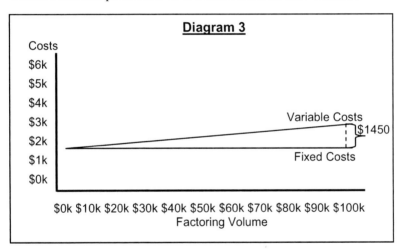

Diagram 3

Step 4. Add Fees. Assuming you average 30-day payments on all invoices, your gross fees are 5% of the $100,000 from factored invoices, or $5,000. See Diagram 4.

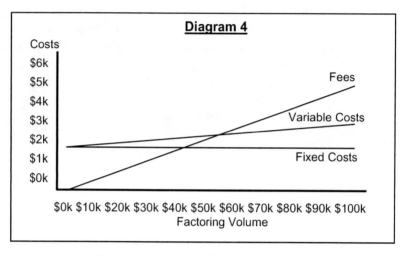

A straight line is drawn from $5,000 in fees on the y-axis at $100,000 in volume on the x-axis, to zero fees at zero volume.

The Break-Even Point is where the Fee Line intersects with the Variable Costs line (which includes the amount of Fixed Costs). The Net Profit, the area between Fees and Total Costs (Variable Costs + Fixed Costs) as you can see in Diagram 5, increases as Fees increase past the Break-Even Point.

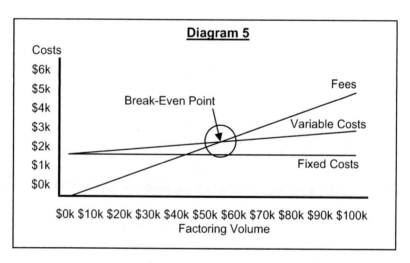

While the diagram above gives you a ballpark Break-Even Point, you can calculate it precisely with the formulas below.

Profit = Factor Fee – Fixed Costs – Variable Costs

Since the Break-Even Point is the spot at which profit equals 0, the above formula for this example becomes:

0 [profit] = $5,000 [factor fee] – $1,500 [Fixed Costs] –$1,450 [Variable Costs]

that is

0 = 5% (Volume) – $1,500 – 1.45% (Volume) –or–
Vol @ BE [Break Even] = $1,500 / .0355 = $42,253.52

The .0355 in the last line above is obtained by subtracting 1.45% (Volume) [Variable Costs] from 5% (Volume) [factor fee]:

5% – 1.45% = 3.55% = .0355

What Ifs

Scenario 1. With your success you decide to pay yourself more and buy a nicer car. You give yourself a raise to $2,000 a month and car payments become $500. Your monthly fixed costs now are:

Salary	2,000
Loan Principal	200
Telephone	100
Car	500
Total Fixed Costs	2,800

Your formula now looks like this:

0 = 5% (Volume) – 2,800 – 1.45% (Volume) –or–
Vol @ BE = 2,800 / .0355 = 78,873.24

Your break-even point is $78,873.24. So to cover the additional salary and car expense you must factor an additional $36,619.62. (78,873.24 – 42,253.52 = 36,619.62) in monthly volume to break even. See Diagram 6.

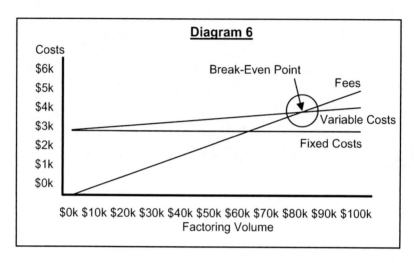

Diagram 6

Scenario 2. Now suppose that competition heats up and you have to lower your fee rate from 5% to 4%. How will this affect your Break-Even Point and profitability?

First recalculate the Variable Cost. Because the factoring fee is less, the broker fee will be less also. The broker fee now is $4,000 x 15% = $600. Variable Fees now are:

Broker Commission	600
Loan Interest	700
Total Variable Cost	1,300

Your new Break-Even Point is:

$$0 = 4\% \text{ (Volume)} - \$2,800 - 1.3\% \text{ (Volume)} \text{ -}or\text{-}$$
$$\text{Vol @ BE} = \$2,800 \text{ / } .027 = \$103,703.70$$

Calculate the formula and see Diagram 7.

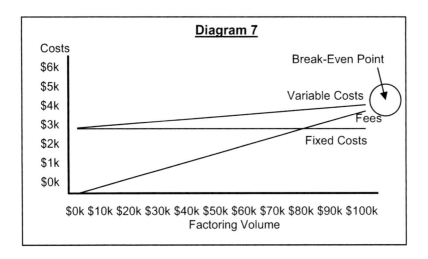

Oops! Your Break-Even Point is now $103,703.70. You will not be able to break even with this scenario with $100,000 in factoring volume! You'll have to either raise rates, and/or cut costs, and/or increase your volume to at least $103,703.70 to break even.

Scenario 3. Recognizing the potential problem in Scenario 2, you are able to secure another $70,000 factoring funds that you have placed in $100,000 worth of more invoices with new clients. The cost of this new money is also 1% of the new $70,000, or an additional $700 per month, plus an additional $200 to pay principal. The new business comes from brokers to whom you pay the same 15% of your factor's fee. You now pay yourself $3,000 per month and decide to keep your car. You believe you can be competitive with a 4.5% factoring rate. Let's calculate and graph what your Break-Even Point is now.

Total Volume	= $200,000
Salary	$3,000
Loan Principle	400
Telephone	100
Car	500
Total Fixed Costs	$4,000
Broker Commissions	$1,350
Loan Interest	1,400
Total Variable Costs	$2,750
Total Costs (Fixed + Var.)	$6,750
Fees are 4.5% of $200,000 =	$9,000

Profit = Factor Fee – Fixed Costs – Variable Costs
0 = 4.5% (Volume) – $4,000 – 3.125% (Volume)
-or-
Vol @ BE = $4,000 / .03125 = $128,000.00

The .03125 is obtained by subtracting 1.375% which is (Volume) [Variable Cost], that is $2,750 / $200,000 = 1.375% from 4.5% (Volume) [factor fee]:

Factor Fee	4.500%
Variable Cost	– 1.375%
	3.125%

Thus your Break-Even Point is now $128,000.00 With this much on the street and no more expenses, you have a healthy profit margin as we can see in Diagram 8.

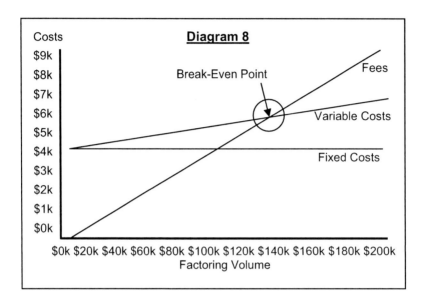

As you can see, it's easy to play numerous "what if" scenarios with this Break-Even Analysis in order to determine what your fees and costs must be in order to break even. It can also help you determine an affordable price to pay for your factoring funds. Changes to your business can be quickly analyzed and profitability determined, both visually with graphs for round numbers, as well as very precisely calculated – literally right down to the penny.

Part 3

Procedures
and
Operations

9
Marketing:
How to
Find Clients

Prospective clients are very close to the new small factor yet the neophyte often doesn't realize it. Locating, recognizing, and then closing prospective clients takes a while to learn. Once your business is established, your name is in circulation and referrals are coming from clients and even strangers, marketing becomes easy. But surviving until you get to that point, which usually takes a year or two, is the hard part.

Business Cards

One absolute necessity is a good business card. Collect as many as you can from all over (other financial professionals, trade shows, hardware store counters, grocery store bulletin boards, anywhere) and study them carefully. Some will be excellent, others worthless. What's your immediate impression when you look at a card? What catches your eye? Does it tell you what the business does? Does it give the person's name and how to reach him? Does anything confuse you? Does art work, logo, or lack of either add or detract? Does it fit the industry or type of work? Would you contact this business if you needed its service? You can learn a lot about what to include and exclude by studying other business cards.

While your card doesn't have to be expensive, it shouldn't look cheap or unprofessional. Consider putting a message on the reverse side, perhaps with a special offer such as finder's fees. Give your card out liberally, but don't print too many at once. You'll undoubtedly want to change the card's look or information two or three times the first year; making more than a few hundred at first will leave you with a lot of expensive bookmarks.

Brochures

Brochures can consume a lot of time and money as you start out. If you're short of both, put more effort and resources into your business cards as you'll use them more often and people are more likely to keep them. Brochures can be helpful but you can probably get by without them. If you do consider them a necessity, make them in small quantities and give to people who specifically request one. Avoid using them in direct mail unless you want to spend a lot of money on something that will end up 98 times out of 100 in trash cans.

A bad brochure can do far more harm than good. Too often, people with a computer assume they can make quality brochures, but turn out ghastly creations made up of poorly written, poorly laid out copy full of misspellings. If you feel you absolutely must have a brochure, you may do best to find a graphic artist who will lay out your brochure. Just be sure to have several people proofread it before you make hundreds of copies, as grammar may not be this person's forte and errors can get by even the pros.

Marketing Methods

Methods of marketing a small factoring business fall into two broad categories, and within each category are numerous strategies. The two categories are **One-to-One Contact** and **Media Contact**. One-to-One Contact is telling an individual or a small number of people, either eye to eye or on the phone, what your business offers and its benefits. Conversely, Media Contact is telling a large number of people at once the same thing – what you do and its value to your audience.

One-to-One Contact is more effective but takes longer to reach a significant number of potential clients. Media Contact reaches many people quite quickly, but provides a far lower percentage of prospects and costs more. An effective marketing campaign will combine elements of both. No matter which method you use, always remember to address how factoring can help your listeners' business. People – especially business owners – want to know immediately the answer to WIIFM (pronounced "Whiff 'em"): "What's In It For Me?" If factoring doesn't solve their problem, don't waste their time or yours with your pitch.

It's very important to always keep in mind the target of your marketing efforts. First focus on businesses which are most factorable. Pursuing retail stores in a mall who sell only to consumers won't get you factoring clients. Isolate a specific industry in which you have knowledge or background, or ones in a specific geographical area. From there, narrow your mark: prospects with a certain yearly volume, those who have been in business for less than five years, those in specific zip codes, and so on.

Don't try to use every method described below; it simply can't be done. Instead, select four or five that fit your personality, style and resources. Then draft an overall marketing plan that outlines your target group, the methods you will use, in what combination, and in what order. Map out a definite time line on a weekly and monthly basis. Also plan ahead financially by determining how much each method will cost and how you will pay for it. Barging ahead with great excitement – yet without a well-conceived and executed plan – can end up an expensive, frustrating waste of energy and time, seriously draining your resources and enthusiasm. This is a separate plan from the one done in the chapter "Charting Your Course," but it is just as important.

Some say you must use a certain marketing method, usually cold calling or direct mail, to be successful. However, if you're not comfortable with these, you'll probably do a poor job and hate every minute of it. Cold calling for people who are very shy or uneasy with strangers is absolute torture. Doing direct mail without knowing what you're doing can be very costly. Take the person who sent out thousands of letters without receiving a single reply, and couldn't understand why. Frustrated, he asked an experienced colleague to read what he'd sent. The colleague immediately saw the problem: he had neglected to put his phone number anywhere in the mailing.

You're more likely to be successful with methods you enjoy that are an extension of your personality and skills. Marketing is very much a "one person's tea is another's poison" kind of thing. Pick the ones that taste best to you, learn how to use them effectively and carefully plan your course. Then go for it!

One-to-One Contact

Friends, Relatives and Acquaintances. Unless you're an orphaned, single hermit, you already have a built-in network that can work wonders. You probably know or are in contact with a much larger circle of people than you realize who can be your very best source of referrals. The fact that these people already know you is your greatest advantage. They know first-hand your reputation, how you treat people and your trustworthiness. These are major issues you must address when working with strangers. But with people who already know you, this hurdle is nonexistent...unless they know you to be a dishonest, greedy, egocentric rat!

Review in your mind all the people in your life's circle, then make a list of people to contact. You might want to look over holiday card lists, rolodex files, people in your neighborhood, directories of your place of worship, civic groups, children's activities, and so on. You can meet or phone them and tell about your new adventure, send a letter, or simply mention it in conversation the next time you're together.

Tell them what you're doing and how it can help business owners. Let your enthusiasm show, and chances are good they might know someone right off who could benefit. If not, ask them to give it some thought and get back to you.

ALWAYS say you give finder's fees, but be sure you've worked out how much that will be before you mention it! 10% to 15% of your gross fee for a year or for the life of the account, for all successful transactions referred, is a common payment for professional brokers. Some factors pay 50% of their first fee, others a flat $50 or $100, and nothing after that. You may want to pay a nonprofessional up to those amounts if a name they furnish turns into a client. People who "sniff out" leads, sometimes called "Bird Dogs" or "Scouts," can be invaluable. The idea of getting money for simply giving you a name will not only silence most skeptics (usually relatives) but motivate some to actually beat the bushes for you. I've had people make phone calls on the spot, even before I told them I'll pay them a fee, simply because they wanted to help a friend – me.

Don't underestimate the potential in this network of people. When I first started factoring, I described what I was doing to a friend, not remembering he owned a small distributing business. He immediately saw the potential benefit to his company (WIIFM) and a few days later called wanting to know more. After nailing down the details of his customers, factoring rates and advances, he soon became one of my first and best clients. He ended up factoring over $100,000 worth of receivables his first year.

Brokers, Larger Factors. When you use brokers you need to have some policies established as to the commission you pay, their role working with you, what information you need about prospective clients, businesses you will and won't fund and your minimum and maximum monthly volume. If they bring you very small receivables (less than $2,500 per month), the amount they'll make in broker fees is pretty puny and it may not be worth the trouble. However, brokers can bring you a lot of business, so treat them well and with integrity. Word gets around brokers' circles very quickly when a factor is especially good or bad to work with.

Larger factors, especially those in your area, can be excellent sources of referrals. If you've referred to a larger factor potential clients that were too big for you, it is only natural for him to return the favor when prospects are too small for him. This relationship is mutually beneficial and can make both of you good money.

Make a point of introducing yourself to local larger factors listed in your Yellow Pages and find out their parameters. If they turn away what you're looking for, say so. If you come off as a professional, there's a good chance they'll give you prospects they turn down. It helps financial professionals enormously, when they must refuse someone, if they can refer to an alternative factor who's likely to help. Be that alternative and you'll have a steady stream of new clients.

Banks. What was just said about larger factors is equally true for banks. Bankers turn down loan requests every day. If someone can't get a loan but is a good factoring prospect, you can make the banker's job easier by being an alternative for the bank's rejected client: "We can't help you, but this person might be able to. Give him a call."

In addition to easing the banker's guilt when turning someone down, you can be a source of new accounts where your factoring bank account resides. Since you deal extensively with deposits into your clients' accounts, it is very convenient for your client to have an account with your bank, especially if the bank offers transfers between accounts without requiring checks. Getting referrals from your bank can be a triple-win: you get new clients, the client gets needed cash, and the bank is a good guy for making it happen, and perhaps, adds a new account to boot.

A few factors and brokers focus exclusively on contacting banks for leads. Certain bankers are more receptive than others. Some view factors as competitors, others see us as scavengers, but some see factors as allies. Some banks have their own factoring division. Deal with them as you would a larger factor: find their minimums and maximums, industries served and avoided, marketing persons and so on – and then tell them how you can help with clients too small to fit their requirements.

The key is to find the right person – corporate lending officer, branch manager, and/or factoring division contact. Then establish a good relationship, make sure he understands how you can help him (WIIFM) and stay in contact. Sooner or later, this can pay off.

Accountants, Bookkeepers and Attorneys. Anyone who has his nose in a business' financial records is keenly aware, usually better than the business owner, when there is a cash flow problem. Accountants, bookkeepers, and attorneys are these very people and the more of them who know what you offer their clients, the more business you can get.

Like bankers, these folks will have varying attitudes about factors, and some will dismiss you out of hand. Many will have only a vague understanding of how factoring works and not appreciate the benefits. Some see factors as loan sharks; and, even if they recommend it, may want their client in and out of factoring as fast as possible because they think it is too expensive or a measure of last resort. Generally such professionals tend to be conservative with financial referrals and may be fearful that recommending factoring could leave them open to lawsuits if the roof later caves in. Getting referrals from people with such an attitude is difficult if not impossible. However, especially if you take time to educate them, some will realize factoring can be exactly what certain clients need and will be happy to refer you.

Having a solid reputation with a handful of "bean counters" and "legal beagles" can have similar win-win-win results as with bankers. You get new a client, the client has her cash flow problem solved, and the accountant or lawyer looks good and now has two people glad to give her new referrals. (WIIFM. See how this works?!)

Networking Groups. Networking groups take various shapes, from established national leads organizations with a consistent weekly schedule, to Chamber of Commerce mixers that meet monthly over a meal with no structured agenda, to informal local groups that do their own thing. Finding a networking group with the right combination of members and good chemistry can be a bonanza. But if it is full of people who can't help you because their sphere of influence doesn't mesh with companies needing a factor, or it's a closed shop/good old boy network, joining or working with this type of group will be a waste of time.

If you use this method, find a group that has a good mix of finance-related members and people who know a lot of people. Look for a friendly accountant, attorney, banker, financial planner, insurance agent, etc. who will be able to give you more leads naturally than people who just service the real estate or housing market.

Some time ago I joined an established networking group called LeTip. Let me describe briefly how it works so you get an idea of what such groups are about. LeTip is a national organization with local chapters throughout the United States. In each local chapter, only one type of business can be represented: one lawyer, one dentist, one real estate agent, one plumber, one whatever. If you're a chiropractor and want to join a group with a chiropractor already in it, you must find another chapter. There are yearly national dues, quarterly dues to cover local chapter expenses and your weekly breakfast, and quarter to dollar "fines" for such things as not having a tip, not bringing a guest, not wearing your name badge, and so on. The whole purpose of the group is for members to give and receive qualified leads every week. A qualified lead is someone who needs a product or service and is awaiting a call from the tip-receiver.

Your group becomes a powerful marketing force that eliminates the need for cold calls. Each week one or two members from the group give a ten-minute talk pertaining to some aspect of their business. The business meeting is conducted during the mealtime, business cards are passed (and accumulated for all members to hand out to potential leads for other members during the week) and the tip bucket is circulated. Each member gives a 30-second commercial and drops his or her written tips into the bucket, giving a copy to the tip recipient. The person receiving the tip then follows up by calling the prospect.

While such a group works especially well for people with small ticket items (florists, carpet cleaners, service businesses, etc.), there are many advantages to groups like this for factors. You're one-on-one with business people with a wide variety of local contacts, and you gain high visibility and the trust of people who can bring you leads. Further, there are regional get-togethers involving several local chapters that will further expand your circle of contacts. Though dues may be somewhat high, one good client can pay for many years' worth of dues. While some professions won't be able to give you leads, good tips can come from unexpected places. The hairdresser in my group referred one of my best clients.

Attend a few groups as a guest and see if any can provide what you need. There are other organizations similar to LeTip. If you can't find them in the phone book, look for them on the web, at business trade shows or ask around. To find a local LeTip chapter in your area, call 800 25-LETIP (800 255-3847) and press 0 or go to their web site at www.letip.com.

Purchasing Agents. Purchasing agents for school districts, city or county government, utility companies, large corporations, and the like have access to a gold mine of information: vendors to whom these entities pay their bills. Remember, the most creditworthy customers that clients can have are business or government agencies that will not go bankrupt or otherwise disappear and who might take thirty or more days to pay. Finding clients who have this type of customer will make your due diligence a snap and let you sleep at night without wondering if you'll get paid. Marketing to vendor lists used by purchasing agents of school districts, utility companies, large corporations, and government agencies is a back-door way to getting the job done, and if you can pull it off, prospecting becomes easy.

Two things to consider: 1) these vendor lists can be voluminous, containing literally thousands of names; and 2) the purchasing agents probably won't be very willing to release the vendor information and may be downright uncooperative. They may say the information is not for the public or they're prohibited from releasing it. In some cases this will be true; in others, it's just too much trouble for an overworked clerk to give you the information. They might be prohibited from accepting a commission and there's no benefit to them for helping you, a stranger (their WIIFM answer is "zero"). Also, refer back to the "Friends, Relatives, and Acquaintances" section above. If you personally know someone who works in an office with this information, she may be more willing and able to help you than she would some stranger. A good, current, huge vendor list like this provides all the marketing leads you can use, and then some.

Seminars. If you don't mind speaking in front of a group, conducting a morning or afternoon seminar can be a great way of obtaining new clients. You'll need to have your ducks in a row, however. Use a well-organized marketing plan which includes at least one method in the "Media Contacts" section to advertise the seminar adequately. Well-placed radio or TV ads may do this best. You'll also need to have your room arrangements, presentation, handouts and other considerations well-organized to conduct a successful program. Done well, you can easily pick up some good clients; done poorly, you can run yourself ragged getting ready or make a fool of yourself to prospective clients. The more seminars you do, the better you'll get. Make your presentation focus on WIIFM primarily, and don't get too caught up in explaining the detailed, specific "ins and outs" of factoring.

Free or nominal fee seminars at a convenient, known location are popular today for getting the word out about all kinds of businesses. Free admission will attract larger numbers, while prepayment of a small admission charge ($10 or $20) will assure a higher percentage turnout of interested attendees plus cover some of your costs. If there is another small factor in your area who has an interest in doing this, or perhaps an accountant or business attorney who would like to advertise her business with you, consider splitting preparation duties, expenses, fees and presentation time and topics. The best times of year to put on seminars are in early fall and the months of January or February. The idea of getting a fresh start with the new year can be an inspiration for people to attend such a meeting.

Trade Shows, Conventions. Keep your eye open for business trade shows and conventions that come to the city nearest you. You can pick up leads from these simply by walking the floor and visiting with other attendees and people in booths of companies that might be good factoring candidates or by getting a booth of your own. Having your own booth requires a fair amount of preparation and expense; but if you know how to do it, a good trade show can bring you enough leads to keep you busy for a long time.

Chambers of Commerce usually sponsor annual trade shows which are a bit smaller. These can be good for learning the ropes of both walking the floor and having your own booth. These are also good places to pick up business cards to inspire your own and for prospects to follow up later.

Cold Calls. If you enjoy the challenge of walking into an office or calling someone stone cold, and if you don't mind hearing nine "no's" for every one "yes," you can get all the clients you'll ever want by cold calling. Find a list of small businesses in your area and do your thing. If you have an industrial business park nearby or business buildings with one to five-person offices inside, you're all set.

Where can you get lists of prospective clients? Several places. Large and small companies (check the web and the Yellow Pages, there are many) sell commercial data bases which provide carefully targeted lists. Credit reporting agencies like Dun & Bradstreet and infoUSA are examples. See the section "Marketing Databases" in the chapter "Factoring Resources" for more information. Chambers of Commerce can be a helpful resource for prospective lists, as can new business listings that are about a year old, from the newspaper or local business journal. These should be in your library and on their web site archives. Also contact home-based business associations.

One method that can be very effective combines cold calling with the fax machine. Pinpoint your audience from the above databases or the Yellow Pages and fax your cover letter giving your pitch.

By law, you must put your company name and fax number at the top of every page of your fax. If you don't, you're sending unrequested and illegal "junk fax." Before faxing anything, call the recipient for permission to send. Keep a log of the date and time of your call and the person's name who authorized your transmission. Without permission and this information, you risk a stiff fine if the person you're faxing raises a fuss. In your pitch letter, be sure to include your voice phone number in your letter for a response! A day or so later, follow up with a call to those to whom you sent your fax. A few may respond before you follow up. These are your hottest prospects! Cold calling this way is a lot more time and cost effective than knocking on doors. It's also less stressful for the meek.

Telemarketing. It can be an expensive alternative to go with a professional telemarketing outfit, but a good telemarketer can keep you very busy with new prospects. You may be able to find an independent who works from home who won't cost an arm and a leg. You'll need to provide the list of businesses that the person will call.

A telemarketer can do your cold calling for you if you think that's the way to get new clients and can't face the 90% rejection rate that goes with the territory. Alternately, you could hire the telemarketer to follow up on your fax calls described above, if you think they'll be more successful than you. Have a contract in writing describing the duties and payment for your telemarketer so there are no misunderstandings or surprises once they start finding you clients.

Client Referrals. Hands down this is the best, cheapest, and most effective advertising you can get. The only problem is, you have to get those first few clients before they can refer people to you! In time, this will probably be the only marketing you'll need to do; meanwhile, work hard at the other ways you've chosen to get to this point. Again, remind your clients every so often that you give finder's fees. Chances are, they'll have a neighboring business, vendor or customer (especially their slower payers, who might have a cash flow problem of their own) who might make good prospects.

Media Contact

Written Articles. If you have a knack for writing, submitting articles to various publications can be a free and relatively easy way to introduce factoring and yourself to a large number of people. While there's no guarantee what you write will get published, county business journals and smaller newspapers are often quite willing to accept well-written articles by a local writer on the subject of factoring, especially if they don't come off as self-serving. If you don't write well, consider contacting a reporter of a business journal or smaller city newspaper for an interview to describe factoring. You take your chances on what will be written, but the exposure can quickly lead to new business.

One of my first clients read an article I wrote in a local business journal. She had never heard of factoring before, called the paper to get my phone number (I foolishly omitted it at the end of the article[2]) and soon became a good client. Conveniently, she lived only a couple miles away which made working with her even easier.

If you have the time and stamina, writing a regular column for a small newspaper or business journal is among the best free publicity you can get. The consistent visibility is what stays with people and a regular column provides this. Again, direct your words to how factoring can help the readers' businesses, not to what you do. Remember WIIFM.

Providing similar articles for business-oriented e-zines can also be effective. Even if your words are printed only once, it's remarkable how long people keep articles before waiting to contact you. The same article above was uploaded to America Online and available there. About two years later, I received a call from a business journal publisher in New York asking for permission to reprint it. Printed media has a wonderful advantage of being clipped and kept by readers for a long time.

Newsletters. Once you have even a few people in your database, consider putting out a monthly or quarterly newsletter. These can take a fair amount of time, but are a great way to keep your name in front of people you know, have met, or you want to remember you. Make it look professional – pay a desktop publisher to lay it out if needed. Send a hard copy or email a PDF format file it to prospects, clients, colleagues, brokers, larger factors, friends and relatives, people whose business cards you've collected, and others who could bring you business. Faxing it (with permission from the recipients), can also cut down production and distribution costs considerably.

Set a regular time to publish, put those dates on your calendar, and follow the plan. Especially to start with, keep your newsletter simple. Even a one-pager can be enough to begin. Include information that will benefit your recipients, updates on your company's services, add a note of humor, and perhaps

---

[2] *Always* include your phone number and email address at the end of such articles. How many prospects did I lose in this instance who were too busy to take the trouble to find me?

spotlight a client or other business with whom you deal. Always keep it upbeat. Remember, the best way to get new business is to remind people what you do and how you can help them and others. The purpose of your newsletter is to make the recipient think of YOU when she becomes aware of a need for factoring.

Classified Ads. Because classified ads are less effective and far more costly to run in large city newspapers, put your classified ads in smaller, weekly publications and appropriate e-zines. Target papers and business newsletters (print and electronic) which cover an industrial, governmental, and/or a small business base in the geographical area from which you want your clients. Classifieds need to run for some time to be noticed and hence can get a bit pricey; but, if they work, they're worth it. Keep your ad simple and to the point: something like, "CASH for invoices in 24-48 hours. Improve your cash flow. Call ABC Financial Services, (253) 555-5555, www.mysite.com." A local or 800 number will induce people to call more than an out-of-area number. Try various publications and revise your words in the ad. See which combinations work best. Set a trial period to run the ads so if they don't work after a month or two, you'll have resources left to try something else. Printed classified ad prices are based on the number of words or lines used, plus the length of time the ad runs. Electronic business newsletters tend to have a flat rate and often well-targeted audience. Figure how to get the most bang for your buck before you start shelling out money.

You might also put classifieds in various trade publications of industries that are factorable; or again, home business publications. These can also be good places to submit articles you've written. A strategically placed ad after an article can further induce someone to call.

Street Signs. Relatively small street signs located near busy intersections with a stop sign or light are also worth consideration. You must keep the number of words to a minimum and lettering large. For example, "CASH FOR INVOICES, (253) 555-5555," is enough to fit onto a two-by-three foot sign, so that most passing motorists will be able to read it. You may want to check your city or county sign ordinances so you're not breaking any law; breaking sign codes that are enforced may result in a nasty fine or having the signs removed and thrown away.

Make your sign look professional. Go to a quick sign shop and ask their advice on materials, color, lettering, etc. before having it made. If there are no legal problems putting them up, a few good-looking signs in strategic locations can be a relatively inexpensive and a very effective avenue to new business.

Magnetic Car Signs. Using a vehicle to advertise your factoring business is a natural. Magnetic signs can be made very inexpensively for around $50 a pair from your neighborhood sign shop, and more if you want a digital graphic[3] or reflective lettering or graphics which stand out nicely after dark when a headlight shines on them. Compare prices if you're quoted a lot more than that for a basic design.

Magnetic signs can be put on or taken off your car any time you want. Test your car door first with a small refrigerator magnet to make sure it sticks; some newer cars have metal alloys that won't hold a magnet. Also be aware that you must keep the car surface clean where the magnet attaches. Dust accumulating between the magnet and the car will weaken the grip and the sign can fall off as you drive along.

Your sign should include a catchy phrase, your company name, and phone number. The phrase might be something like "CA$H for Invoices in 24 hours," "Alternative Financing for Business," "Improve Business Cash Flow," or something similar to grab motorists' attention. Keep the wording simple and the lettering easy to read: motorists will have to rely on memory or a hastily scribbled note to record your information. Make it as easy for them as possible; too much information is unreadable.

Magnetic car signs are an excellent way to advertise to local prospects as that's who will read your sign every day as you

---

[3] Digital graphics are a blended mix of colors printed on a sign, as opposed to one color vinyl letters or designs. Digital technology is used to print graphics and logos with color gradients, very intricate designs, and photographs.

make your commute, do your errands, even drive to leisure activities.

Use a magnetic sign on a vehicle that's neither too expensive-looking nor a heap, as your vehicle is a statement of your business practices and success. The only down-side of this marketing method: you need to keep your car clean.

Vinyl Vehicle Lettering. Tasteful lettering and graphics on your car, van or pickup's windows, sides, and/or back have the same advantages of magnetics; the only difference is it costs a bit more and once it's on it stays there – unlike a magnetic that can go on and off any time.

Vinyl can be removed from a vehicle without permanent markings. Yet you need to think of this as a more permanent look on your vehicle, and therefore you need to think this through more carefully than magnetic signs.

Vinyl lettering makes your vehicle a full-time "company car." It's easy to leave it on (compared to the magnetic surface you need to keep clean) but you need to consider this: are there ever times or places you want to drive without identifying who you are or what you do?

For example, if you're factoring on the side and have a full-time job where your co-workers see you come and go, advertising your side business this way may not set well with your boss.

If such issues don't matter however, vinyl lettering can give your business a look of permanence, show you're serious about it, and set well with prospective clients. Prices will depend on how elaborate the design, square footage of surface coverage, and your use of digital graphics or reflective vinyl – which may be worth the extra cost. Expect to pay around $50-100 for a very simple ad to several hundred or even a thousand dollars for something elaborate. Tell the sign shop your budget and they'll give you an idea of what's available for your price range.

Just like a magnetic sign, keep the design simple and the wording sparse, Avoid intricate logos that will be time-consuming for the sign shop to reproduce or install, as this will increase your cost. Again, this is great "bang for the buck" advertising with the exposure it gives you, especially if you drive a lot. I was once asked how many trucks I had in my fleet because this person saw my vehicles with their signage so often. I had a "fleet" of one and just drove around town a lot.

Public Speaking. If a sea of faces staring at you while you talk doesn't intimidate you, public speaking can be another free and highly effective means of finding business. Civic and business groups which meet monthly usually have a speaker at each meeting. Invariably, the person in charge of arranging speakers is looking for someone to fill a slot. Find out who this person is for your local Lions Club, Rotary, Chamber, home-based business association, and the like, and offer your services. Just as with putting on seminars, you must be prepared and appear as a knowledgeable professional, or your public speaking event can be more damaging than beneficial.

Here's an idea to use if you're invited to speak before a group. Bring many business cards with you with one specially marked on the back. Pass them out as you begin your talk. When you finish, give a door prize (perhaps a certificate for a meal for two at a nice local restaurant) to the person who ends up with the marked card. Done effectively, you may have interested prospects call the next day or two; you'll also have a good chance of getting invitations to speak to other groups.

Internet Web Site. The day is here where you need to have a web site to be considered legitimate, or at least serious about your business. Most larger factors have web sites and after reading several, many look somewhat alike. Those that stand out – with unique innovations or services, a special look of professionalism and confidence, even humor done tastefully – will have more appeal to prospective clients and be more likely to generate a response.

With a web site, you're likely to get some inquiries from prospects shopping for the best deal or who don't meet your parameters. Many will want to know about getting cash but don't have a factorable business or any business at all. Be careful to pre-qualify responses from your web site because you can waste a lot of time answering inquiries from people who turn out to be non-prospects.

The number of people who access the Internet is mind-boggling. Try to get on as many search engines as you can but be careful of spending a lot of money for them. Many will give you a free listing, while others can be quite expensive. You can also pay other services to submit for you, but you may not know how effective this is.

Many web hosts offer a certain number of search engine submissions with a subscription to their service. Look into whether this is offered and which search engines are included, as you search for a web host. There are free web hosts out there which will require their banner be posted prominently on your site. These same hosts offer low-cost web hosting with the banners removed. Monthly costs for such hosts can be from about $5 to $50 per month. If you don't mind banners on your site, look into banner exchanges which can drive traffic to your site. Some hosts will charge set up fees, others don't. More expensive hosts are out there but for your purposes as a small factor you shouldn't need to spend too much.

Shop around for a web host and web designer if you need one. In general prices can vary widely and it's easy to drop a couple thousand dollars for web design and end up with very little for it. Be sure your site looks professional and is exceptionally well done, or the impression you leave could be similar to a poorly organized and badly presented seminar – multiplied by thousands of people checking you out.

Internet Financial Exchange Sites. These have developed enormously over the last few years and can be a great source of business leads. These are sites which match businesses needing funding to businesses providing funding. A few deal only with factoring while many provide a dizzying array of financing needs and products.

Few will allow you to freely browse their databases of businesses looking for money, which gives you an idea of how many and the kind of prospects they list that will fit your parameters. However when you join (usually free for funding seekers, and fee-based for the funding providers) you then get the information needed to contact the prospect and close the deal. The fees are reasonable and deals you find here should easily cover the fees. If they don't you can cancel your membership as they're usually not long term. See the Section "Factoring Exchanges" in the chapter "Factoring Resources" for a list, description of, and links to some of the ones best suited to small factors.

Email Databases can reach large numbers of prospects but may also be considered spamming if not done properly. Unrequested email is easily ignored, so carefully word your Subject line so it is read by the recipients and not considered a get rich quick scheme, hot air hype, or a possible virus. Also, when sending a mass emailing to businesses, many will probably go to unfactorable companies. See how precisely your email list can target recipients before using such a service. Refer to the section "Opt-in Email Databases" in the chapter "Factoring Resources."

Direct Mail Postcards. Gurus of marketing often say direct mail is the only way to go. However, as mentioned in an earlier chapter, this can be very expensive. Good, attractive designs, mailing lists, postage, printing, and paper costs add up fast. Then too, it takes a lot of time to get the mailing ready. Much direct mail (considered "junk" by recipients) that comes in an envelope doesn't even get opened, so use a mailing that nearly always is read: postcards. They cost less to mail, less to produce, and are far more likely to be read than the nicest letter on fancy stationery with an expensive brochure included.

More importantly, use some eye-catching graphics, cartoons, fonts, and/or colored paper so that your mailer grabs the reader's attention immediately. You have approximately three seconds for the reader to decide if what you've sent is worth reading. Something that tickles the funny bone or clearly speaks to his need (WIIFM) will greatly increase your chances of winning that three-second decision.

Postcards are most effective if they are mailed in a series, about one to three weeks apart over a one- to three-month time span, to the same recipients. Develop a plan, carefully target those who will receive your mailing, and follow through completely. Be sure to budget adequately. Timing your mailings can be important. Events requiring cash flow–first of the year (fresh start), spring (tax time), other months quarterly taxes are due, and seasonal needs for your target businesses–should be considered.

Response rates are generally low for direct mail (2-3% is considered good), so don't send out 10 postcards and expect your phone to ring. Get your list ready, mail out 100 or more cards per week (check with the post office for quantities needed for bulk rates) and be systematic in your coverage. If you mail out too many at once, you could have trouble handing the volume of response, so plan accordingly. If you don't want to buy a bulk rate permit (costing several hundred dollars), find a small secretarial service who has one who will make it available for a fee. They should put on the labels and take care of the mailing at a reasonable price. The post office can be very picky about bulk rate mailings, so know what you're doing or find someone who does before you prepare your first mailing.

Radio/Cable TV Ads. These can be powerful media. Ads designed and placed on radio and TV may not be as expensive as you think. Call various radio and cable stations to get an idea of how much 30- and 60-second spots are. Prices will vary widely with the size and audience of the station, hours of the day, time of year and number of times you advertise. After the year-end holidays (the good time for advertising a seminar you're putting on), rates are often lower because most advertisers have exhausted their marketing budget in the December blitz and the media company needs revenue.

Radio and TV personnel are usually available to help you in making your ad or presentation come off professionally. While you may not want to use this media as your very first marketing method, once you know what you're doing in the factoring world they can be a very effective means of reaching new clients.

A company called ResultsMedia provides advertising spots to radio and TV specifically for factoring companies and brokers to attract business. Each spot is customized with your company name, phone number and web site address. Their library includes

30-second television and radio spots for factoring, medical receivables, factoring seminars, as well as business notes, home mortgages and home mortgage seminars. With each spot you receive unlimited rights in every market.

For prices and additional information call Melissa Gatchel-North at 817-469-6400 or email at mgatchel-north@msn.com. Joey Spurlock is the Executive Producer and can be reached at 214-728-8710 or jspurlock@aol.com.

Business/Trade Journal Ads. Printed advertising can be costly and needs to run many times before it's even noticed. Consider what publications your target audience reads and price how much printed ads are in these. Generally, printed advertising is one of the more expensive means of reaching prospects for the number of responses you get. But because it's fairly easy and people like to see their company's ad in print, many neophytes do this early in the game, spend a lot of money...and then try other methods more successfully.

Yellow Pages Ad. What was just said about Business/Trade Journal Ads also applies to Yellow Pages ads. While this gives you the look of credibility in major phone books, these ads can cost an arm and a leg every month and not result in the desired end: prospects calling you ready to factor. Smaller, independent Yellow Pages phone books won't cost as much and may be the way to go if you feel you must advertise this way. While you may get some clients with a Yellow Pages ad, you're more likely to get inquiries from people shopping for rates, calls from other factors wanting to learn about the competition, and pitches from people trying to sell you something.

Radio Guest Spots. Acting as a radio guest is another method to try once you're established and confident in the factoring world. You can get tremendous exposure as a radio guest. A few inquiries will lead you to the people or stations you should be calling, and this wide exposure costs nothing more than the calls. Start by doing an internet web search looking up "radio guide" or similar key words to point yourself in the right direction. As you learn the ropes, you'll improve your presentation and can use the experience to tout your expertise as a "frequently interviewed radio guest." Pretty impressive.

10
Common Mistakes

There are numerous mistakes new factors can make early in their business. Unfortunately, you may not realize the potential hazard of what you're doing. While there are no doubt more than those described below, what follow are mistakes I've observed others make or have made myself.

Giving Up

The first mistake is to get discouraged and give up too quickly, especially if you start full-time instead of gradually. Often people new to this business make little headway finding clients the first several months. Many people take over a year or more before they actually close deals and begin to make money. If this happens, realize it's normal and that you're not a complete incompetent, even though you may feel like one at times.

Also realize there will be episodes, even after you've been at it a while and have a good group of clients, when you'll have bad days, lose money, or make mistakes and feel like throwing in the towel. This is especially true during the slow seasons of factoring: the summer months and December. Don't give up. Keep at it. Be diligent and your efforts will eventually pay off. This is the kind of work that takes months, sometimes years, for the seeds you've sown to come to fruition. Discouragement can be your greatest enemy when you begin any new endeavor, especially factoring.

Getting Sidetracked

In the course of looking for (and finding) clients, you will inevitably run into requests for loans or venture capital, acquaintances who offer multi-level opportunities, and numerous other "attractions" which can lure you away from factoring. It is very, very easy to get sidetracked by these, and your business will not fare as well if you wander off the path. Be able to say, "No thanks," stick with factoring, and do it better than anyone else.

The proverbial, "Jack-of-All-Trades, Master-of-None" result is all too common among people who get sidetracked. Lack of focus will retard the growth of your factoring business while you chase after venture capital or other money for a prospect. Requests for loans and venture capital are easy to come across, but extremely hard to place with a funding source. One local venture capitalist told me he funds about 1% of the requests that come across his desk, all of which are presented in carefully constructed business plans.

Unless you already have experience and multiple contacts in a related cash flow business, stick to factoring and stay clear of brokering loans or venture capital. There's plenty of business out there for the small factor who does nothing else.

Inadequate Due Diligence

Once you have survived the first two pitfalls, giving up and getting sidetracked, you will have clients…and then, watch out – other mistakes can befall you! The next of these is to fail to do adequate "due diligence."

The tricky part about this necessity (when you start out) is not knowing what adequate due diligence is. Even with directions to follow, there is a queasy feeling most of us get the very first time we do something new. Because of our inexperience, we don't know exactly what we're doing or supposed to do; moreover, we don't know how much we don't know. This is especially true with due diligence which requires reading credit reports and related material, and trying to determine if someone will be a good client or customer. The best approach is to have an experienced colleague review your due diligence before you agree to take on a client or customer or before you advance funds. See the chapters entitled "Due Diligence" and "Credit Reports" for help in this area.

A mistake I've observed is the tendency of an inexperienced factor to overlook a customer's true credit worthiness. The new factor may be fairly thorough in checking out a client, but often learns little or nothing about the client's customers. As these are the ones paying the invoices you're buying, it is critical to know as much as you can about them too. In credit reports, look for payment trends; number of days past due; occurrence of bills sent to collection; comments by other vendors; general risk guidelines; bankruptcies; positive, neutral and negative account profiles, and so on. In particular, look for judgments against this company or individual and be extremely wary of factoring a prospect with past judgments.

As you read the report ask yourself, "What is the general picture painted in this credit report? How stable is this business? Is this someone who will pay his bills? (They're going to be my bills, after all!) How long will he probably take to pay? Do I want to wait that long?" Check out the customers, at least the major customers, as well as the clients!

Not Saying "No"

Many people, especially those who want to help others, find it hard to say "no." It can be even harder when you've struggled for months to get your business under way, find that first client or two to factor, and can almost taste your first fee. At this point, all you have are your instincts to guide you, because you don't have much experience.

If a potential client and/or his customers have terrible credit reports (or none), and you have an uneasy feeling in the pit of your stomach in some intangible way, listen to your instincts. Too often, people who turn out to be flaky at best or crooks at worst have burned new factors right out of the starting gate. (A few notable examples are provided in the book *Factoring Case Studies,* the third book in *The Small Factor Series.)* You may be tempted to accept someone questionable because you don't want to say no, and don't want to start all over again finding another new client. Always remember: there are other fish in the sea. If you get a bite from a prospect who ends up making you nervous, let him go and put your line back in the water. For some reason, interested prospects tend to come in waves, and you may well get another bite quickly from someone who could be a far better catch.

Accepting a Client as a Favor

This goes hand in hand with "Not Saying 'No.'" At some point in your factoring business, you will very likely be presented with a prospect who, based on your due diligence or simple gut feeling, you would ordinarily decline as a client. However, extenuating circumstances may sway you to accept this prospect as a favor to someone.

Here are three scenarios.

1. The prospect comes from a broker who has brought many good clients in the past and you want to keep this broker happy, so you'll do her a favor and approve this client.

2. The questionable prospect is your favorite aunt's next door neighbor, and she's told you how much this person would benefit from your help. She's also told him what a great person *you* are and how your service will benefit him. Since this aunt is a dear woman you've loved since you were in diapers, you decide to do her and the neighbor a favor and accept his account.

3. A charming prospect just tugs your heart strings in such a way that you'll overlook some glaring shortcomings to her account and take her on because you just inexplicably feel like you should.

Be very careful of letting your heart rule your head in such circumstances. When you are inclined to turn someone away, you usually have very good reasons for doing so. The extenuating circumstances – your relationship with the broker, your affection for your aunt, or your desire to help a winsome prospect – may lead you to overlook very good reasons for rejecting the account. But when you step back from these emotional elements of the decision, you may realize that accepting this client is just not a good idea. In fact, it's probably a downright *bad* idea.

Most factors who have accepted new clients as a favor to someone usually end up regretting the decision. Consider very carefully whether this is one of those times that your head needs to rule your heart.

Being Under Capitalized

This can creep up on you whether you have $10,000 in factoring money or ten times that much. You constantly need to have a good handle on how much money your clients are going to need for advances and how long their accounts take to pay. If you're off on either of these, you can end up in a very embarrassing situation.

Take the small factor with $10,000 to use as advances. He takes on a client who has only one customer who wants to factor $2,000 every other week, and who swears up and down his customer always pays in 30 days. After a month, $4,000 is out. The first invoice is paid, but the next two drift into 45 days each. Another invoice with the same client/customer is factored, but then the client takes on a new customer he wants to factor. Now more advances are needed and the factor has a cash flow problem himself. He must scramble to come up with the funds to meet his client's need.

The above scenario can play if you have one client or a dozen. Factoring, by its very nature, enables companies to increase business. That means their invoices will grow in size, number, and frequency. If you're not in a position to meet that need for more and more funds as demand increases, your reputation as a "money person" can go down the tubes. Don't take on more than you can handle – both in the number of clients and the volume they factor. If you expect your client base to grow, be positioned to fund that growth, and you'll be a savior in their eyes. There is nothing more embarrassing or stressful than to have clients submit invoices and expect advances in 24 hours...and you can't come up with the money. If the phone or fax rings and you hope it's not a client wanting an advance, you're under funded. Believe me, that's under fun.

Advancing Too Much to Start

Your greatest risk with most clients will be the first funding you provide. You have no first-hand experience with receiving payments, of the client's and customer's honesty and integrity, or that the payment will come to you instead of the client. All of these put you in a vulnerable position. So prudence dictates that the first advances to a new client should usually be the smallest advances they receive.

However (especially when you're first starting out), the tendency is to move ahead more quickly than cautiously and to get the client under contract. Fight the temptation to give more than is wise. Make it clear that you will only advance so much, and no more, until you start to receive customer payments. Once a track record is established and you feel comfortable with your client's customers' payment patterns, you can gradually ease your earlier restrictions. Remember the Cardinal Rule of Money: don't risk more than you can afford to lose.

Payments Not Sent to You

You want to have all payments sent to you for one primary reason: you have a better chance of getting paid. With local clients, you may be slightly safer in allowing them to pick up payments, and they may be able to get them sooner. However, allowing payments to go to all clients routinely should never be done. You can lose a lot of money if only one client receives and keeps payment due you. Never rely on her saying she's going to "pay you back" – she may become very hard to find. This happened with one client I had (with her first and only invoice I bought) who was a published author in the medical field. A mutual friend who was a member of her church referred her. My daughter even babysat for her. Sounds like a good risk, right? Someone you'd think will keep her word and pay you? She skipped town owing me and a number of other people a collective pile of money.

When a client willfully and intentionally pockets a payment for a factored invoice, it constitutes criminal fraud because that client is literally stealing twice what is yours: first the advance she's already received, and second the payment for the invoice you own. When you bought the invoice it became your property and is no longer hers. Make sure every client fully understands this. Also make it clear from the start that such activity is a criminal offense you and your attorney take very seriously.

The other reason not to allow payments to go to the client is the simple fact that an honest mix-up or human error can easily occur. The client, client's spouse, secretary, bookkeeper, or whoever gets the mail may not realize that an invoice was factored and innocently deposit its payment into their account. Several weeks later when you haven't received payment you end up charging the client a larger fee. Your loss is that your factoring money hasn't turned as quickly as possible to make more money for you, and your client's paid an unnecessarily higher fee. The headache and loss of income is bad for both of you. This reason alone is good for explaining why payment must come to you.

Be clear from the beginning that payments will always come to you or you won't be able to be their factor. Sweet and simple. If they balk, you may allow the customer to make the check out to the client and send it to your address or lock box; just be sure you have a power of attorney in your client contract and – especially – that your bank will let you deposit checks made out to clients. Above all, make certain that your address appears prominently on the invoice as the "Remit to" address. This is discussed further in the chapter, "Record Keeping."

Poor Follow-up on Late- and Non-Payers

Because this is one of the most important aspects of your ongoing factoring business, the chapter "Preventive Maintenance" is devoted to it. Overlooking follow-up on late- and non-paying customers is a not only a very common but a very costly mistake.

As anyone who's ever collected money knows, the longer the wait to receive payment the less likely you are to be paid. Collection agencies have statistical graphs that illustrate this and the results are indisputable.

Therefore, the wise factor will carefully monitor how long customers take to pay bills and will take regular, definite steps to assure payment is made. When you don't make a point of regularly checking on payment status for overdue debt, all too often the debt will be ignored and can become impossible to collect.

For example, I had a client with two long-overdue invoices. Eventually the client was confronted on a very consistent and direct basis. After checking into what had become of these payments, the client stated that one of the customers claimed to have paid the invoice. The client and customer traced the check and found it was made out to the client's company and cashed. What had happened? Several months earlier, with the client's permission, an employee of the client had gone to the customer and offered a 25% discount if the customer paid the invoice immediately. The check was made out to the client's company and given to the employee...who promptly cashed it, pocketed the money, and never returned to work. The client agreed she still owed my company the money, but this problem could have been avoided if I had been in close touch with both client and customer as soon as the payment was overdue.

A good way to handle slow pays is discussed in the chapter "Preventive Maintenance." Once your business is under way and you have money on the street, refer to this chapter, understand and consistently practice what it suggests, and your company will be far more likely to succeed. The old saying fits perfectly here: the squeaky wheel gets the grease.

Chaining Clients

The business of one of my clients was to locate and arrange new accounts for janitorial service companies. His customers, the janitorial services, paid him the first two months' worth of billing for accounts provided, after which all income was the customer's (janitor's) to keep. The client wanted to factor one of his janitorial service customers who in turn wanted to factor some of the accounts the original client had secured. It sounded like a good deal: in a sense, two clients for the price of one.

However, the companies being cleaned didn't pay for the janitorial service, and the janitorial companies therefore didn't pay me for the invoices factored for the original client. The domino effect took place and all three of us ended up with a mess. If it had worked well, wonderful; but chaining clients like this is doubly risky. If the customers who paid the janitorial services were tried and true, it should have worked. Lesson: don't do transactions like this unless you have a solid history showing that the customers at the end of the chain have always paid and will continue to pay their bills in a timely and dependable manner.

Over Concentrations
and Lack of Limits

In the chapter, "Reducing Your Risk," we look at client and customer concentrations. Look at the charts in that chapter of client concentrations. Note the risk involved in putting too many eggs in one basket: i.e., if the basket spills, most of your eggs are history. Avoid over-concentrations. A new factor had $100,000 in factoring money and took on his first client who was soon factoring $80,000. All of this was concentrated in one customer. The things that could go wrong with that arrangement are enough to make one shudder.

Don't hesitate to put limits on how much you'll have in outstanding advances with a given client and customer. Make sure the client understands your limits. It's up to you to enforce them. Not doing so can lead you to the over-concentration problem just mentioned, as well as becoming under capitalized.

No Structure to Pay Yourself

Unless you need absolutely no income from your factoring business, arrange your company's budget from the start to pay you something, even a nominal amount, every month. If the fees you collect are routinely put back into the business and you never enjoy the fruits of your labors–at least a little – there can be a psychological side effect which is not healthy, especially if this is your full-time work. You need to feel that your efforts are benefiting your clients and providing you income. Nothing can sap your enthusiasm for work and the enjoyment of running your own business like working your fingers to the bone and not making a dime of take-home pay. The worker deserves his wages: that includes you.

The temptation as your business grows and you accumulate clients is to channel all net income back into advances. That can be a necessity at times (and a definite sign of under capitalization), but it's a bad idea to do this regularly. Make your salary a part of your operating budget, pay yourself every month or every other week, and make your business revolve around you...not the other way around. Talk to your accountant about the best way to structure this. If your fees are not enough to pay you what you need or have established as goals, you must either obtain more funding and/or clients, cut expenses, charge higher fees, or reconsider whether factoring will meet your income needs.

Making Loans to Clients

You will be looked upon by your clients as a person of means because you're providing cash they don't have. As a result, a few clients may ask you for loans instead of or in addition to factoring. This is especially possible if your client is in financial trouble, gets hit with an unexpected tax bill, or experiences some kind of financial crisis – medical expenses, lawsuit, divorce, car/truck/mortgage/building balloon payment due...you name it.

First, he may come to you and ask for a relatively small loan, perhaps $1,000 or $2,000, just to get him out of this temporary situation. Because he's a good client, honest and hard-working and you like him, you want to help. So you loan him the money, probably at an interest rate far lower than your factoring fees.

That crisis passes and then a few months later another problem arises. He's behind in his truck payments. If he doesn't have $3,000 in the truck dealer's hands by noon tomorrow, he'll lose his truck which is vital to his delivery business. If he loses his truck, he'll go out of business and you'll lose both the client and the $2,000 you're still owed from the first loan. Against your better judgment, you loan him another $3,000. Two months later...five months later...six months later...one crisis after another is met with more nervous requests. The tension in his voice is clear. By this time you're more than several thousand dollars into this client but if you pull the plug, the house of cards will come crashing down, he'll be out of business and you'll never see your money again.

Refer back to the section on saying "No." Avoid getting into a situation like this by declining such requests right off the bat. You are a factor, not a lender. You buy invoices, you don't lend money. If your client would like to factor some receivables to get out of a bind, you'll be glad to find a creative way to help; but you don't do loans. Period.

If you start loaning money, you won't make as much in interest as you would from factoring (even if they pay you back). And you'll have less factoring money available. You stand to lose a lot in the long run if the above scenario develops, and unfortunately it's quite possible. Again, stick to one thing and do it well: factoring.

Giving Advances on Invoices for Work Not Yet Completed

This can happen very easily with even your best clients, and with clients who are either new or have been factoring for some time. It will creep up on you if you let it.

Similar to making loans described above, a client will come to you saying there's an unexpected bill or he wants to make a special purchase to help his business, maybe some new equipment he can get at a great price if he grabs it right away.

Knowing you don't do loans, he asks if it would be okay to give your advance for an upcoming invoice now rather than when the work is done and the invoice is ready to send. The invoice may be for next week's work or perhaps next month's work. Obviously you won't be able to verify the invoice because the work's not finished or perhaps not even started.

But he pleads that helping him in this way will really get him out of a jam, or really enable him to make more money with that new equipment. Especially if he's been a good client for some time, you honestly expect him to complete the work as usual; after all, the invoice will be to a regular customer who is routinely factored and a good payer (maybe). Why not help him out, after all? He's honest and a good client and you like to help people.

If you agree to do this most of the time everything will work out smoothly. But it only takes once for a snag to develop. What can happen? Just about anything, though none are likely. The client might be injured or fall ill and not be able to do the work as expected. A family emergency can arise (death of a parent, a child is severely hurt or very ill...you name it) which takes the client out of town or away from work for a few weeks–precisely the time he *would* have done the work for which you just advanced him. Worse, the client could have a heart attack or be in a serious car accident or anything else catastrophic and just drop dead. Not likely, but not impossible.

Heaven forbid, if your client turns out to be a crook and is smooth enough to gain your trust after working with you for some time, he's also learned your operation's vulnerability. He's figured out this is a perfect way to fleece you, pulls it off, and is long gone or declares bankruptcy by the time you realize what's happened.

Again these are unlikely scenarios but stranger things have happened. The longer you factor the more likely you are to get a request like this. Sooner or later, someone will ask for it so be ready with your answer.

On the other hand, none of the above scenarios may happen at all. Life will more likely carry on quite routinely. However, what will this early advance do to his cash flow next month? Because this advance will not be forthcoming then, will he be able to pay regular bills, meet payroll, or pay for some unexpected expense that crops up then? If he can't you'll likely find him on your doorstep asking to do the very same thing again, and when this becomes a pattern you have a problem.

Abusing factoring like this is a big reason clients go out of business due to cash flow problems, even when they're factoring. Larger and more experienced factors simply don't advance on invoices before the work is complete; neither should you. Make it your policy not to advance on *any* invoice until the work is finished and is signed off by the customer or can be verified. Period. (Just like you don't do loans. Period). Make this clear from the very beginning so he never even thinks to ask in the first place…though he very likely will ask anyway just to test you. Kind of like your kids.

Standing by this policy protects you both from intentional fraud and from situations which truly are not expected but which put your money at risk anyway. You'll feel a little like a parent turning your teenager away who's asking for money to go somewhere fun, but you need to be firm.

What's more, when you say yes just one time the precedent is set. It'll be harder to say no the next time and chances are high your client will ask you to do it again if you've said yes just once. Count on it.

Purchase Order Funding

It is very common for prospects to think the only receivables they have to factor are purchase orders. These are orders from a customer for work to be done, but which has not begun. Thus, there is no invoice generated yet, and no completed service or product for you to verify with a customer.

Sometimes factors will advance against purchase orders, but usually decrease the advance to perhaps 50 to 70%. The advance is sent to the client's supplier, not the client. When work is eventually completed and the invoice is cut, the factor then buys it from the client for the remaining 30 to 10% of the advance (the total advance now equals 80%). It becomes a normal factoring transaction from there.

Often with government transactions, all you'll have is the equivalent of a purchase order. While the government is obligated to pay (in their own sweet time) as long as the client delivers, the same is not necessarily true with business purchase orders. This makes funding purchase orders, especially with a new client, terribly risky, and you are wise to avoid doing so.

Early in my business, I funded a new client's three purchase orders from some nurseries that had ordered wholesale trees from him. There was no supplier for my client since he dug the trees up in the mountains himself and the advance went to him. He delivered the trees to the nurseries which they acknowledged receiving; unfortunately, the nurseries later claimed the trees died and they refused to pay. Because my client guaranteed his products, the nurseries didn't have to pay for them. Worse, he had a bad year, no personal financial reserves, and therefore couldn't make good the money he now owed me. Eventually he ended up in bankruptcy and I lost everything advanced him. It was an expensive lesson in purchase order funding, as well as buying receivables for perishable goods.

Being Rushed

It is very common in this business to run into potential clients or brokers with potential clients who absolutely MUST get funding by tomorrow or sooner, or dire consequences will befall them. This can be a two-edged sword, but by and large be careful with people who want money too quickly.

While you want to find clients who have sincere cash flow problems which put them in a pinch (which is why we're in business), never allow yourself to be rushed. You must act expeditiously with new clients, as unnecessary delays can cost them money and create further problems. However, rushing to help someone out of a crisis (usually of their making) may not be in your best interest. Someone who needs instant money may be either

1) a bona fide good prospect
2) a prospect with poor management skills and therefore questionable as a good client (see the section, "Making Loans to Clients")
3) a prospect who knows hurrying up the process can cut corners to his benefit, or
4) a con artist ready to take you for a ride.

If the prospect wants you to hurry up your procedures, beware. Don't be rushed. Take the time necessary to do the due diligence you feel is needed. If the prospect isn't willing or able to wait for this, she probably won't be the kind of client with whom you want to work. If she's legitimate, she can almost always wait a couple days for you to do your homework. While you should move quickly, don't short-circuit your background checks: you may end up getting burned.

Not Following Your Own Rules

The times I've run into trouble factoring are when 1) because of my inexperience, I took on clients or customers I didn't recognize as bad risks, and 2) I didn't follow my own rules. While you're in this business to help others and make a decent living, you'll do neither if you can't separate your heart from your head when tough decisions must be made.

Count on it: you'll have people with hard luck stories that can tear your heart, prospects with good customers but one nasty glitch, and all sorts of circumstances which force you to decide: do I accept this situation or not? This chapter outlines rules I've made to avoid making costly errors; you will develop your own rules. But if you have rules and choose to ignore them, your risk of losing money or even your business is greatly increased. Establish and test your parameters, limits, types of businesses you'll fund, and whom you'll turn away and why. Once you have a good set of guidelines, follow them. Being firm does not mean you're cold, calculating, and heartless; it means you'll be around for the next prospect you can truly help.

Failure to Plan

The chapter "Charting Your Course" provides guiding questions to point you in the direction you wish to take your factoring business. While this manual doesn't provide similar specific questions for a marketing plan, it's not a bad idea to commit this part of your business to writing as well. These are the two key parts of piloting a successful ship.

While you probably don't need to plot every detail years in advance, failure to plan, at least in general terms, is planning to fail: trite but true. Compose the map you will follow, make adjustments for detours as they appear along the way and you'll arrive at your destination a lot more smoothly and quickly than if you just wing it.

Poor Record Keeping

Accurate, organized record keeping is vital to your factoring service, and a separate chapter is dedicated to it. It may appear to your clients that you don't do much – just verify invoices, advance money, wait to get paid and give rebates. But in order to keep this financial information accurate and accessible (as well as client, customer, co-factor, and broker data), you have to be well organized when it comes to keeping records.

Unless you intend to have only one or two clients, and work with a small number of brokers, you'll need a computer with a good data base for the above organization. You'll certainly need good and flexible factoring software and adequate financial software to track your business. You'll also need to have your filing cabinet(s) systematically organized and leave a good paper trail backing up what you have stored on your computer. If you don't, and your computer goes down, or you need proof of an invoice or check or hard copy of some aspect of a transaction, you'll be stuck. That's not to say you need paper copies of every little thing; just be so organized that you'll be able to quickly pull what you need.

Poor record keeping makes you look unprofessional to clients, customers, and colleagues. It can cost you dearly if there are ever tax questions, or a dispute as to whether an invoice was mailed, payment received, rebates paid, and so on.

Inadequate Software

If you have no more than two or three clients, you can probably track your factoring information on spreadsheets and be satisfied. However, as your client base grows, you will quickly outgrow spreadsheets and wish you had started with software written expressly for factoring. A selection of programs is available and the chapter "Factoring Software" is dedicated to this subject.

I started my business with spreadsheets for tracking factoring transactions, but it became unwieldy by the time I had about six clients. When I reached a dozen, it was a terrible burden on my time and energy. Once I started using database software written specifically for factoring, hours of entry and reporting work were lifted which enabled me to dedicate more time to other aspects of the business. I only wished I had started using this approach in the first place.

11
Reducing Your Risk

Factoring Fundamentals, Book 1 of this series, contains a section with three chapters which discusses the risks factors face and how to minimize these risks. Rather than repeat that information here, let's expand on some of these points and add a few more.

Protect Yourself

There are several measures you can take which will provide protective shields. Remember, however, the potential for loss remains an ever-present aspect of factoring. The purpose of the following steps is to *minimize* risk; you cannot *eliminate* it.

Avoid Over Concentrations

Without question, this is by far the most important safeguard you can implement, and harks back to the Cardinal Rule of Money. If you religiously follow all other risk management practices but overlook this one, you can still lose big time and be out of business in a heartbeat.

The policy of many larger factors is to never invest more than 10% of their funds in any one client, and they closely monitor their concentrations with customers and invoices as well. Watching concentrations is a critical method of limiting risk, and a similar policy for a small factor is wise. Charts 7 through 11 show various client concentrations.

As you study the following pie charts, ask yourself: "What will happen to this factor if any one or two of these accounts (pie wedges) go bad? Will the loss seriously harm or even kill the factor's business?"

Chart 7 is a fairly common example of a new factor's client concentrations. Having a very small number of clients makes spreading risk around somewhat difficult. If the client with 54% of the factor's funds were to defraud the factor, not make good on large invoices, or otherwise not repay the factor, the loss would be significant. However, the same misfortune happening with the client holding 13% would not be as harmful to the factor.

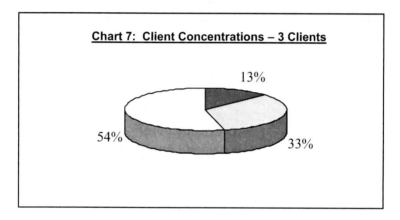

Chart 7: Client Concentrations – 3 Clients

In Chart 8, the small factor has added two clients and has spread her concentrations safely.

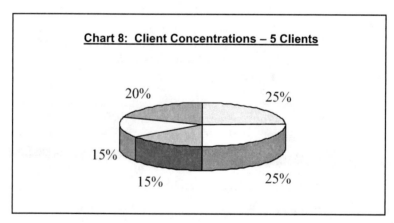

Chart 8: Client Concentrations – 5 Clients

In Chart 9, a risky imbalance has occurred. If the client representing 60% of the business were to have problems, 60% of the factor's money would be in jeopardy. Don't let yourself get into a position such as this.

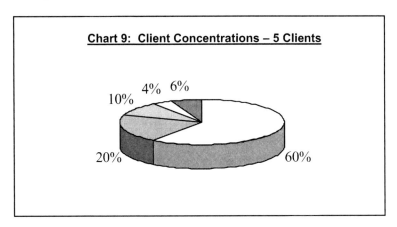

Chart 10 may represent a typical small factor's distribution of funds. The factor's resources are overly concentrated in the client holding 35%; otherwise, the risk is fairly well distributed.

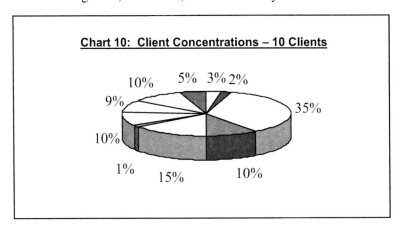

In Chart 11, the factor has grown considerably and now has 25 clients. This chart shows an excellent distribution of funds, keeping risk to a minimum in all accounts. This represents safe concentrations among all clients.

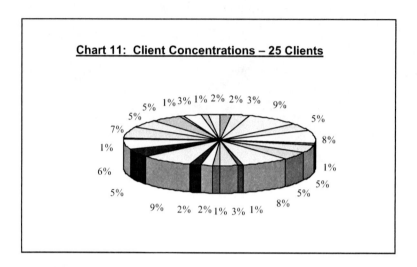

Chart 11: Client Concentrations – 25 Clients

Set Credit Limits

The logical way to avoid over concentrations is to set limits on the credit you extend to clients. Likewise, set a limit on the total money invested in the invoices of any customer, and establish the dollar amount of the largest invoice you will buy. This protects you from having too many eggs in any of these baskets, as mentioned earlier.

Most medium-sized factors will not accept clients factoring less than $10,000 per month. In my own business, I have turned this rule upside down. To limit my exposure, especially with new clients (where a factor's risk is often greatest), I set initial client credit limits at $10,000 and accept only clients who start factoring with monthly volumes *less* than $10,000.

This goes against traditional factors' thinking but I have found this practice to be not only one of the best safety valves I've ever used as a small factor, but leads to referrals from larger factors when they must turn away deals that are too small for them. What's more, when a client reaches a certain level of factoring volume (in my case, I set it at $25,000 to $30,000 on a consistent factoring basis), I either bring in another small factor to participate with me, or simply hand the client to a larger factor (the same one who referred the client earlier, if that's where he came from). This limits my total exposure with any client to $30,000, and keeps me from risking what is, to me, more than I can afford (or just choose) to lose. For further thoughts about this subject, see the article from *FactorTips* entitled "A Small Factor's Thoughts about Big Factors' Concerns," reprinted in the Appendix.

Once a client has been incubated with me, finding another factor willing to take the account is not difficult. If the client was not originally referred to me by a broker, I receive a nice broker commission from the larger factor.

If a broker brings you a client who then outgrows you, do your best to protect that broker's interest when referring the client elsewhere. This is simply a matter of fairness to the broker and also good business for you: the broker will appreciate what you're doing and be inclined to continue referring new business to you.

Set Time Limits

The longer factoring companies are in business, the pickier they often become about selecting their clients. A very experienced and successful factor located near me usually will not take on a new account that takes longer than 30 days to pay. After he's worked with that account for a while, he'll accept customers who take longer to pay.

Set time limits that you'll accept as "prudent" with your clients. The longer they take to pay, the less are your chances of collecting. When you're waiting for checks to come in – especially when clients have new invoices coming up they want you to fund – even 30 or 40 days can drag on and seem like a very long time for money you're waiting to receive.

Factor on a Recourse Basis

Recourse factoring means if a client's customer does not pay an invoice for *any* reason, the client is responsible to cover this nonpayment. Non-recourse factoring means if a customer does not pay for reason of insolvency or inability to pay, the factor will take the loss. However, with non-recourse factoring, if an invoice is disputed by the customer, the client is still responsible to the factor.

Because of the obligation of the client to repay factors under a recourse relationship, the argument is made that recourse factors are lending money to their clients. After all, if a customer doesn't pay an invoice, the client must pay the factor back either in the form of cash, a new invoice, deductions from advances or rebates, or a combination of these. This repayment raises the issue of usury, with which you must be familiar.

Usury is the maximum interest than can be charged by law on a loan and each state has its own usury laws. In many states these laws are different for business and consumer loans. Some states are very general about what they consider usurious business rates, while others are very restrictive. For example, in Washington state a lender can charge anything a business borrower agrees to in writing. A usurious rate can be claimed only if there is no written and signed agreement as to interest or fees. In other states business usury is a fixed percentage, as low or as high as 10%, 24%, or 36% APR, depending on the state.

Some argue that factoring should be considered exempt from usury because no loans are being made – the factor is buying receivables for a fee, not charging interest on a loan. However, when recourse occurs, the client must make up the advance and fee earned: is this "paying back a loan" and therefore subject to usury laws?

In some states this is not an issue as long as you meet the state's usury requirements. For example, say one state's laws require there to be a signed contract between two businesses, but any interest amount is allowable. If factor does business with a private individual on a recourse basis, that factor could be in violation of usury because the contract is between a business (the factor) and a private party (the client). But if both parties are businesses, the factor can charge any fee ("interest") which the client agrees to in writing.

However, in states with more strict usury laws, the factor fee becomes an issue because usurious interest amounts are usually a lot less than the APR of a factor's fee (5% factoring fee per month equals 60% APR). If a factor operates in a state where usurious interest is above 18% APR, that factor could be considered to be charging usurious rates. If that factor were to end up in court with a client, a judge could level severe penalties against the factor.

The state in which the factor operates determines which usury laws are to be applied. Obviously you need to learn your state's business usury laws. To find these, do an internet search looking up "usury" and the name of your state. Look for the actual laws in the state's constitution if you can find it. If you can't find specific information, contact a knowledgeable business lawyer and ask what the laws are. If he doesn't know, ask where you can find out.

If your state's usury laws make recourse difficult or impossible you should provide non-recourse factoring. As long as your state allows it, you're safer to factor on a recourse basis. Non-recourse can cost you some advances and fees unless all your clients' customers are rock-solid – and some of them may not be. If your client gets large enough that you need to broker him, providing non-recourse through a larger factor can be a selling point for handing him off to one. Again, you're looking out for his welfare and he'll appreciate that.

Because your client will bear the loss of a bad invoice, recourse factoring provides you the following safety nets:

1. Clients are less likely to dump bad customers on you.

2. Clients are even more interested in collecting, besides wanting to keep their fees lower.

3. You'll get your fee and advance back even if the customer doesn't pay, assuming the client has the means to make good on the unpaid invoice. Be sure your contract specifically states the recourse nature of your factoring relationship, unless this is precluded by the usury laws in your state.

With recourse factoring you need to do a thorough job of due diligence with your clients as well as their customers. If the customer isn't good for the invoice and your client can't make it good either, you still end up eating the loss. Recourse to the client is only as good as that client's ability to pay. Obviously doing your homework before you begin is the name of the game with recourse factoring – and even more so with non-recourse.

Make it clear to your client that he should never factor customers about whom he has the slightest doubts regarding their ability or inclination to pay. Neither of you want to factor poor-paying or exceptionally slow-paying customers. Making up unpaid invoices hurts his cash flow badly (which is why he's factoring in the first place) and can dig him into a deep hole with you.

Establish Reserves Beyond the Advance Holdback

When you advance 80%, you have a built in reserve of 20%, from which your fee is taken. However, if the invoice doesn't pay you're still potentially out the 80% you advanced. What do you do if this isn't paid by the customer and the client can't cover it?

Exchanging for a new invoice, deducting from advances and rebates, outright cash payments from the client, or a combination of these are the common answer. Yet each can create a cash flow problem – a problem he knows too well already, and the reason he started factoring in the first place.

A simple work-around to this dilemma is to establish a separate reserve account. Make very clear to the client why and how you do this. When a customer short pays or doesn't pay, tapping the reserve will often take care of the shortfall. If there is still more owed than is in the reserve, taking the remainder from advances, rebates, cash, or new invoices doesn't have quite the bite as before.

When I finish explaining this reserve, many prospective clients say, "That's a good idea" and are happy to cooperate. This is what I tell them:

> "Establishing a separate reserve account will protect both of us if your customer short pays or doesn't pay at all. To safeguard against this risk, we will create a reserve account from a small portion of your rebates which acts as a 'rainy day' fund, and here's how it works.

"As you know, I give you a 75% advance and keep a 5% fee when your customer pays in 30 days. That means when a $1,000 invoice pays, I'll reimburse myself $750 for the advance, keep $50 for the fee, and owe you the remaining $200. I will provide a rebate of 15% or $150 right away, and put aside the other 5% or $50 into your reserve fund, and build the reserve up to a certain level. Ordinarily the reserve is 10% of your credit limit, so if your credit limit is $10,000, we'll build up your reserve fund to $1,000. The $50 from this invoice goes into your reserve fund, and when the reserve reaches that $1,000 cap, you receive your full rebate from there on.

"Setting aside a little from each payment will provide $1,000 to cover unpaid or short paid invoices, and we'll draw from this fund first before requiring you to trade a new invoice, take the money from a new advance, or withhold money from you your rebates.

"If we need to use the reserve, we'll build it up again from future customer payments. When you are finished factoring, the reserve is yours and will be paid you in full."

Clients who have factored before usually see the wisdom of this procedure. Potential clients who see how it protects their cash flow appreciate the prudence behind it. Besides, they're getting most of their rebate back anyway. Accountants or attorneys with very sharp pencils might suggest to the clients they're paying the equivalent of somewhat higher fees because they don't receive their full rebate until a later date. However, these people in particular will also see the wisdom of an added cushion against short payments and non-payments. This added protection benefits both you and the client.

Due Diligence

Proper due diligence, public records searches and filings, and credit searches on appropriate parties are critical for limiting your risk. The next three chapters are dedicated to these subjects.

Incorporate or Become an LLC

While this is another expense, it's a good idea to do when you move from brokering to factoring and/or have some serious money on the street. The reason is simple: as a sole proprietor, if you go bankrupt or lose a lawsuit, all your personal property can be used to make the debt payments or restitution due. If you are incorporated or an LLC (Limited Liability Company), your personal property is better protected. Also, as you make more income from factoring, tax laws will benefit you more this way. LLC's provide better flexibility and protection than partnerships and are often recommended by attorneys. Finally, having "Corporation," "Inc.," or "LLC" at the end of your business name makes you sound like a force to be reckoned with and, in turn, gives you more credibility. Check with your attorney and accountant to determine which entity best fits your situation.

Key Person Insurance

Talk with an independent insurance agent about key person insurance. This is usually a term insurance policy that pays a beneficiary or beneficiaries (your spouse, estate, or business lenders) in the event you die or are incapacitated and can't work. Not having this may discourage private lenders from putting their money in your business if you work solo or your company wouldn't function without you. Having this insurance not only shows you're responsible, but that their investment is more secure in your company. They will be impressed if you can demonstrate the ability to repay them even if you're not around or can't physically continue to work.

What's more, if you're married this provides a major benefit to your surviving spouse. It provides him or her with cash in hand to can pay off any debt and continue your business if they so choose.

Liability Insurance

This is not cheap and may not be something you can afford right away, but it is definitely worth having sooner or later when you're factoring and dealing directly with people's money. This is business insurance that covers someone suing you for giving bad advice or doing something they claim harmed their business and cost them money. Given society's penchant for suing the pants off anybody for anything, this is another means of protection you must consider. Check with an independent insurance agent regarding coverage and costs in your particular situation. It costs around $2,000 a year to carry; it could cost you everything if you don't.

Credit Insurance

This is insurance larger factors sometimes purchase to protect themselves from a catastrophic loss. I say "larger factors" because the minimum factoring volume to make this insurance cost effective is around $1 million. If your volume is less, your best insurance as a small factor is to religiously follow the risk management methods in this series, particularly avoiding concentrations in any client, customer, and invoice, and keeping a fairly low cap on the total volume you will allow for these.

If your volume is large enough credit insurance provides your business with protection against customer nonpayment because of insolvency, slow payment, or inability to pay. Most credit insurance carriers require coverage on your entire portfolio, rather than just those customers you're most concerned about.

Premiums are calculated as a percentage of your sales, and the rates vary depending on the history and historical debt loss of your company and customer base. Typically the cost is less than 1% of sales. The level of indemnity usually ranges from 80% to 100%, depending on the policy you select, your experience, your portfolio, and your premium target. Like any other insurance, deductibles are in place so there is little point in filing a claim on smaller accounts which fall under the deductible amount. In general, credit insurance is used against catastrophic losses, not smaller, routine losses most small factors are likely to experience.

Be aware that using this type of insurance usually means your credit insurance company must approve all your clients' customers. In turn that means your carrier will become your underwriter for determining which customers you can and cannot factor. Some factors will be glad to give this responsibility to the carrier; others may not want to lose control of this important part of their business. Choosing between the two becomes a management decision once your business reaches this level, if it ever does.

The advantages of credit insurance are:

- Protection against large bad debt losses
- Pre-approved coverage for large accounts
- Ongoing account monitoring which provides early warning of potential credit risks
- Ability to secure better financing terms for working capital by offering your lender insured receivables as collateral.

EULER ACI is a carrier that covers factors' accounts receivable. Founded in 1893, this is a large company with branches across North America and around the world. To apply, you complete an application and forward it with a recent aging of your receivables to a EULER ACI agent or broker for a quote. To find a representative, call 877-909-3224 or go to their web site at www.eulergroup.com.

Trust Is the Name of the Game

With all of these risk management tools in mind, let me reiterate a key element of factoring. You must act in every way and at all times so that your clients hold you in complete and utter trust. You must never do anything to violate that trust or the need for liability insurance may be urgent!

Your client must trust you as she would her banker, accountant, lawyer, doctor, pastor, and anyone else in whom she entrusts the welfare of her life and business. If there is the slightest doubt about your character, integrity or business expertise, she will pull away and you won't keep that client as a client very long (or get referrals).

If your motives are pure – if you are putting your client's needs above your own selfish interest (notice I did not say your need to be secure and profitable; be clear about the difference) – you will develop loyalty that will pay for itself ten times more than any advertising budget. Think about the professionals with whom you deal and those you completely trust with your important business and personal affairs. Why do you trust them? Go and do likewise.

12
Due Diligence

What Is "Adequate" Due Diligence?

Someone once asked me, "Why do due diligence costs vary so much among factors? Some charge nothing, while others require $100 to as much as $500 or more just to check out a prospective client. What does it take and how much does it really cost to do adequate due diligence?"

My answer: what constitutes "adequate" due diligence is in the eye of each factor. And I posed a counter-question: Why is due diligence even necessary? The answer is this. Factoring is a business that involves risk to operating capital. A factor's income is based on fees received for factored invoices. These fees pay for services the factor performs, plus the risk the factor assumes in advancing funds against a client's receivables. A factor's working capital – advances and earned fees – can be quickly lost in just one bad debt.

Suppose a prospective client comes along and is interested in factoring with you. In order to decide if you want to invest your money in this prospect's business, you want to learn as much as you feel is necessary about this company, its history, its customers, and its management's skills. You perform due diligence to learn these things. The purpose of due diligence is to limit risk. While due diligence carries no guarantee that money will not be lost in the course of factoring, it provides indications as to which clients and customers will be less risky and have fewer complications, and thus be more desirable. When your due diligence is done, you decide if you want to take on this client's receivables – this risk – or pass. Just how much and what kind of due diligence you feel is "adequate" is up to you.

Due diligence is one of the more difficult aspects to learn when becoming a factor of small receivables. It is imprecise, subjective, and provides no guarantees you won't get burned.

Recognize that the purpose of due diligence is to *limit* your risk, not *eliminate* it, and to help you determine which other precautions to take to further limit risk after factoring begins. (For those precautions, see the chapters "Reducing Your Risk" and "Common Mistakes.")

The purpose of this chapter is to point out the subjective nature of due diligence, present what is commonly done by other factors, and invite you to decide how extensive your due diligence will be. Will your process be carefully planned and carried out, very loose and easy-going, or somewhere in between? You decide. You're the boss.

Starting Your Due Diligence

Generally speaking, you will probably want to learn about the honesty, business experience, debts, lien positions, and financial position of a client – not to mention what gets the most hype: the financial health and stability of the customers.

Most factors start with an application form. By reviewing this information and asking questions for clarification, you'll determine whether or not the prospect fits your parameters. That is, are this prospect's monthly volume and invoice amounts and quantity in your range, are you comfortable factoring receivables in this industry, is the geographical location acceptable, and so on.

The more new prospects you consider, the more you will have a sense for what due diligence needs to be performed on each. Some factors routinely run the same due diligence on all prospects; others do more in-depth searches with certain prospects than with others. What follows are the various due diligence tools available.

Often prospective clients are in a hurry to start factoring and understandably become impatient with delays caused by due diligence. While you need to respond to their need, you also need to protect your funds. One of the peculiarities I first noticed about larger factors when I began brokering was how extremely careful and unwilling they are to be hurried. There is a good reason for this: when they were not careful and were hurried in the past, they got stung.

Also, when I first told a larger, experienced factor to whom I had brokered some transactions that I was beginning to factor small deals myself, he congratulated me and then immediately asked me if I were doing recourse or non-recourse. When I said recourse only, he made a point of telling me to:

- get business financial statements
- get personal financial statements
- get personal guarantees
- continue to verify invoices.

You can choose to skip these if you want to close a deal quickly – you're the boss, remember – but you live with the consequences in any event. Let's look at each.

Business financials (balance sheets and income statements) for the last couple of years will tell you how much a client has coming in, going out, where his money is tied up, and overall how stable, and therefore how safe, this company will be to factor. If he is new and doesn't have these, your risk is increased. Not only do you know little about him financially, you may be dealing with someone inexperienced in business and/or with his product or service. He (like you learning to factor) will no doubt make costly mistakes as he learns. This is where your gut feeling about the person comes into play – does this business owner strike you as someone who has what it takes, or not?

Personal financials (a statement of net worth – total assets and total liabilities – and income taxes paid) will tell you how much personal income she makes and what she has to fall back on. The reason you want to know this is so you are assured she personally (apart from her business) has enough to cover invoices that go bad. This also helps you determine a limit as to how much you want to factor her in a given period of time, as well as a limit to the total amount of credit you want to give (which is also based on how stable her customers are).

Personal guaranty (one of the signed documents which is part of your application packet) states precisely this: regardless of what happens to his business, your client will personally make good on any money owed you. This gives you greater protection if his business flops, provided he has the personal resources to pay what you're owed. Occasionally a business owner will balk or even refuse to sign this; you must decide if no signature here is a deal killer. If there are problems collecting in a recourse situation and the owner hasn't signed a personal guaranty, you may have great difficulty recovering the debt. Make sure, however, the business owner's personal resources are sufficient or a personal guaranty is worthless. Also be sure that they do not state the title of their position in the company and that the company's name is not by the signature. This is important to distinguish that they are guaranteeing personal funds, not business funds.

All principals of the business must sign this document for you to be fully protected. They need to be clear that this puts them on the hook personally to ensure you are paid, even if their company is incorporated. If the business is in a community property state, the principal's spouse or principals' spouses must also sign it. Check with your attorney regarding the laws in your state. If you must do non-recourse factoring, this document may not be necessary; but remember, you have less security if there are problems. Again, ask your attorney what to do for your particular situation.

Continue to verify invoices. This can be one of the more tiresome tasks of factoring, but it's frequently educational. Verifying invoices is simply calling up the customer when you receive an invoice to factor and:

- asking if the product or service has been received in good condition
- asking if the customer is satisfied with the product or the work done
- making certain the payment will come to you.

Doing this can save both you and the client a lot of hassles down the road when you learn (as does happen) that something went awry and the customer in fact *doesn't* intend to pay the bill. In fact, the customer probably wouldn't have told your client there was a problem until a month or two later, if at all. Thus you serve as a quality control agent – another benefit of factoring.

Only after the invoice is verified (and if there is a problem, after it's resolved) do you provide the advance on an invoice. This is why it may take a day or two before the advance is forthcoming. Verifying invoices by faxed letter can save a lot of time and offers documented proof of acceptance by the customer.

The document "Notice of Assignment/Certificate of Acceptance" can be an excellent tool for routine verifications. A shipping receipt, bill of lading, or other proof of work done or product received (time cards for a temp agency, for instance) – properly signed by a responsible party at the customer's business – can also provide verification.

Other Tools

There are other due diligence tools a small factor does well to employ: aging reports, UCC-1 filings, credit reports, and background searches

Aging Reports

If your prospect can provide you with aging reports, get them. These are a gold mine of information concerning their customers and how long they take to pay. They can help enormously in deciding if you want to accept a prospect as a client, which of his customers you do and don't want to factor, and if you'll give him different advances or rates than usual. If an aging report shows they have nothing but extremely slow- or non-paying customers, and/or a huge number of very small invoices, you may simply decline him right away and save a lot of expense and time with further due diligence.

Not all clients will be able to provide you with an aging report, but always ask for one. Most computer business accounting programs come with these reports, especially a Current Outstanding Receivables report. This shows who presently owes the client how much and for how long, and will give a good indication of which customers shouldn't be factored (usually 90-day-plus payers).

In addition to a report of Current Outstanding Receivables, a report of Closed Receivables and their aging is especially valuable. That is, try to get a report that will give a year's history of paid invoices (sorted by customer and payment times) with the invoice amounts. If the customers maintain their past payment patterns, you'll see pretty easily which ones are best to factor and be able to predict future payment patterns for customers on Current Outstanding Receivables report. In other words, if certain customers have histories of paying in a week, others in a month, and others in three months, the best ones to factor are those who pay in a month.

Aging reports can vary widely in how they are laid out on paper, but the basic information is pretty similar: name of customer, perhaps their address and phone number, invoice amounts, and length of time out. The length of time is usually divided into columns named "0 – 30 Days," "31 – 60 Days," "61 – 90 Days," and "Over 90 Days." Some aging reports will add a column for Current (within terms) before the "0 – 30 Days" column, and some will add a column of "90 – 120 Days" before the final column, "Over 120 Days."

On the following pages are a sample Current Outstanding Receivables aging report and a sample Closed Receivables aging report for the fictitious Acme Services Company.

Try this exercise.

1. Review only the first report. Which customers are you likely to accept with only this information?

2. Now review the second report and compare the information here to that in the first report.

3. How does the second report further inform your decision?

4. Would you change your decision on any customers now?

Chart 12: Aging Report – Current Outstanding Receivables

Acme Services Company

Customer	Inv. #	0 - 30	31 - 60	61 - 90	91 +	Total
AAA Business Svcs	1355			500		500
253 555-1443	1378		1,575			1,575
	1488	350				350
	1565	900				900
		1,250	1,575	500	0	3,325
Barry's Berry Farm	1285		2,500			2,500
360 555-9889	1556	3,000				3,000
	1766	1,000				1,000
	1790	4,000				4,000
		8,000	2,500	0	0	10,500
Delightful Deli	1200				225	225
206 555-1345	1256				295	295
		0	0	0	520	520
Never Never Land Sales	4562	2,500				2,500
509 555-PPAN	5661	4,500				4,500
	5862	7,000				7,000
	5955	3,000				3,000
		17,000	0	0	0	17,000
Pink Elephant Advertsg	2599			1,000		1,000
206 555-9873	3700	1,000				1,000
		1,000	0	1,000	0	2,000
Reverb Music Store	1014				25	25
206 55BLAST	1022				50	50
	1032				35	35
	1532				60	60
	1544			50		50
	2554		15			15
		0	15	50	180	235
Total Outstanding Rcvbls		**27,250**	**4,090**	**1,550**	**700**	**33,590**

Chart 13: Aging Report – Closed Invoices, Last 12 Months

Acme Services Company

Customer	Inv. #	0 - 30	31 - 60	61 - 90	91 +	Total
AAA Business Services	445	400				400
253 555-1443	586	595				595
	599	350	750			1,100
	701	500				500
		1,845	750	0	0	2,595
Barry's Berry Farm	253	1,000				1,000
360 555-9889	456		2,500			2,500
	625				1,500	1,500
	755		2,000			2,000
		1,000	4,500	0	1,500	7,000
Cascadia Clinic	654			500		500
253 555-0988	786		1,500			1,500
		0	1,500	500	0	2,000
Never Never Land Sales	452	1,500				1,500
509 555-PPAN	564	2,500				2,500
	753	6,000				6,000
	783	8,500				8,500
		18,500	0	0	0	18,500
Oscar's Cans & Liners	15	25				25
509 555-SCUM	35		75			75
	77	50				50
	105	100				100
	155		25			25
	236	35				35
	350	50				50
	369	60				60
		320	100	0	0	420

Chart 13, continued

Customer	Inv. #	0 - 30	31 - 60	61 - 90	91 +	Total
Pink Elephant Advertising	125		500			500
206 555-9873	159		1,000			1,000
	456		750			750
	756		500			500
	789		1,250			1,250
		0	4,000	0	0	4,000
Reverb Music Store	456	500				500
206 55BLAST	754		150			150
	788				50	50
		500	150	0	50	700
Samson's Gym & Hair Salon	156		250			250
206 555-SNIP	265			450		450
	354	100				100
	568		300			300
	686	100				100
	782			500		500
	793				750	750
	825		350			350
	835	75				75
		275	900	950	750	2,875
Ursula's Umbrellas	56	500				500
206-555-DRIP	156	500				500
	265	500				500
	387	500				500
	444	500				500
	489	500				500
	500	500				500
		3,500	0	0	0	3,500
Total Closed Recvbls.		25,940	11,900	1,450	2,300	41,590

UCC-1

The next tool is the UCC-1 (Uniform Commercial Code) form, which places a lien against a client's collateral. This is described in detail in the chapter, "UCCs."

Credit Reports

Another tool is a credit report on the client, customers, and/or their principal(s). There are a number of credit reporting companies out there, and the one(s) you use is up to you. Dun & Bradstreet is the best known and gives extremely thorough reports. Once you've been factoring a while, you may want to move up to D&B's services. However, there are some disadvantages to D&B for the beginning factor.

1. They're expensive. The larger the report you wish to retrieve (larger means more information), the higher the cost.

2. There are a lot of companies who are not listed in D&B. This is especially true of very small companies, many of whom you are likely to factor.

3. Much of the information in D&B reports is supplied by the companies themselves, which makes the very information you're looking for suspect in some people's minds.

For your purposes as a beginning small factor, carefully review the credit reporting resources in the next chapter. Compare prices and features offered, such as small business and personal credit reports (you'll want both), UCC-1 searches, other lien and judgment searches, what credit reporting company they use (D&B, Experían, Equifax, etc.). Get as much information from each as you can, and you should be able to find a service that best fits your needs. Most provide a free sample report online that can be quite instructive.

Meanwhile, you might consider obtaining Experían (formerly called TRW) credit reports through National Association of Credit Management (available to anyone). The NACM offers numerous resources to members including collection services, a newsletter, educational workshops, discounts with Airborne Express and long distance rates, and more. Each credit report will cost around $10 to $20 and up, depending on the number of reports you order per year, how much information is provided, how you access the information, and if you provide credit information on clients' customers. You may want to have your client share or absorb the cost of these when they apply. Just be sure you make it clear what their cost is and why you need the information. If you obtain credit information on a customer, the client will be more than happy to learn what you find.

If you're considering factoring a very young company, there probably won't be a business credit report available. Hence a personal credit report on the principal(s) can often tell you what you need to know. Experían calls such an item a "Small Business Advisory Report." The assumption in this case is how they pay their business bills will be reflected in how they pay their personal bills. You need written permission to run a credit check on a private individual; you don't need permission to run one on a business.

You certainly want to run a credit check on customers they want to factor. This is the most basic due diligence. Remember the invoices are only as good as the customer's ability to pay. Charging back invoices because a customer doesn't pay is not only a pain in the neck, but you could end up harming your client's cash flow or even lose money yourself. Credit checks on customers also serve to verify a client's word that someone is a good, regular payer. You may find in their credit report that "it ain't necessarily so."

Experían has a very helpful tool for this purpose. It is called an "Intelliscore Report." This report is a one-page summary of everything found in a business credit report. Most full credit reports and Intelliscore reports frequently refer to something called Days Behind Terms, or DBT. If a client gives a customer 30-day terms and the customer pays in 45 days, that customer is 15 DBT. Information summarized in the Intelliscore report includes current and monthly average DBT, highest DBT in past 6 months, and worst ever DBT. Also listed are the trade account balance from number of trade lines, average balance in the past 5 quarters, recent high credit, and median credit. Rounding out the data are number of: bankruptcies, judgments, liens, collection accounts, original UCC filings, and years on file. Last are the legal balance and SIC Code.

One of the best features of the Intelliscore is a ranking score from 0 to 100. The higher the score, the lower the risk. If a business has a score of 90 to 100, they might be considered "A" quality; 80 to 90 is "B," and so on. Thus, you can tell from this one-page summary information if you want to purchase invoices to this customer. If the customer's Intelliscore is 98, they're a prime customer. If it is 14, you'd be wise to recommend your client put them on COD if they choose to do business with them. You, however, must pass on purchasing invoices to them.

At the bottom of the report are the reasons for negative ratings, such as reported late payments, insufficient information, inconsistent payment behavior, and so on. Finally, at the very bottom is a line for you to fill in stating the credit limit you assign to this customer, and your signature.

Remember, an Intelliscore is a one-page summary of a business credit report. To run a full report, you get all the above information in detail plus further information on positive, neutral, and negative credit balances, a list of UCC filings, bankruptcy information, industry DBT patterns, and much more. I've seen Experían business credit reports anywhere from a half-page to dozens of pages in length, though most are in the five- to ten-page range.

If I want to know as much as possible about a prospective client, I might run a full credit report on the client's business, or on the client personally if little or no information is found on their business. If I find a history of judgments, significant tax lien problems, long-standing problems indicating severe financial mismanagement, criminal history, or other significant red flags, I will turn the prospect away. However, realize that few people who come to you will have sterling credit reports. That's often a reason they can't get bank loans or funds from other sources. What we are looking for is a pattern that suggests the business owner is honest, reasonably proficient at running a business, not likely to become a problem account, and of course has good paying customers. If the individual looks responsible, has customers who are creditworthy and pay in our preferred 2-week to 2-month window, chances are good we will accept them as factoring clients. However, before doing so, we want to be as sure as possible there are no stones left unturned.

Background Searches

Some factors utilize other means of looking further into a client's character, financial solvency, liens, and more. Numerous investigative companies offer a variety of background and lien search services that may be helpful to utilize.

These companies usually provide UCC and tax lien searches, judgment searches and pending litigation searches at county and federal levels, plus criminal background checks. There are many companies with web sites that provide background searches and other due diligence services for you; some are mentioned in the next chapters.

Due Diligence Costs

Due diligence costs depend on the source from which the information is obtained. Financial statements and aging reports given from the client are free and thus a good place to start. Checking references is also a low-cost means of obtaining information. Cost of UCC searches and credit reports will depend on the size and type of information desired and the company from which it is retrieved. Also affecting costs are whether you supply information on your customers' payments histories to the agency. With all the above considered, credit reports can cost anywhere from very little to well over $100 for a full-blown credit report (see the next chapter). One hopes the information in credit reports is accurate and up-to-date, but unfortunately this is not always the case.

This is where due diligence costs escalate quickly, depending on the number of searches you need to feel your due diligence is "adequate." Further, if you wish to contact a client's accountant, attorney, and/or business references, this can be time-consuming and the cost of your or your staff person's time needs to be calculated. Finally, if you decide to accept this prospect as a client, you have costs for searching and filing a UCC-1.

Clearly, thorough due diligence takes time and money. Some factors consider these expenses the cost of doing business and absorb all or a portion them. Others cannot afford to spend hundreds of dollars apiece on several new prospects each week, only to find they were "tire kickers" and not really serious about factoring. However, charging a prospect – especially a very small business – all or even just a portion of these costs may discourage some from factoring. On the other hand, charging at least some out-of-pocket reimbursements can quickly distinguish prospects who are serious from those who are "just looking."

Some factors consider in-depth searches undependable and no more predictive than a coin-toss, and therefore worth neither the trouble nor expense. I knew of one very successful factor who simply ran a lien search on the client and checked D&B ratings on customers, period. Is that adequate? Well, "adequate" due diligence is in the eye of each individual factor.

When deciding how much due diligence to perform in your business, perhaps the best question is this: "What is adequate due diligence for *my* peace of mind with *this* particular client?" Remember, the purpose of due diligence is to *reduce* risk. Nothing can completely *eliminate* it.

Other Considerations

The thought of going through such a rigorous due diligence process may raise a question: "Will asking prospects for all this paper work kill a deal?" In some cases it may – especially for very small accounts. If you're afraid it will, you need to judge if the account is worth the risk and how hungry you are for the business. If a prospect acts like you're snooping or wonders why you need all this information, turn the tables and ask, "If you were going to be investing several thousand dollars of your money into the business of someone you don't know, what would you want to know about this person?" I asked a hesitant client this very question and his immediate reply was, "Everything." Understanding your perspective helps prospective clients see you're only trying to protect yourself – something any business owner appreciates.

On the other hand, all this may be overkill for exceptionally small accounts. If you're going to factor someone for $2,000 or $5,000 a month and you know it'll never be more than that, you need to consider whether losing this amount is worth the risk of not spending a few dollars to run the check. This is especially true if the person is previously known to you as being "as honest as the day is long." In this case, you may choose to skip some of these precautions. If you do this, you can certainly close deals in a hurry and turn your money over quickly. However, if a client grows more than you expected and you then want the protection the paperwork provides, going back and doing this later will be more difficult than if you had done it when you first considered the new account. The client may justifiably wonder why you didn't do it back then in the first place.

Also be very clear that even though you have known someone for a long time, or a person is honest through-and-through, you can still lose money with him or her. While fraud may not be a risk with such a person, there are a number of circumstances that can befall an honest client: past debts, investments or business deals gone bad, divorce, illness, injury...you name it.

If your prospect needs the cash badly enough – and many do – he'll gladly sign any papers you put under his nose, especially if he believes doing so will supply the cash for his cash-starved business. Closing deals like this are a breeze and enjoyable. Just be sure you are comfortable with the findings of your due diligence, whatever it may be.

186 – Factoring Small Receivables

13
UCCs

Most people with little exposure to the world of finance, loans and factoring are quite ignorant of the Uniform Commercial Code (UCC). Yet once this door opens a crack they find a whole unexplored world there, and it can be somewhat daunting.

What Is the Uniform Commercial Code?

UCC stands for Uniform Commercial Code, which is a branch of law that has to do with debts owed by one party to another. Any time one person or company provides money to another person or company, the one providing funds understandably wants assurances he will be paid back. The law makes provision for this in the Uniform Commercial Code.

Each Secretary of State's office in the country has a division that handles UCCs. When the party who provides money to another seeks greater security of repayment, the providing party will complete a UCC-1 form and is referred to as the "Secured Party." The person or company receiving the funds is called the "Debtor" on the UCC-1 form. When this form is completed and registered with the Secretary of State, a lien (pronounced "lean") is put in place which secures the collateral of the secured party. The collateral is whatever the secured party says it is on the form, which is authorized by the Debtor.

When this lien is filed, the information becomes a matter of public record. Think of it as a nationwide bulletin board, notifying everyone that the secured party has first rights to the collateral if there is ever a problem recovering the money. Why is this important?

When everything goes smoothly, a UCC filing is unnecessary. A borrower pays back her bank loan with regular payments, is never late, the bank gets its money back, and everybody is happy. Likewise, a factoring client's customers pay their invoices, the factor gets his money back, and everybody is happy. In such transactions a UCC filing has no significance.

However, such perfect transactions do not always occur in the real world. If a borrower defaults on a loan and declares bankruptcy, the bank stands to lose the remaining unpaid principal. If a factoring client has outstanding invoices that are uncollectible and the client's business declares bankruptcy, the factor stands to lose just like the bank. Having a UCC filed – and having it filed before anyone else – will provide some protection to these secured parties.

Let's use an example. When they started the factoring relationship, Factor A filed a UCC-1 form which secured the accounts receivable and assets of Client B. They factor for a period of time, when unfortunately Client B falls on difficult times and ends up with $200,000 worth of debts he cannot repay. His assets are only $100,000. Sadly, Client B feels the only way out of the problem is to declare bankruptcy, which he does.

However, Factor A has purchased $25,000 worth of Client B's receivables. Some of these invoices are paid by the customers, but $20,000 is determined to be uncollectible and Client B is of course unable to pay them. Without a UCC filed, Factor A loses the $20,000.

However, Factor A filed the UCC and did so before any other secured party, thereby placing himself in "first position." When the bankruptcy is complete, the determination is made that there is a total of $70,000 in remaining assets in Client B's company, which must be distributed to its debtors after court costs and attorneys fees. Being in first position, Factor A is first in line. He receives the $20,000 owed, and Lender C, who is in second position, is next in line to receive what she is owed. If Lender C is owed $75,000, she will only receive the remaining $50,000 in assets, and the rest must be written off as a loss. In this scenario, parties in third or lower positions are out of luck.

As you can see, debtors are paid back in the order of their UCC filing position, which is determined solely by filing date. The first to file is in first position. Bankruptcy disbursements are not made by simply determining the amount everyone is owed and splitting up the assets equally between them. The remaining goods go to those first in line (after the trustee and attorneys are paid, that is). If Client B's assets were determined to have been only $15,000, Factor A would have received $15,000 and lost the remaining $5,000. Lender C would have been completely left in the cold.

Also, holding a lien protects the lien holder from garnishment by other debtors. Suppose you have a lien against a client's receivables. If that client owes someone else money and that person tries to garnish the client's receivables, you not only own the receivables in the first place, you are in first position and the receivables are protected.

I had a client who was a printer and who owed money to a paper company that did exactly this – the paper company tried to garnish his receivables which he had factored with me. It was nice to have my attorney deal with the situation, and he appreciated the proper paperwork I had done – my UCC-1 was properly filed and in hand, plus the signed factoring documents were in my files. The paper company had filed no liens and even though they had a judgment, they were out of luck in this case.

Therefore, as you can well understand, any factor or bank will want be in first position with every one of its clients. If a client wants to factor and already has a bank loan or line, the bank has no doubt filed a UCC already. If the bank can be persuaded to subordinate at least part of its position (the accounts receivable) to a factor, the factor will likely accept this client. If a bank will not subordinate, the factor will be required to take a second position and will probably decline the deal.

Likewise, the presence of tax delinquencies, judgments, and the like usually involve liens which will put the parties involved in first position. Unless these situations can be worked out – and sometimes they can, particularly tax liens – the deal will probably not be doable for the factor. No first position usually means no deal.

UCC-1 forms are available the web sites of most Secretaries of State, from a company called Registre, Inc. (Tel. 763-421-1713, web site www.registreinc.com), and from most of the UCC filing and service companies described later in this chapter.

Revised Article 9

In July of 2001, the Uniform Commercial Code underwent significant revisions that affect factoring transactions. These changes are usually referred to as "Revised Article 9" or "RA9" of the Uniform Commercial Code. Generally speaking these changes made UCC procedures more uniform across the country, and much easier to file. However you must be careful to file correctly or the protection the Uniform Commercial Code is intended to provide will be lost.

You must be aware of the following points which are now in effect under Revised Article 9.

1. **Company Name**. Using the correct, full name of your client is very important. In many states, a slight variation in the name can make a filing ineffective. Therefore you should obtain copies of a business' organizational documents, including a copy of their state registration certificate, to determine the client's correct legal name that is registered with the state. Trade names and DBA's are not effective. For Sole Proprietors, the full, complete name of the owner should be filed, such as "John Jacob Smith," rather than "Jack Smith" or "Smith Enterprises." You should verify the name with a driver's license or Social Security card and have a copy of this documentation on file.

2. **Signatures**. Obtaining the client's signature on the UCC-1 form is no longer necessary with RA9. You are only required that the client *authorize* you to file the UCC-1 Financing Statement as the Secured Party. Be sure your contract uses this language.

3. **Where to File**. All filing is now done in the jurisdiction in which the client is located. Dual filings (state and local) have been eliminated except in the case of real estate fixtures, which your factoring transactions won't include. How do you determine where the client is located? It's not quite as simple as you might think.

   • Filings for **corporations, LLCs,** and **limited partnerships** are done in the state of their organization. That is, if a company is located in Missouri and incorporated in Delaware, the UCC is filed in Delaware. Therefore you need to see the first page of the articles of incorporation or equivalent to get both the exact name and the state of organization.

- Filings for **non-registered organizations** like general partnerships and joint ventures are filed either a) at its place of business if it has only one location, or b) in the state of the chief executive office if it has more than one place of business.

- Filings for **sole proprietorships** are done in the state in which the owner's principal residence is located. Therefore if a sole proprietor's office is located in Portland, Oregon, but the owner resides in Vancouver, Washington, the filing is done in Washington state.

If it is not clear which is the proper jurisdiction, you should file in each jurisdiction that might be the client's place of business or residence.

UCC Filings

Filing fees vary from one state to another and cost from around $5 to $84, with most in the $10 to $25 range. Specific UCC requirements in each state are available from the web site of each Secretary of State. They're also reviewed in a book entitled *Uniform Commercial Code and Related Procedures Guide,* also published by Registre, Inc.

The national UCC-1 form is found in this manual in the chapter "Record Keeping." In many states you can file online at the state's web site. An extremely helpful web page is provided by a company called Capital Services at http://www.capitolservices.com/stateLinks.asp. This page lists all the Secretary of State sites alphabetically, with links to each of these sites' key pages.

The first due diligence you perform is to discover if there are tax liens filed by IRS or the state against the business, and any other liens filed against the prospect's assets. If there are, you will not be in first position until the debts have been satisfied and a release or subordination (UCC-3) filed.

How do you know if a lien is on file? First ask the prospect, who may know. However, never rely solely on this. UCC-1's are a matter of public record and you can simply do the research yourself by using credit reports that display lien filings and/or public records searches. These can be made easily on the internet.

There are many companies which offer UCC searching and/or filing services for a fee. Let's look at several of them.

Public Records Search Companies

Accurint

A relatively new player in the field is Accurint, with information you will find valuable, easy to obtain, and quite inexpensive compared to its competitors.

Accurint (http://www.accurint.com) is a registered trademark of Seisint (www.seisint.com), an information management and technology company located in Boca Raton, Florida. Seisint was founded in July 1998 and Accurint launched as a Seisint Product Division in May 2001. Seisint maintains information from a variety of public and private sources about U.S. subjects and businesses.

To do this, Seisint has built an enormous repository of data which includes more than 1,000 different data elements regarding 280 million subjects and 20 million businesses in the United States. Seisint acquires its data from nearly 400 public and commercially available sources. Its sources include nationally known compilers, specialty compilers, consumer and business transactions, and public records.

Accurint's ability to deliver high-quality matches and find rates is impressive. Its technology allows searches to be performed much more cost effectively than alternatives. Given a few pieces of information (e.g. a phonetically spelled name and the city of a previous address), Accurint can rapidly retrieve a complete and accurate identification of an individual, including current and historical addresses as well as associative links (relatives, associates, and neighbors).

Accurint is a web-based service that can be accessed with a User ID and Password. There is no other software needed, and any updates and upgrades are generated automatically and behind the scenes upon login.

Accurint claims to have the most in-depth information on U.S. individuals, and after using its resources for a while, you are inclined to agree. They say their associative links, historical residential information, and the relative data are deeper and more comprehensive than other commercially available database systems presently on the market.

Accurint boasts the following characteristics:

- *Response Time.* Accurint query responses come back virtually instantly, and reports are generated in under four seconds.

- *Timeliness of Data.* Data is updated as often as daily, depending upon the data source. Queries and reports are always run against the most current data, so there is no need to wait until the end of the month or the end of the quarter to obtain current information.

- *Configurability.* The user can control what results are included in his reports, and his preferences can be saved as a default setting.

- *User-Friendliness.* Based upon customer testimonials, Accurint is the easiest system on the market to use.

Accurint also has available a Directory Assistance option containing telephone numbers from every state in the U.S. The telephone numbers are updated every 24 hours, translating to real-time phone feeds.

Like the other companies in this chapter, Accurint does not provide credit reports as do D&B, Experían, and BusinessCreditUSA. However Accurint does provide easy and by far the most inexpensive searches (as low as 25 cents) for

UCC filings, corporate records, bankruptcies, tax liens, judgments, and personal assets of your potential clients. Other information Accurint provides makes this a great resource for locating people who owe you money and have skipped out. These tools are well worth the little time it will take you to learn to use them.

Accurint provides free on-line training to customers wishing to learn the most efficient and cost-effective methods of searching. For a very personable and helpful tour of Accurint's web site, call Helen Fries (pronounced "Freeze") at 888-332-8244 x4777. She will be glad to introduce you to Accurint's many tools.

While Accurint provides an inexpensive means of searching for UCC filings and other public record information, you are not able to submit UCC filings through Accurint: it is limited to public record searches. There are many companies who specialize in providing UCC search *and* filing services, and each makes the process quite smooth and efficient.

KnowX

A web site called KnowX.com provides quick access to comprehensive public record information at a relatively low cost. Its site is divided into five sections: Background Check, Assets, Locator Tools, Ultimate People Finder, Professional Licenses, and Ultimate Business Finder. The Background Check section is of most interest to the small factor: from here you run the following public information searches (as well as many others):

- Bankruptcy
- Judgments
- Lawsuits
- Liens
- UCCs

From the Ultimate Business Finder you can run D&B Business reports and Experían Business Reports (more on these in the chapter "Credit Reports") but there is no price saving here. KnowX is best used for the above public record information, especially if you want to compare public records information with Accurint or a credit report, in particular one of the less expensive ones like BusinessCreditUSA or D&B's Credit eValuator.

There is no subscription cost or registration fee to open a KnowX account; you pay only when you run a search. Registering is required to run a search and doing so provides credit card information for quick orders when you want them.

To run a search you simply sign in and click on the type of public record information you want (UCCs, liens, or whatever – each is a separate search). Preliminary search costs range from free to $7.95 per database, and you always receive a price tag before you order so you know what you're paying and can cancel out before it's too late. Once you ok a search you will be charged the search fee whether records are found or not.

After you complete a search and items are found you get a summary of matches. If you're looking for other UCCs on a client and nothing is found you can stop there as that's what you wanted to know and it hasn't cost you much to learn that. If matches are found, detail records are available on each of the company matches located. To obtain a Detail Record (another $2.95 to $7.95 per record) click on the link and you'll again be given a price tag. Say Ok and you'll be given the details of the UCC or lien filing, judgment or bankruptcy or whatever you're looking up. This detail will tell you, among other things, who recorded the filing and what the collateral is (look for the same as what you'll be filing in your UCC to see if you'll be in first position on those assets). If you're looking up a judgment or tax lien it will include how much the entry is for and if it has been discharged (paid). If you want to look up several record details at once you can "buy them all" for a discounted price.

KnowX prices for the searches in which you'll be interested as a small factor are below.

Database	Search Price	Detail Record Prices	
		Indiv Record Price	Multi-Record Discount Price
Background Check	9.95	7.95	29.95
Bankruptcy	2.95	7.95	19.95
Corporate Records	Free	4.95	12.95
Judgments	2.95	7.95	19.95

Liens	2.95	7.95	19.95
Lawsuits	2.95	7.95	19.95
Owners & Officers	Free	9.95	19.95
Professional Licenses	Free	9.95	15.00
The Ultimate Business Finder	Free	3.95	9.95
The Ultimate People Finder	Free	2.95	9.95
UCCs	2.95	7.95	19.95
Experian Business Reports	1.50	57.00	N/A
D&B Business Reports			
Search Summary	Free		
Comprehensive Report		123.00	N/A
Supplier Evaluation Report		108.50	N/A
Business Information Report		37.00	N/A

KnowX is good when you want a quick public records search to compare or verify the information in a credit report or Accurint. It costs $2.95 each to learn that there are no liens, UCCs, and so on recorded – which is what you're hoping for. However, make sure you have the *exact* spelling of the company's name: these searches are quite fussy right down to commas, periods and spaces. One mistyped character and a record won't be found, so be sure you first get it correctly from your client and then type it correctly when you run the search. Likewise, if was entered incorrectly in the filing you'll only find it if you duplicate that spelling.

While KnowX searches are relatively inexpensive, the lower cost of Accurint and that site's greater flexibility in phonetic and partial name searches make that service the first place to go. However, KnowX is easy to navigate, intuitive to use, and can be a good double-check if you need one. Logon at www.knowx.com.

Each company below offers similar services with prices that are significantly more than Accurint and KnowX, but similar to each other. You'll need to decide if the convenience and professional services these companies provide are worth the extra cost, or you'd rather save some money by searching and filing on your own. However, you will benefit from touring each company in this chapter to decide for yourself.

UCC Search and Filing
Service Companies

UCC Direct Services

UCC Direct Services' main product is called iLienOnline, which houses a vast, proprietary microfilm library of state-level UCC documents drawn directly from local and state sources. Having been in the business over 25 years, UCC Direct Services says they provide the "most accurate and efficient public record searching and UCC filing available from a single source," their iLienOnline service.

This system enables you to either outsource your UCC activities or file yourself. iLienOnline includes UCC filing preparation, document ordering and the online search process. Since it is web-based, there is no software to install, no complex training, and no compatibility issues.

iLienOnline's search features allow you to:

- Customize group searches and search across multiple jurisdictions simultaneously
- View online images of results retrieved directly from states' records, right on your computer
- Create personal default settings to quickly access frequently searched jurisdictions
- Gain immediate access to UCCs, Corporate Charters, Bankruptcy and Real Property Filings, Tax Liens, Judgments, and Assumed/Fictitious Names
- Pinpoint the exact location and obtain real-time status of a UCC online, 24 hours a day.

iLienOnline's filing features include:

- Quick validation of key filing data such as names or Organization IDs to help ensure filing accuracy
- A date-entry wizard to minimize re-typing and save time
- The Intelligent Auditor, which checks compliance with new RA9 requirements
- AuditCheck, which automatically reviews filings for missing information

- The ability to track expirations and create subsequent filings using stored portfolio filing data
- "Quick views" which provide a snapshot of all your UCC filing activities at every step.

The home page is www.uccdirect.com; to talk to a representative call 877-258-8158.

Capitol Services, Inc.

Capitol Services, Inc. has been in business since 1978 and provides complete UCC, tax lien, judgment and pending litigation searches, combined with multi-jurisdictional filing assistance. Based in Austin, Texas, Capitol Services has offices in six cities around the country, each with its own 800 number.

The company's web site provides a lot of helpful and educational information about UCCs. The home page provides an easy link to their online services, which include:

- *Order Entry* – submit orders for searches, retrievals and filings
- *Project Tracking* – monitor the progress of your current projects as well as completed projects
- *Invoice Reprint* – locate, review and reprint past invoices on your account
- *Forms Library* – locate and download state forms required for creating and/or qualifying entities.

There is also a link to UCC filing forms, where you prepare and submit the forms over the Internet.

Capitol Services, Inc.'s prices are as follows:

State or County UCC Search	$20
UCC/Tax Lien/Judgment Search	$35
UCC/Fixtures/Tax Lien/Judgment Search	$50
Litigation or Bankruptcy Search	$35
UCC Filing	$20

Capitol Services, Inc.'s home page also has a link to RA9 information that provides informative articles and PDF format UCC forms are there for the taking.

As mentioned earlier, this site has a page which lists and links you to the sites of all 50 Secretaries of State – one of the handiest web pages any factor can ever want. Go to www.capitolservices.com, click the Secretary of State link, and there you are.

Diligenz

Diligenz provides a nationwide web-based due diligence search and document retrieval system. Logging on to www.diligenz.com gives you a comprehensive UCC database and film library with 24/7 access to corporate and legal information. You can search and view documents within seconds on your computer screen, and print or have them e-mailed, faxed or mailed to you at the touch of a button.

If web access is not available; Diligenz Direct Dial is a 1-800-dial up service that provides access to document search and retrieval services without using the Internet. Such users can submit their requests through telephone, fax, mail or e-mail orders. Their trained search professionals conduct thorough and reliable searches, frequently discovering DBA's, misspellings and deviations of debtor names. Diligenz charges the same search fee whether you do the work or they do.

Diligenz offers a complete Corporate Search service for verifying the status of a company and retrieving certified copies. Corporate Searches are easy to use: simply type the name you're searching to see the exact legal name under which it is filed. Document filing and follow-up services help you take it from there.

Diligenz purchases information directly from the states rather than purchase data through third parties, which eliminates most incorrect and out of date information. Monthly updates via the Web help you track and audit your filings. Management tools ensure that you comply with Article 9 changes and speed up your turn-around time.

Diligenz' filing system uses Web wizards to help you complete your UCC forms accurately. Filings are confirmed and the status can be tracked. Reports remind you of upcoming filing expirations.

Diligenz' unique, simple fee structure on many state UCC searches and document retrievals make it easy to predict your costs. There are no set-up fees, monthly fees, software fees, fax fees, or rush charges. Diligenz charges per transaction; there is no contract to sign. Services include complete set-up, training and ongoing support at no additional cost. Here is a summary of their charges.

Filing: $10 service fee charge for any state, plus the state's charge for filing.

Searches:

Lien Searches:

UCC County, Federal & State Tax Liens, Judgments

First Search	$25.00
Second Search	$20.00
Each Additional Search	$15.00
Per Page Fee	$1.50

Corporate Document Retrievals:

Good Standing Certificate	$15.00
Articles of Incorporation	$15.00
Corporate Annual Report	$15.00

Filing Tracking:

Life of Filing	$2.00
Termination Tracking	$2.00
Notification of New Filing	$3.00

Litigation Search:

Civil or Criminal	$39.00
Per Page Fee	$1.50

Bankruptcy Search	$25.00
Per Page Fee	$1.50

Business Credit Report	$25.00

UCC Searches:

UCC Search Charge	UCC Document Charge	Good Standing Search
	$14 or	
$21 for the	$1.50 per page	$16 for the
following states:	is available for:	following states:
Arkansas	Alabama	Arizona
Delaware	Arkansas	Delaware
Hawaii	Delaware	Hawaii
Indiana	Hawaii	Indiana
Louisiana	Indiana	Louisiana
Michigan	Iowa	Maryland
Montana	Kentucky	Michigan
New Hampshire	Louisiana	Minnesota
New Jersey	Maine	Nebraska
New York	Massachusetts	New Hampshire
North Dakota	Michigan	New Jersey
Rhode Island	Missouri	New York
South Dakota	Montana	North Dakota
Tennessee	New Hampshire	South Carolina
Vermont	New Jersey	South Dakota
Virginia	North Dakota	Utah
Washington DC	Rhode Island	Washington DC
West Virginia	South Carolina	West Virginia
Wyoming	South Dakota	
	Tennessee	All other states:
All other states:	Utah	$11
$14	Vermont	
	Virginia	
	Washington DC	
	West Virginia	
	Wyoming	
	All other states:	
	$14	

Diligenz is located in Mukilteo, Washington. Telephone is 800-858-5294.

All-Search & Inspection, Inc.

This company began in 1983 and its services include UCC and Corporate Filing and Retrieval, Real Estate research,

Registered Agent Services, Liens and Litigation research, Federal and Bankruptcy court searches, Tax and Insurance services, and more. Searches can be performed in every federal, state, county, city and town in the U.S., and every province and local court in Canada. For more information go to www.all-search.com or call 801-984-8160.

AmeriSearch

Located in Sacramento, California, AmeriSearch is a public records search and filing company that serves the legal and financial communities. Established in 1992, this firm has developed a nationwide network that obtains information quickly from federal, state or local government agencies. They conduct business by phone, fax, e-mail and a comprehensive web site.

Its UCC/Lien services include:

Secretary of State Services
- UCC Searches
- Tax Liens
- UCC Filings

Local (County) Searches
- UCC Searches
- Tax Liens
- Abstracts of Judgments
- Mechanic Liens
- Lis Pendens
- Fictitious Business/Assumed Business Names
- Filings

AmeriSearch requires no contract or monthly minimum. Below are some of the company's prices.

UCC/Lien Search & Filing Services

State UCC Search (Certified/Uncertified)	$25.00
California Comprehensive UCC Search	$35.00
Local Level (County) UCC Search	$25.00
Local Level (County) Tax Lien/Judgments	$25.00
Filings (Local & Nationwide)	$15.00

UCC monitoring and preparation services are available.

Court Records Research

State Court Record Search	$30.00
Federal Court Record Search	$30.00
U.S. Bankruptcy Search	$30.00

Other Services

Email (per page)	$1.00
Faxing (per page)	$1.25
Copies (per page)	$1.50
Overnight Courier – Priority	$16.50
Overnight Courier – Standard	$13.00

To open an online account, call 800-877-2877. The web site is www.amerisearch.com.

ChoicePoint

ChoicePoint is a large company that offers many services, among them the UCC searching and filing capabilities factors use. Its product of interest is The LienGuard System (www.lienguard.com), a patent-pending, complete electronic solution for the entire UCC process. This service offers a reliable, fast and low-cost way to expedite handling searches and filings over the Internet.

At the time of this writing, services available on the LienGuard system are:

- Original Financing Statements – UCC-1's
- "In Lieu of" filings
- Amendments – UCC-3's
  - Continuations
  - Assignments
  - Terminations
  - Partial Releases
- Due Diligence Services
  - UCC Searches
  - Corporate Records Searches
  - Tax Lien Searches
  - Judgment Searches
  - Bankruptcy Searches

To find out more about LienGuard or ChoicePoint, Inc. in Alpharetta, Georgia, call toll-free 866-281-6860.

Pacific Corporate & Title Searches

Pacific Corporate & Title Searches started in 1987. Its members can fill out UCC-1 and UCC-3 forms online and electronically submit them. You need to be an online member and you need to have Adobe Reader installed on your computer.

Below are the services PCTS provides which pertain to factoring.

Account Monitoring
- Provides timely and accurate reporting of Tax Liens to alleviate any potential problems with the 45 day IRS lien issue.
- Monitors recent UCC filings to report the breaking of negative covenants.
- Keeps customers informed on the filing of other miscellaneous liens such as mechanics liens, abstracts of judgment, Notices of Bulk Sales, and Liquor License Transfers.

Nationwide Corporate Document Retrieval
- Plain or Certified copies of any item on file for an entity
- Good Standings/Legal Existance
- Plain or Certified Officer Statements
- Tax Status Letters

County Services
- UCC Filing Search
- Tax Liens & Abstract of Judgment
- UCC Filings
- Legal Publication Services
- Fictitious Business Name Search
- Fictitious Name Filing & Publication

Litigation Court Services
- Superior Court
- U.S. District Courts

- Branch Courts
- U.S. Bankruptcy Court

Uniform Commercial Code
- Secretary of State UCC Filings
- Secretary of State UCC, Tax Lien & Judgment Search
- Certified UCC Search
- Plain UCC Search*
- Library of California UCC filings on premise*

* Searches and copies available via online system as well.

Pacific Corporate & Title Research can be reached at 800-230-4988. Their web site is www.paccorp.com.

As you can see, there are more than enough means of obtaining UCC information, running searches, and filing UCC financing statements. Which resources you use are up to you. You can choose to do the searches and filings yourself, thereby saving some funds; or you can conserve time and concern over the accuracy of your own independent searches by using one of the search and filing service companies mentioned in this chapter

But UCCs are just part of a factor's due diligence. Knowing how to read credit reports, and what to do with the information contained in them, is next.

14
Credit Reports

The internet has made pulling credit reports remarkably easy. In this chapter are some of the better-known business credit reporting companies, how they can be accessed via the internet, and some of the costs involved. This information will give you more than enough to get started.

Dun & Bradstreet (D&B)

Dun & Bradstreet is a venerable icon of business credit reporting. For most small factors much of what D&B provides may be more expensive and more complete than you need. However, there are certain D&B rating scores which are well known to the credit management industry and you should at least be familiar with what they are and what they mean.

Every quarter D&B publishes a massive listing (at $753 it contains four volumes that are each about the size of a metropolitan telephone book) of all the U.S. companies in its database. These are sorted by state and city so you must know where a company's headquarters are located to be able to find it in the book. This listing includes the company's name, sometimes its telephone number, year the rating was applied, and the rating itself.

The rating is coded with a combination of letter or letters and a number that can leave you feeling quite ignorant without an explanation. The rating is assigned by D&B based on information collected on a company.

One rating is the ER (Employee Range) rating. Some businesses do not lend themselves to classification so D&B assigns these an Employee Range symbol based on the number of people employed. No other credit significance should be attached to this symbol.

As you can see below, a Rating of "ER7" means there are between five and nine employees in the company. "ERN" means D&B does not have information indicating how many people are employed at this firm. Below is the key to D&B's ER ratings:

Rating	# of Employees
ER1	1,000 or more
ER2	500-999
ER3	100-499
ER4	50-99
ER5	20-49
ER6	10-19
ER7	5-9
ER8	1-4
ERN	Not Available

If more information is available to D&B a Rating Classification is given based on a company's balance sheet; added to this is a Composite Credit Appraisal determined by D&B that assesses the firm's creditworthiness. The Rating Classification is a letter or letters, and its Composite Credit Appraisal follows this with the number 1 through 4. The Composite Credit Appraisal is based on analysis by D&B of company payments, financial information, public records, business age and other factors.

As you can see below, a company with a rating of 1A1 reported a balance sheet of $500k to $750k and was assigned a Composite Credit Appraisal of "High." The most desirable classification for a client's customer would be a 5A1 rating. A company with a rating of GG3 would be less desirable to factor, but at least would be rated by D&B. A huge number of U.S. companies are not rated or listed in D&B.

Rating Classification (Balance Sheet)				Composite Credit Appraisal			
				High	Good	Fair	Limited
5A	$50,000,000		and over	1	2	3	4
4A	10,000,000	to	49,999,999	1	2	3	4
3A	1,000,000	to	9,999,999	1	2	3	4
2A	750,000	to	999,999	1	2	3	4
1A	500,000	to	749,999	1	2	3	4
BA	300,000	to	499,999	1	2	3	4
BB	200,000	to	299,999	1	2	3	4
CB	125,000	to	199,999	1	2	3	4
CC	75,000	to	124,999	1	2	3	4
DC	50,000	to	74,999	1	2	3	4
DD	35,000	to	49,999	1	2	3	4
EE	20,000	to	34,999	1	2	3	4
FF	10,000	to	19,999	1	2	3	4
GG	5,000	to	9,999	1	2	3	4
HH	up to		4,999	1	2	3	4

Another D&B rating is 1R or 2R. This also is based on the number of employees and is assigned to businesses that do not supply D&B a current financial statement. A "2" is the highest Composite Credit Appraisal such companies can receive. The classifications are as follows:

Rating Classification (# of Employees)		Composite Credit Appraisal		
		Good	Fair	Limited
1R	10 employees and over	2	3	4
2R	1 to 9 employees	2	3	4

Sometimes you'll find a company with a Rating Classification but without a Composite Credit Appraisal number. That is, a company may be rated "BB–" or "2R–" with no number 1 through 4 following. This means the information available to D&B does not permit them to classify the company within their Rating key. Some reasons for using the "–" symbol include deficit net worth, bankruptcy proceedings, lack of sufficient payment information or incomplete history information.

D&B's Paydex Score gives you an instant overview of how a firm pays its bills as reported to D&B and helps determine how quickly they're likely to pay you. Obviously this information is very useful for a small factor. The Paydex is a 1-100 numerical score of payment performance, calculated using up to 875 payment experiences from trade references reported to D&B.

The D&B Paydex Score is as follows:

Paydex	Payment
100	Anticipate
90	Discount
80	Prompt
70	Slow to 15 Days
50	Slow to 30 Days
40	Slow to 60 Days
30	Slow to 90 Days
20	Slow to 120 Days
UN	Unavailable

The payment comments above may be understood this way.

Anticipate: Payments are received prior to date of invoice. (Not much point in factoring these!)

Discount: Payments are received within trade discount period. (These may pay too soon to make factoring worthwhile, but if the client wants to factor them anyway, these are very strong customers.)

Prompt: Payments are received within terms granted. (What you want to see as a factor.)

Slow: Number of days beyond vendor's terms, e.g., "Slow 30" means payments are 30 days beyond terms. (In other words, if they are given 30 days net and are "Slow 30" the client is waiting 60 days to get paid.)

As you can see Paydex scores in the 80's and 90's are most desirable for customers whose invoices you are considering buying. Scores below 50 indicate a customer whose invoices you probably are better off not buying because they will take too long to pay.

D&B has a dizzying array of credit and marketing products from which to choose. For a newcomer this can really be overwhelming, yet their web sites are geared toward their customers' specific needs.

Larger factors with more sophisticated credit reporting needs will want to browse their Products page from their main menu. Go to www.dnb.com/us and click the Products button. From there click the Assess Risk link and you will be presented with many risk assessment tools D&B provides. However, these are more costly than most small factors will choose to pay.

Thankfully, D&B has developed products for small business which are more suited to the needs of small factors. While the affordable product provides much less detail, the prices are more in line with small factors' budgets and generally provide the information you'll need. Small factors will prefer D&B's site called "D&B Small Business Solutions," which is accessed at www.sbs.dnb.com. There, look for three links which say:

Click here to see a Sample Comprehensive Report
Click here to see a Sample Electronic Business Information Report("eBIR")
Click here to see a Sample Credit eValuator Report

Click each of these in turn and you'll see sample reports of D&B's offerings for small businesses. You'll benefit from taking the time to view these samples. Here's a summary of what these reports provide.

The **Comprehensive Report** has been offered by D&B for some time, and is quite thorough. This report combines D&B's proprietary statistical scoring with business, payment, and financial information all in one report. The Comprehensive Report is designed to provide customers with the current profile and future outlook for an account. With the Comprehensive Report you can:

- Get an instant snapshot of a business
- Understand a businesses overall performance
- Make faster credit decisions
- Analyze information
- View the D&B Rating (e.g., 4A3)
- View the D&B Paydex

The **Electronic Business Information Report (eBIR)** provides the same information as the Comprehensive Report, but is created for the internet user and is quite handsome compared to its older brother, the plain vanilla Comprehensive Report. The eBIR's information is divided into 5 tabs which are Overview, History & Operations, Payments, Banking & Finance, and Public

Filings. It's easy to find whatever information you want by clicking on the appropriate tab.

The Comprehensive Report/eBIR is, indeed comprehensive. So is its price as you'll see below. If your small business can afford to spend this kind of money routinely, you're doing exceptionally well. However, for most small factor the Credit eValuator Report is probably a much better fit.

The Credit eValuator provides a one-page report with three sections:

- Risk Summary
- Company Profile
- Legal Filings & Other Important Information

The **Risk Summary** includes a gauge with an arrow pointing to the green, yellow, or red section of a ... well, a "Risk Meter" if you will. This semicircular gauge is labeled "Risk of Late Payment" with the green area taking up the left half of the semicircle and labeled "Lower Risk." The yellow and red areas take up the right half and the end of the red part is labeled "Higher Risk."

An arrow simply points to a color somewhere between the two ends of the semicircle to indicate risk. There is no accompanying numeric (0 to 100) or letter (A, A-, B+ etc.) score, just a pointing arrow.

Below this gauge is an explanation of how the score was determined, stating "Risk of late payment is based on the following prioritized factors in addition to other information in D&B's files," and then the factors are listed which produced the rating.

The other part of this Risk Summary section shows a large arrow pointing either up, sideways, or down and is labeled "Payment Performance Trend." Below this arrow is the text, "The payment performance trend for this company is..." and then it reads either "Improving," or "Unchanged" or "Declining." Further text then describes the payment activity that reflects the most recent information in D&B's files.

The second section, **Company Profile**, lists some basic information about the company: Chief Executive's name, Line of Business, Type of Business (Corporation, Sole Proprietor, etc.), Years in Business, Annual Sales, Employees Here, and Employees Total.

The third section, **Legal Filings and Other Important Information**, gives the public records filings you want to know: Bankruptcies, Judgments, Judgment Amounts, Liens, Suits, Negative Payment Experiences, and Payments Placed for Collection. This section and the first contain the most important information you're looking for.

Also on this page are tabs to the left which allow you to keep Tracking Folders of earlier reports you've run. Very handy and a nice feature.

To access these reports you select from three different membership packages. You can also obtain Credit eValuator reports directly through newer versions of QuickBooks®. Simply open the QuickBooks® Customer Navigator and click the Credit Check button (which has a small graphic of the Credit eValuator's gauge). You'll be invited to select a membership plan before obtaining your first report.

Here are the prices according to the membership level (Gold, Silver, or Basic) you choose.

Credit Services	Gold	Silver	Basic
Credit eValuator Reports	4 free report per month	2 free reports per month	$19.99 each
Additional Credit eValuator Reports	$12.99 each	$12.99 each	$19.99 each
Comprehensive Report	$99.00 each	$117.00 each	$117.00 each
# of companies you can store & track in your Tracking Folders	Up to 150	Up to 75	Up to 15
Monthly Membership Fee	**$39.99/month**	**$24.99 /month**	**No Charge**

Experían

Formerly called TRW, Experían is a well-known and often used source for credit reports. Searching Experían's web site database is free. Start browsing their web site at http://www.Experían.com/Experían_us.html and from there follow the links to business credit reports.

Experían provides numerous types of reports, from very basic company information to more complete. When comprehensive information is available, they provide a full Snapshot report, including a credit risk category, for $19.95. Full reports cost more. When little information is available, a limited report without the risk category costs $8. When there is no information about a business, there is no charge.

Below is a summary of some of the various reports provided by Experían.

<u>Snapshot Report</u>

The Experían Snapshot report provides seven types of data:

1. *Company information*
Includes the company's name, address, phone number and Experían file number. The year the file was established on Experían's database will be displayed when the company's incorporation date is not available.

2. *Snapshot credit categories*
Classifies the company's current credit status into one of five categories:
- Acceptable
- Caution
- Warning
- Serious risk
- Bankruptcy

The status assigned by Experían is based on the company's current payment behavior and the presence or absence of collection data or derogatory legal filings.

3. Legal filings
Summarizes any bankruptcy, tax lien and judgment filings gathered from federal, state and county courthouses nationwide.

4. Detailed collection filings
Includes information gathered from a nationwide network of collection agencies. The report provides the collection agency's name, the amount placed for collection and the date the account was submitted to the collection agency. If this information is extensive or shows a pattern of irresponsibility you'll do well to avoid buying invoices to such a company.

5. Payment behavior
Summarizes the company's credit relationships and payment performance. This information is collected from suppliers nationwide.

6. Payment trends and industry comparison
Compares the company's payment performance with other businesses in the same industry to help you make a more accurate risk evaluation. (Requires payment information to be available to Experían for at least the past six months.)

7. Company background
This information can include the type of business, number of employees or sales figures, where incorporated and key officers.

A sample report is available for your review on their web site at www.Experían.com/product/bis/sample.html.

Experían Intelliscore^{SM} Report
    Experían Intelliscore is a credit risk scoring service, providing small factors an easy, quick way to screen prospective accounts.

    Intelliscore is an analytical system that measures the likelihood of derogatory payment performance and identifies a business' credit risk. Intelliscore models are based upon trade, demographic and public record data. The Intelliscore report lists key factors that affect the score, including derogatory public record data, payment performance, credit experience and industry background information.

Intelliscore also can help you identify potential credit or payment risk among prospective customers. By screening high-risk accounts prior to buying their invoices, you can reduce risk.

There are two Intelliscore models:

- Commercial Intelliscore – is used across all industries based on companies of all sizes throughout the country. This is the report well suited to your needs.
- Small Business Intelliscore – integrates information on the personal credit history of a business owner with the credit history of his or her business. This produces a single business credit risk score.

Intelliscore Features:

- A single credit risk score
- Action items, which you may fill in or ignore
- A percentage ranking of the risk level of the business compared to all other businesses. This is the 0 to 100 score which is extremely helpful in deciding whether or not to purchase invoices to this company.
- If applicable, a summary on the business and its owner including trade payment and public record data.

Business Summary Report

This report provides a quick evaluation of low-balance accounts. Business Summary is a low-cost summarized credit report that allows you to make assessments of your low-balance transactions of less than $1,000. The summary analyzes the account's current trade experiences, determines the presence or absence of collection data and derogatory public record filings, and then classifies the account into one of the following categories:

- *Acceptable*: The company actively uses credit and pays its bills no later than nine days late, on average.
- *Caution:* If the company actively uses credit, the risk category is based on the current payment performance

and/or legal records on file. If the company does not actively use credit, it may pose increased risk.

- *Warning:* Derogatory payment performance information and/or derogatory legal records exist on file for the company.
- *Serious risk:* The company has seriously derogatory payment performance and/or seriously derogatory legal records on file.
- *Bankruptcy:* The company previously filed for bankruptcy.

Pricing information

The following prices are for the database search (not including applicable state and local taxes). Prices for the above reports are considerably more and not listed on the site unless you open an account. The following searches are included in most of the above reports at no extra cost. To search them separately on Experían's web site the cost is:

UCC search	$16
Corporate Records search	$12
Bankruptcy – tax lien – judgment search	$10
Fictitious Business Name (DBA) search	$10

BusinessCreditUSA

A smaller and lesser known player in the credit reporting world, but one worth considering by small factors, is BusinessCreditUSA. This company is a division of infoUSA Inc. (NASDAQ: IUSA), a public company with more than $300 million in annual revenue and 2,000 employees nationwide. They have been compiling an "accurate and current" database of over 14 million North American businesses for some 30 years and spend over $40 million yearly gathering, compiling and updating their database.

BusinessCreditUSA provides free initial searches on these 14 million businesses and have a standard charge of only $5 to pull a credit report on any business you find. They also offer promotional discounts when you buy credit reports in quantity, which vary from time to time. For example, at one point they were $4 each if you bought 100; at another time they were $3.50 each if you purchased a State Business Credit Directory CD for $350 (100 credit reports were included); at still another time, they were $3 if you bought 50. These promotions don't last long and change frequently so watch for them and take advantage of the better ones when they occur – you can save a lot on this important part of your operation.

BusinessCreditUSA describes itself as the "ideal source" for information on small businesses. Compared to the other guys you sure can't beat the price. While their information is not as comprehensive as their competitors' more expensive credit reports, this should be all you need for checking out both clients and customers in your due diligence searches. What's more, these credit reports provide more information than D&B's Credit eValuator, but at one-fourth the single report price of D&B. If what you find here is complete enough and accurate, you need not go much further.

Their credit reports are intended for

- Verifying business existence and stability factors
- Confirming information on new accounts
- Learning about current & prospective customers
- Pre-qualifying prospective customers
- Generating sales leads
- Finding fax, telephone and address data

Running a credit report doesn't get much easier than this. Go to www.businesscreditusa.com where you'll find a simple little form to fill in.

Step 1 – type in the company name or telephone number or Executive's name.

Step 2 – type in the city (optional) and state, then click Search.

Talk about a no-brainer. You then get a list of matches and to read the one you want click on its name, then click a button saying View Report, and give your credit card information if you don't have an account set up. You don't have to have an account to access reports but you do need to pay the $5 to get a report. If no records are found you don't pay anything. Having an account means you just don't need to give your credit card information each time you want a new report; you just enter your email address and password, then when asked how you wish to pay, click "Deduct 1 Report From My Account." The number of reports remaining and used are there for you to see.

A sample report can be viewed by clicking the Sample Credit Report link on the main page. All the items on the report include:

- Name, address, telephone & fax of the company
- Credit Rating (a letter grade like a report card) and a numeric rating of 0 to 100.
- Years in this database
- ABI#
- Sales Volume (range of dollars)
- County
- # of Employees (range of numbers)
- Metro Area
- Location (as in single or multiple)
- Stock Symbol if publicly traded
- Web Site Address
- Management Directory which includes names and titles of officers
- Lines of Business and SIC Code
- Public Filings (Tax Liens, Judgments and Bankruptcies)
- Headlines
- Competitors in the Area (with names and addresses)

All this for $5 or less! As long as the information is accurate and up to date I don't know how you can beat this. The fine print at the bottom is worth reading. As do most credit reporting agencies, they say the information provided is believed to be accurate but is not guaranteed. Then in red letters there is a long paragraph which includes the following:

"Our Credit Rating Codes are indicators of probable ability to pay. They are based on business demographic factors such as number of employees, years in business, industry stability, barriers to entry, and government data. We recommend that these ratings be used primarily as a starting point and should not be the sole factor used in making a credit decision."

They go on to suggest you get more information from bank and trade references, credit bureaus, and anywhere else you think appropriate before making a credit decision. Not bad advice. However if you find this information reliable (and there's no other way than to compare it to what you find from Experían, D&B, and your own experience) this can fill your due diligence needs very nicely. As of this writing, I've used BusinessCreditUSA for over a year and have found the credit ratings on target.

They also provide a place for you to give your experience with a particular business. This provides them further information to apply to their Credit Score and is there for the world to see. You are asked to rate the business on a scale of 1 to 5 (or N/A) on the following:

- Customer Service
- Pricing
- Quality of Work
- Performance
- Overall Credibility

Then they ask if you would recommend this business to a friend (Yes/No) and provide a field for you to write a longer message. You then leave your name and email address and choose whether to have these included in the posting of your evaluation. However, most of the businesses I've searched have no such experiences posted.

Meanwhile back at the home page there are also links to several business services. There are numerous links to each of the following:

- Marketing Services
- Debt Collection
- Employment Services
- Financial Services
- Business News
- Industry Resources
- Payroll Services
- Web/IT Resources
- Business Resources

All in all the information you'll find here is the easiest to understand, the easiest to access, and by far the least expensive. You won't find specific payment histories as you do the larger reports of Experían and D&B so you'll need to go there if that information is important. However, what this does provide is very concise and clear, and may be the best place to start your due diligence as you look into factoring a new client and customers. BusinessCreditUSA will also help you understand the more the sophisticated data found in D&B and Experían as you begin to use credit reports.

National Association of Credit Management (NACM)

For those who plan to run a fair number of credit reports and want additional benefits, joining NACM can be the way to go. This is an association whose Business Credit Services members receive numerous benefits including reduced rates on credit reports, educational offerings, collection services, and much more. In some regions, the only way to obtain Experían reports is through NACM, which means you must join the organization to obtain Experían reports.

Costs for membership and services vary from region to region; many but not all regions provide Experían reports. To find what is offered and to join, contact the affiliate in your area. Each will tell you the various types of credit reports they provide, as well as costs for annual dues and the reports.

If you pull a moderate number to many credit reports in the course of your business, NACM may be more cost effective than getting the information directly from Experían. But if you pull very few, the membership dues may cost more than what you save in discounted credit report costs.

While offerings differ from one region to another, those branches of NACM that provide Experían credit reports usually have the information most small factors will need. To find your regional office and/or its web site, go to www.nacm.org, click the Membership link, then the List of Affiliates link or Affiliates Web Sites link.

USSearch

USSearch is a company that offers numerous background investigation searches, most of which you will not need unless you want to find skeletons in the closet of just about anybody. If you think your life is not an open book in this day and age, go to this site and get an education on public information and how easy it is to get. But for your purposes as a small factor there is one link of interest.

The link is to D&B's reports. Except for the Credit eValuator Report, these are available to purchase here, very easy to navigate, and there samples of these D&B reports which are easy to find and view. There is also a very helpful chart that lists D&B's reports (but again, not the Credit eValuator report) across the top, and down the left column lists purposes for which you might be running a search. The grid in the middle provides check marks to show which reports scratch which itch. Prices are the about same as you pay for the same reports directly with D&B. You need to open an account with USSearch (no cost) at which time you give your credit card which will be used for every report purchased.

To open this chart, open the home page (www.ussearch.com) and click on the Business Services tab, then the Business Background Check tab. From there click Learn More under the D&B U.S. Company Profiles section. Clicking Samples and Descriptions opens a new window in which you click a text link with the words "View a comparison of the six D&B Business/Credit reports." This opens a chart called "Which D&B Report Do You Need?" and includes links to samples of each of the D&B reports listed. This chart is very nicely done, though getting there could be easier.

Again, USSearch is probably not a site you will use as much as others because their costs are the same for similar information. But this chart helps you understand D&B's more expensive reports quite clearly.

Observation

Clearly there is far more information available to the small factor than one can possibly use or even need. The information is presented in this chapter so you know what's out there and can get an idea of what is useful without being overwhelmed by what you can get.

Credit reports that you choose will be determined by:
- the number of clients you have
- the number of customers they have
- the amount you have or wish to spend on credit report information
- your comfort level with buying invoices based on credit information you have or don't have.

Refer to the previous chapter on just how much due diligence is really needed for the level of business you do and the comfort level you need. Overall, you will probably get enough information to make good decisions from one or a combination of a few of the following:

For clients
(UCCs, Judgments, liens):
- Accurint
- KnowX Background Check
- BusinessCreditUSA
- D&B Credit eValuator
- A UCC search and filing service company (e.g. UCC Direct Services, Capitol Services, Inc., Diligenz, etc.)

For customers:
(Credit reports):
- BusinessCreditUSA
- D&B Credit eValuator
- Experían Intelliscore

Public records such as UCC-1 filings, liens, bankruptcies, and judgments are found from Accurint and KnowX, and are included on the credit reports from BusinessCreditUSA, and D&B Credit eValuator. All of these cost less than the larger reports from D&B and Experían in which this information is also found. These public records can also be searched and filed through various companies that provide UCC search and filing services discussed in the previous chapter. UCC searches can also be done at the sites of many (though not all) Secretaries of State for a fee.

For a "quick and dirty" due diligence process, you can run

1) a BusinessCreditUSA credit report on your prospective client's customers, and

2) an Accurint search on the client's business for UCC filings, plus searches for personal tax liens, bankruptcies, and assets.

This will give you an idea of whom you're dealing with (both client and customer), and can be done inexpensively in a matter of minutes. For those small factors whose limits and exposure are low, this may be enough due diligence while costing very little. If you're dealing with significant funds, you'll no doubt want to be more thorough.

It's a sound practice to check UCC-1 filings annually to see if a tax lien or other UCC-1s have been filed against your clients, or with customers with whom you have a lot of funds outstanding. Tax liens have priority over UCCs even if the tax liens are filed later. Checking this once a year will inform you if your collateral is at risk because your client hasn't told you about a tax problem that has arisen, or a customer has been dinged with new judgments or other problems since you last checked. Hopefully your client will keep taxes and other obligations current with the cash flow factoring is providing. Making this annual check can be a bit costly but if you turn up a problem it can more than pay for potential losses because your lien position, or client's or customers' finances, weren't as stable as you assumed. Most credit reporting agencies such as D&B and BusinessCreditUSA sell a service which provides automatic updates if data changes on companies you've checked in the past. Such updates usually are part of the package with the UCC search and filing services.

What kind of credit report searches (called underwriting) do larger factors do? It varies of course but a common practice when considering new customers is to first look up their D&B

rating in the 4-volume rating book. If it is a 3A company or higher, that is sufficient for acceptance. Some factors consider any D&B Composite Credit Appraisal with a 1 or 2 as good enough to look no further. Others consider a Paydex of 80 or higher to be a no-brainer. Meanwhile, if scores are lower than these or the firm is not listed in D&B, they will often run an Experían Business Credit Report which costs less than D&B's Comprehensive Report but usually gives enough information to make a good decision.

If too little or no information is found a bank and trades search is done. That is, the customer's bank is contacted to get an average bank balance and NSF history. That's usually all the information you can get from a bank and you must show them signed approval from the customer before they'll give it to you. Depending on the bank official responsible for providing the information, some fax it back in a day or two. Many others are painfully slow, taking as long as three or four weeks to return it. Follow-up calls are unfortunately necessary to light a fire under such people.

Trade information is usually obtained from at least three vendors of the customer. You'll request the vendor's experience with invoice terms given, payment history, maximum trade line given, and date of last purchase. This is pretty standard credit application information and if you do them often enough to warrant, you can develop a form to fax them with the customer's name and provide blank lines for them to fill in next to each piece of information you seek. Getting these back can also take a while but vendors are usually better about returning them than bankers. The customers have a relationship with your client that this customer's bank obviously does not have, and the customer wants to maintain good rapport so there's incentive for them to get this done (back to WIIFM again).

As you can see, getting bank and trade data can take a long time and be very tedious. It's usually the least favorite job of the person who gets stuck with it in the large factor's office. If you can't find adequate credit report information on a customer and don't want to bother with the hassle of a bank and trades search (and I won't blame you if you don't), you may simply decline buying invoices to this customer because "not enough information" was available for you to make a sound credit decision. Which is true.

"Not enough information" is a common and legitimate reason companies turn down credit requests and factors refuse to buy invoices. This also gives the client a good reason for requiring COD terms with the customer, in which case this customer won't be factored. If the client wants to do business on this basis neither she nor you have placed funds in jeopardy with a customer who has no credit history and may be a credit risk.

Alternately, you could agree to factor such a customer on a trial basis. During the time that it takes to establish a good payment history (perhaps two to six months) you might give a 50% advance, charge a higher factoring fee, and allow a shorter than usual recourse period, perhaps 60 days if you usually give 90. Once you're comfortable with the payment history, you can provide a better advance, fees, and recourse period.

However, be careful of your exposure with customers like these. Closely watch your concentrations with unrated companies and keep an eagle eye on their aging reports to track their payments. If you don't they can fall behind and getting paid can become a nightmare. That's what the chapter "Preventive Maintenance" is all about.

15

Factoring and the USA Patriot Act

The events of 9/11 have changed our country dramatically, and the factoring industry has been touched as well. Previously, factoring was subject to little if any government regulation. However, with the enactment of the USA Patriot Act by Congress in the aftermath of this event, the new regulations imposed will have some impact on how factors operate.

The entire text of the USA Patriot Act can be found at http://www.epic.org/privacy/terrorism/hr3162.html. In the next few years, how this law is to be implemented will become definite and clear cut. At the time of this writing, however, the specifics of these regulations are in the process of being worked out, so some of the information that follows is a bit vague.

There are two sections of the USA Patriot Act which affect factors: Section 326, Verification of Identification, and Section 352, Anti-Money Laundering Programs.

Section 326 states financial institutions, after being given adequate notice, will have to:

A. verify the identity of any person seeking to open an account to the extent reasonable and practicable;

B. maintain records of the information used to verify a person's identity, including name, address, and other identifying information; and

C. consult lists of known or suspected terrorists or terrorist organizations provided to the financial institution by any government agency to determine whether a person seeking to open an account appears on any such list.

The first two provisions of this section should already be done on a routine basis during the course of your due diligence. The third step should be simple once such lists are available.

Section 352 refers to Anti-Money Laundering Programs. Money-laundering is a criminal act whereby the origin of illegally obtained funds (drug money, stolen money, money for terrorist activities, etc.) are intentionally obscured and made to look legitimate, usually by creating a complicated money trail that is difficult to trace. Criminals who launder money usually use innocent and honest citizens and businesses as conduits, which give the criminals an appearance of legitimacy. However when their illegal actions are discovered, the crooks quickly disappear and leave the honest and upstanding people or businesses holding the bag.

Section 352 has four elements with which a factoring company will have to comply:

A. the development of internal policies, procedures, and controls (in other words, each factor will need to write an anti-money laundering program tailored to its operation)

B. the designation of a compliance officer within the factoring company

C. an ongoing employee training program

D. an independent audit function to test programs.

Part A says a factoring company will have to design an anti-money laundering program. At first blush this has an ominous tone of a lot of work being foisted on already-busy factoring operations. However, Treasury has made it clear they do not want to put any factors out of business with excessive requirements. They are just carrying out their mission of creating a practical and effective implementation of the law.

Factors will need to develop written internal policies, procedures, and controls for checking out clients and customers. Practically speaking, this means you'll need to write down your due diligence procedures for checking out new business. This can actually be a good thing for those who are a bit casual about these procedures: having a written policy can actually make your operation more efficient and lead to fewer mistakes.

You will also need to name a compliance officer, provide training for employees, and undergo independent testing. The compliance officer will be the person who can answer questions from employees regarding the Anti-Money Laundering Program, and who is the contact point for the government. The compliance officer does not have to be a full-time position nor be from within management of the company. For one person businesses, which include many small factors, the owner will be the compliance officer.

Training will be provided which the compliance officer will need to attend, and in turn pass along the information learned to other employees. This training will teach where and how money laundering activities are likely to occur. Persons in a factoring company who are responsible for transactions in which funds are exchanged will be trained by the compliance officer.

Testing must be done to make sure the company's Anti-Money Laundering Program works. The testing must be done by someone other than the compliance officer. If two or more people are employed by the factoring company, the testing does not need to be done by a person outside the company. How this will be implemented in one-person shops remains to be seen, however.

Your Anti-Money Laundering Program will need to be applied to clients and customers. The program will also need to be applied to a factor's sources of funds or investors. Exactly how that will be done is uncertain at this point. In any event, you certainly don't want to use laundered funds for your working capital.

Because the USA Patriot Act and its implementation is both new and undefined for now, many factors may be wary of the regulations they fear it will generate. However, the good news is the International Factoring Association (IFA) is in regular contact with the Treasury Department and is drafting, at Treasury's request, a set of guidelines for factors to follow to be in compliance.

As of this writing, preliminary guidelines (which have not been formally adopted by the IFA nor approved by the Treasury Department) instruct factoring companies to:

1. Review, where possible, all incoming forms of payment attributable to factored invoices. Irregularities may include but not be limited to:
   - third party payments
   - money orders
   - cash payments
   - foreign checks or drafts (including correspondent bank transactions), or
   - physically remote and/or frequently changing locations of check issuing banks.
2. Identify seemingly disinterested, over-eager applicants.
3. Identify factor clients continually retiring/rolling transactions without corresponding receipt of direct payment instrument from the account debtor.
4. Conduct a preliminary investigation of any irregularities including the report of any unexplainable circumstances (of the above) to proper government authorities.

As you can tell, the government is asking factors to help them detect unlawful money-laundering activities and report them. As suggested in #1 through 3 above, what factors need to especially watch for are:

- Prospects who wants to be a client badly and are not asking about the economics of the factoring arrangement.
- Clients who continually pay off transactions with their own money.
- Clients who continually pay off transactions with third-party checks.
- Customers who continually pay transactions with foreign checks.

In addition to the above "watchdog" activities, the IFA recommends that factors maintain a written record to provide proof, upon governmental inspection, of the firm's compliance with practices mentioned above. They will want to document dates of compliance concerning

1. Training
2. Exception reports and applicable conclusions/actions
3. Audits and resultant reports, which should be retained for any desired governmental inspection.

As you can see from the tentative guidelines above, most factors should be able to follow them without difficulty. No doubt boilerplates will be developed that can be easily adapted to any factoring organization. Ample time will be provided for all organizations to comply.

We need to keep in mind the purpose of the law: to prevent terrorists and other unsavory people from using unsuspecting people and businesses like factors to launder illegal funds. That is not only in our country's best interest, but in our interest as honest business owners and citizens. How we accomplish this will require that we establish and follow definite, written procedures – which we should be doing anyway to ensure the success of our companies.

The fear that factors will have unduly heavy burdens placed on them is unlikely to occur. In fact, I see the strong possibility that beginning or small factors will actually develop improved procedures and policies as a result of this legislation. How? Simply by being required to write the procedures down, making sure everyone in the company understands them, and by testing them.

232 – Factoring Small Receivables

16

Preventive Maintenance

Not long ago my car was overdue for an oil change. When I finally got around to taking care of it, the oil that came out was dark, dirty and pretty ugly. It contrasted starkly to the clear, clean oil that went into the engine to replace it. Not only was the old oil dirty, there wasn't much of it. My car usually takes four-plus quarts but there were probably no more than two quarts drained out of the engine.

Simply put, I wasn't taking proper care of my car and if I had let this go much longer the engine could have been in very bad shape. Anybody who owns a car knows the value of such simple preventive maintenance as regular oil changes…especially if you've had to pay for repairs that regular maintenance would have made unnecessary.

Your factoring business needs some regular preventive maintenance too. It's pretty easy and inexpensive to do, just like an oil change: you must follow up on the slow paying customers of your clients. You can spend all the time and money you want getting accounts set up with proper due diligence, careful checking of credit reports, and so on…but if you don't do what's necessary to keep your receivables running smoothly, all that earlier work may be wasted.

Think of it as going out and buying that nice, new expensive car you've had your eye on for a long time. What is it – a Mercedes, Lexus, BMW, Cadillac, Jaguar, a sports car, a classic antique? Whatever it is, do you have a picture of it in your mind? Ok, now imagine yourself spending time and energy researching the consumer guides and learning everything you can about the car's features and benefits. See yourself shopping around at various dealers, negotiating the best deal possible, and then finally driving your dream car home with a happy smile on your face and sense of satisfaction inside. And now imagine driving this work of art everywhere you go, and all your friends and everyone you drive by staring and admiring your beautiful new machine. What a great feeling! And now imagine driving this fantastic car everywhere for the next four years…and *never once changing the oil*. Aaaugh! Who in their right mind would do that?

Well that is exactly what factors do who spend large sums on nice office equipment, expensive software, planned marketing campaigns, fancy web sites, thorough due diligence, and all the bells and whistles…but then never make calls to customers who are late paying their overdue bills. It makes as much sense as never changing your dream car's oil.

It is very easy to just let your clients watch your aging reports and make calls to their slow paying customers. After all, you reason, these clients are on recourse and if the bills don't pay in 60 or 90 days you can take a charge back against future advances or rebates. Right? Yes, but wrong thinking.

One of the most important services you provide your clients is tracking their accounts receivable and knowing their customers' payment habits. That is, over time you will learn which customers pay like clockwork in 2 weeks, which take 30 or 40 or 50 days as a normal course of business, and which ones are completely unpredictable. Often clients can tell you what length of time is normal for many of their customers, so be sure to ask.

When you learn these payment habits and find a blip on the radar – like a 2-week payer is suddenly at 35 days, or a 30-day payer has slipped to 45 – this is the flag to alert you they need a call. Being on top of slow payments this way is crucial to your value as a factor, and if your clients' cash flow dries up because of slow payments due to *your* being lax on needed calls, their business may soon be in peril. And guess what – that in turn puts your investment in their invoices in jeopardy.

Perhaps you think you're too busy with other more important things to do anything as mundane as calling slow payers to see what's happened to the money they owe you. Well you know what? Changing your oil is pretty mundane too. Do you skip that?

The more consistently you follow up on overdue payments the more likely you are to catch problems and get paid. Collection calls – I prefer to use the term "check-up" calls – are very important to both you and your clients and need to be handled professionally. If your manner comes off as threatening or heavy-handed you can alienate the customer – which is a very reasonable concern most clients have when they first consider factoring.

The great majority of overdue bills are late not because the customer is unwilling or unable to pay. With good due diligence you will usually avoid such customers. Most bills are not paid on time (my guess would be around 80%) because the accounts payable clerk responsible for paying a bill doesn't have the invoice.

This can be due to being mailed to an incorrect address, or incorrect routing to them, or they simply lost it, or just about any reason you can think of. Believe me, you'll hear them all. Therefore when you make a check-up call, it's best to use the following approach.

If the customer is a large company call and ask to speak to the accounts payable department; once you're there ask to speak to the person who handles the payables for this particular client. Accounts are often distributed among payables clerks alphabetically: Mary handles companies whose names start with A to D, Bill handles E through H, and so on. If the customer is a smaller company ask to speak to the person who handles their bookkeeping. Get right to the person who cuts the check so you don't waste a lot of time explaining who you are and what you want to people who can't help you.

Once you have the right person, say, "Hello, I'm _____ and I handle the receivables for ABC Widget Company. I'm showing an invoice that's getting a bit old and I want to make sure you received it. Can you help me with this?" This engages the person by enlisting their help to solve your problem, rather than making them defensive with the blunt, accusatory approach of "Why haven't you paid this bill yet?"

After taking a moment to check, most of the time she will say she "never received it" or "has no record of it" and if you can just fax or re-mail her a copy of the invoice she'll take care of it right away. (Be sure you keep invoice copies!) Check to see you have the correct fax or mailing address as that may be why she never received it. Then again, there's a good chance she just lost it.

Be sure to write down the name of the person you talk to and keep a log of these calls – date, time, and who said what. If you don't have software to track these conversations you can use the Telephone Log below.

<u>Telephone Log</u>

Date	Time	Company	Person's Name	Tel./ Ext. #	Re: Client	Message

You should end the conversation with a rough estimate of when to expect to receive the payment. If she's evasive or won't give you one, that's a red flag that you may not get paid so watch that customer carefully! Inform your client when a customer concerns you this way, as he may want to put the company on COD or cease dealing with it altogether. You probably don't want to buy any more invoices to such customers.

If the bill still hasn't been paid a week or two after you expected you now know whom to call. You phone that person back to "follow up on the payment status" of the invoice you spoke to her about earlier. Armed with your Telephone Log information you'll have exact dates and what she said. This will make you come off as professional and on top of things, which makes an impression on people who pay bills.

If there's another reason an invoice hasn't been paid besides "I never received it," the payables clerk or bookkeeper can usually tell you: it's not been approved for payment, someone has been on vacation, they're short handed and behind, something was wrong with the product or service, and so on. Sometimes the invoice and/or check must cross several desks and it just takes a while to get signed and mailed (common with factored customers). Other times the check will have already been scheduled for next week's print run and is all set to go, but just won't get mailed until then. Again, log this information and follow up if you don't receive payment in a reasonable time based on the information given.

A friendly relationship with the payables people at customers' companies can not only make your job easier and your (and their) day brighter; it can also ensure you get paid in a timely fashion. That can go a long way to keeping your client's (and thus your own) business solvent, plus you will be a hero in your client's eyes. You'll make him look good, save him money, keep his and your cash flow stable, and maintain both of your businesses on firm footing.

Get in the habit of regularly watching your receivables agings and make needed check-up calls to people with overdue bills. Account managers at large factoring companies understand this as a key part of their job and they spend a lot of time doing it. This kind of monitoring and follow up had a lot to do with what made their company big. Translate: check-up calls make you money.

If payables staff and bookkeepers come to know you as friendly and also diligent, they will be sure to pay your clients' invoices in a timely manner when those invoices arrive…and frequently before other invoices that are also awaiting payment.

So keep your and your clients' businesses running smoothly with the routine preventive maintenance of regularly watching customer agings and making timely check-in and follow-up calls. It's a painless way to avoid what can become costly repairs that never should have been needed in the first place. Do this long enough and consistently enough and maybe in time your factoring business will provide the funds for that dream car you've always wanted. Remember the nice feeling as you pictured yourself driving it home?

Just remember to change the oil.

17

Factoring Software

As mentioned in a previous chapter, there are good computer factoring programs available and you will make life easier on yourself down the road if you start your business using one. I started my factoring business using Quicken to keep my business finances, Excel to manage factoring records, and a regular database for general records. (I've since graduated to more robust programs but those worked for starters.) Working this way can be adequate if your budget is tight and/or you only have one or two clients and don't expect to gain more. However, if you're serious about factoring, you'll definitely want to invest in a professional software package written specifically for the factoring industry.

You can spend unnecessary hours and exorbitant costs in developing custom-made software for your business; thankfully, that is not necessary unless you're especially picky about what you want your software package to do (or unless you have a Macintosh that won't run Windows software).

Before you grab the first piece of factoring software you find, study what's out there. You'll want to use a package that will meet your needs now and in the future. If you invest many dollars and countless hours in inadequate software, you may eventually find it doesn't do what you want and then need to transfer or re-enter all that information into another package. This is not most people's idea of fun.

One software vendor, Distinctive Solutions, offers a series of helpful evaluation questions to review before purchase. They are reproduced below with Distinctive Solutions' permission.

Factoring Software
Evaluation Questions

Purchasing software to handle your portfolio is one of the most important decisions you can make. Inadequate software will not only cripple your organization, but your clients. This may open you up to unexpected litigation and major legal expenses. The following are important items that should be covered before any money is spent purchasing software.

Will the software handle your portfolio? If the software you plan to purchase does not handle your portfolio, it is not useful to your organization. Look at both your current portfolio and your growth plans. Make sure that the software can handle at least 90% of your needs without modification.

Can you try out the software? The best way to determine if the software will work for you is to install the software on your computers and try it in your organization. Make sure the software vendor will release the software with a money back guarantee. This not only lets you work the product in a production environment, but will exhibit that the software vendor has the faith in their product to stand behind it. Viewing a demo disk may give you a brief overview, but will not let you know how the software will actually work in your organization.

Who is using the software? Check with the vendor's referrals! Will the software company give you a complete user list, not just a list of a few of their handpicked clients? Can you call the users at random? What do the users report on both software performance and the customer support?

How does the company handle customer support? This cannot be stressed enough, Customer Support is a very important part of the overall software purchase. Is the vendor's customer support department well trained on the software and industry specific questions? Do you have to pay for each customer support call? What hours is the customer support department staffed?

Does the software stay current with the industry? Purchasing quality software can be one of the best educational tools you can get for learning about new developments in the industry. Is the software adequately maintained to keep up with changes in the industry? Will you be billed for new releases?

Are you adequately covered if the software is no longer supported? Review your contract. What happens to you if the software company cannot support you? Do you have access to the files and source code?

What is the background of the software company? The company that provides your software will be your partner; find out who they are. Is it an individual, or a group of people that understand your business? How long have they been around? Do they have an office or are they run out of an individual's home?

Price. What is included in the purchase price? Are there fees for extra modules? Is training included? Remember that it is cheaper in the long run to purchase software that is designed to handle your portfolio both now and in the future than to try to convert your portfolio to a new system, or spend your time apologizing to clients for inadequate reports.

As of this writing, I am aware of the packages described below. Each vendor provided all the information in the pages that follow, so if each one is described as "the best" you'll understand how that can be. I suggest any new factor considering purchasing software study each package carefully and determine which best suits his or her needs and circumstances. This is one of the most significant investments in your factoring business you will make in terms of dollars paid, the amount of time you spend with it, and the image of your company it projects.

Features and prices will continue to change over time so refer to each company's web site or contact the software vendors for the latest information on their products and prices.

For the purpose of full disclosure, the author has contributed significantly to the development of one of the following software packages (BluBeagle™ Suite) and is part owner of its company, Factor Solutions, Inc.

FACTOR/SQL

Software and Vendor: Factor/SQL by Distinctive Solutions, 555 Chorro Street, Suite B., San Luis Obispo, CA. 93405-2396. Tel. 805 544-8327 x6, fax 805 544-3905; Email: bert@dissol.com. *Web site:* www.dissol.com

System Requirements: Pentium III or higher, 128 mg RAM, 100 mg hard disk space, for network system on Novell 3.x and 4.x networks, NT or 2000.

Price: $9,500 single user system; $11,000+ network system.

The granddaddy of factoring software companies, Distinctive Solutions has produced a complete and comprehensive factoring system. Distinctive Solutions has been in business over twenty years and writing factoring software purchased by numerous factors for about sixteen, giving it a big jump on much of the competition in terms features and familiarity with the factoring industry.

FACTOR/SQL is Windows based, web enabled, easy to use and can accommodate portfolios of any size and complexity. It is designed to handle all aspects of a factoring operation, from manual or electronic input of invoices, to comprehensive fee structuring. There is even an interface with Word to handle all of your reporting needs. There are interfaces to various G/L packages including Peachtree and QuickBooks® to keep your accounting records, plus a host of reports, lists, and letters. Written in Delphi utilizing a SQL database, this software has an impressive list of users with sales to over six hundred users who in turn have contributed to its features. Its customers range from startups booking their first factoring client to some of the largest factors in the world.

Distinctive Solutions President Bert Goldberg is very willing to offer a variety of innovative payment packages. One of the easiest for start up factors is the pay as you grow plan. You can receive the fully functional system for $1,000 down and $500 every time you add a new client (up to twenty clients). You can take as long as you need to pay for the system. In this way you can pay as your portfolio grows. An annual maintenance contract, for fee of 20% ($1,900 for the single user system, payable quarterly), is highly recommended and provides software updates (usually coming twice a year) plus a 24-hour help line.

Rather than using a demo, which has proven to be very limited, the scope of this software requires a different approach. Goldberg personally gives a very thorough and helpful walk-through of all features directly on your computer via the internet. Once your machines are connected, he displays on his computer the full-blown program as you simultaneously see it on yours. Doing so takes an hour and allows you to appreciate the comprehensiveness of the product. If you decide to purchase the software, a two-day training course is offered at Distinctive Solutions' site (San Luis Obispo, California). Your cost is transportation, food, and lodging. For an additional fee, their training staff will come to you.

As a further selling point, the company sponsors a major factoring conference in which factors from all around the world gather to discuss how they do their factoring business (see the chapter Factoring Resources). This conference is open to all factors, not just Distinctive Solutions customers. The American Cash Flow Association allows continuing education credit for its members who attend Distinctive Solutions user conference.

The company has no plans for a scaled down version of the software. Goldberg believes software that controls not only the Factors business, but the finances of the clients should not be scaled back, and factors should not rely on limited functionality type products with the payment plans offered and the completeness of the system. You can get started with this system for $1,000, which includes two days of training plus $500 for each client. Purchasing the recommended annual maintenance contract means you're paying $3,400 for software to factor your first client, not counting travel to California plus expenses for two days of training.

Features

The following is a partial list of some of the features available with FACTOR/SQL. To fully appreciate the systems flexibility and ease of use, a demonstration is recommended.

- **Full EDI capability** allows you to upload both Invoices and Payments directly into the system.

- **General Ledger Interface** into the General Ledger Package of your choosing.

- **Verification processing** via phone or verification letters.

- **Easy to use Schedule screen** with Add it Now feature allowing you to enter new Debtors on the fly.

- **Payment entry** with searches by Client, Debtor, Invoice ID and Amount. A check may be applied to any number of Invoices. Non-Factored amounts may be tied to specific invoices.

- **Accruals of Income and Reserve Amounts** are available at any time.

- **Extensive Fee Capability** allowing you to charge fees based on:

  - **Incremental Rates based** on buckets of time. Twenty-two buckets are provided.

  - **Daily Rates** allows you to charge client fees based on a fixed rate or a prime. May be charged on the Invoice or Advanced amount, Full amount or Unpaid Balance, Compound Interest and varying Days in Year.

  - **Fees on Net Funds Employed** allows you to charge a fee based on Net Funds Employed in conjunction with an Incremental or Daily Rate.

  - **Float Fees** on Business or Calendar Days.

  - **Fees tied to invoices** allowing you to use different rate tables for each Client's invoices.

- **Up front fees** may be earned immediately or Accrued until the Invoice is closed.

- **Reserves** may be held until the Schedule is closed.

- **Fees charged on an Invoice by Invoice basis** or when a threshold is reached.

- **Late or Finance fees** may be charged to the Debtor.

- **Default charges** (i.e. Wire, Expedite) will display at the time the schedule is entered. Amounts may be deducted from the Advance or Client's reserve.

- **Credit and Concentration Limits** notify you when you are getting close to a Client, Debtor or Account's credit limits. Unique tracking feature monitors Debtor exposure across all Clients.

- **Unlimited User Defined Tickler system** allowing you to track any date sensitive items for Clients and Debtors.

- **Special Reserve** allows you to hold a greater portion of your Client's reserve for contingencies.

- **Investor Tracking** allows you to tie Investors or Participants to the invoices.

- **Broker Commissions** are calculated and reports are printed for you automatically.

- **Comprehensive Collection Module** allows you to help your Clients with their collections.

- **Unlimited Comments** for Debtors and Invoices.

- **Check Printing** for Advance and Reserve disbursements. Check layout is defined by you.

- **Full Security** is available allowing your users and Clients to log directly into FACTOR/SQL and view only the data that they have authority to view.

- **Internet Connectivity** allowing you to run FACTOR/SQL via the internet.

- **Comprehensive Help Feature** and excellent User Manuals are also provided.

- **Full Spreadsheet Interface** in the Spreadsheet or Report Writer of your choosing.

- **Client/Server Based** utilizing COM architecture for the fastest and most secure Networking available.

- **eFactor module** allowing your customers to view information, run reports and enter invoices over the internet.

FactorSoft

Software and Vendor: FactorSoft by Bayside Business Solutions, Incorporated, 23852 Pacific Coast Highway, #909, Malibu, CA 90265. 310-455-7520 (voice and fax); 800-567-4580 U.S. and Canada. Email: info@factorsoft.com
Web site: www.factorsoft.com

Pricing
Version Types and Support Levels
Prices Effective January 1, 2003
FactorSoft Enterprise Lite Edition - The Enterprise Lite Edition is network compatible and runs on the Microsoft
MSDE database engine, a 'lite' version of Microsoft SQL Server. Support is available by fax, email and telephone.
Price: $ 12,575, includes 5 user licenses
Additional 5-user license packs: $2,575. 1 additional pack available, for a total of 10 users.
Optional Subscription: $4,575, plus $975 per user pack, annual subscription after the first year. Includes continued upgrades and support.
Installation and Training: $1,200 per day. Travel and other expenses are billed separately

FactorSoft Enterprise Edition - The Enterprise Edition is network compatible and runs of the Microsoft SQL Server database engine. Support is available by fax, email and telephone.
Price: $24,575, includes 20 user licenses.

Additional 5-user license pack: $4,975.
Installation and Training: $1,200 per day. Travel and other expenses are billed separately
Optional Subscription: $9,575, plus $ 1,975 per user pack, annual subscription fee after the first year. Includes continued upgrades and support..

FactorSoft Enterprise for Oracle - Enterprise for Oracle is network compatible and runs on the Oracle 8i PL/SQL database engine. Support is available by fax, email and telephone.
Price: $ 36,575 includes 20 user licenses.
Additional 5-user license pack: $5,975.
Optional Subscription: $14,575, plus $2,375 per user pack, annual subscription fee after the first year. Includes continued upgrades and support.
Installation and Training: $1,200 per day. Travel and other expenses are billed separately.

FactorSoft Web Interface Module - Based on Microsoft's Internet Information Server (IIS) technology, the FactorSoft Web Interface offers the security, flexibility, and scalability you need to transmit data on the Web, providing clients the ability to query your database to retrieve selected report information, and upload new debtor information and invoices at will. Use of this module requires FactorSoft Enterprise Lite or higher.
Price: $9,575, plus $1,275 for ActivePDF report printing software (third party software)
Optional Subscription: $3,575 annual subscription fee after the first year. Includes continued upgrades and support.

FactorSoft Imaging Module - This integrated FactorSoft scanning solution, which requires the Enterprise Edition, provides reduced paper filing and instant data retrieval, fast data entry, quicker response to questions, and easier distribution of requested documentation.
Price: $ 6,575
Optional Subscription: $2,575 annual subscription fee after the first year. Includes continued upgrades and support

FactorSoft TrakFax Module - This integrated FactorSoft faxing solution, which requires the Enterprise Edition, is an add-on product that provides automated importing of faxed invoice information. Faxes sent to your computer faxing system can be automatically imported into FactorSoft creating schedules (batches) automatically including the faxed image. TrakFax requires the FactorSoft imaging module.
Price: $ 6,575
Optional Subscription: $ 2,575 annual subscription fee after the first year. Includes continued upgrades and support.

Regardless of which version is initially purchased, the original purchase price will include the first year's subscription. This subscription entitles the user to continued support and all upgrades.

The subscription renewal price will be locked in for at least two years based on the price at the time of purchase, as long as the subscription is kept current. Upgrades to the next version level will be priced at the current difference in price.

Custom programming, on-site training and installation services are available at additional cost, including travel, and or other expenses. Please contact us at 310.455.7520 x105 for more information regarding these services.

FactorSoft Product Features at a Glance

Windows 98/NT/2000/XP Compatible
FactorSoft is a full 32bit Microsoft Solution written in Microsoft Visual Basic, requiring Windows 98/NT/2000/XP.

Microsoft Office Integration
You can use any of the Microsoft Office 2000/XP products to access the data components of the system, giving you the ability to define your own reports and queries. FactorSoft also has direct export capabilities for Word and Excel.

LAN/Wan Scalability
Whether you're a single user, have a Windows peer-to-peer network with two computers, or run a 100-user Windows 2000

network with Back Office and SQL Server, FactorSoft is fully scalable, so your system and your business can grow.

Security

Users belong to groups. With these groups, you have the ability to set up users with only the functions you want them to perform. Groups are set up based on how you do business. Users who are not authorized to perform certain functions will not see those functions on their screen, giving you complete security.

Tickler Files

FactorSoft creates tickler files from information that you enter as notes. If notes are posted as requiring follow-up, credit renewal, or UCC expiration, they appear on the appropriate day for the relevant user as a tickler.

Multi-Currency

With FactorSoft, you can have portfolios denominated in any currency, with the ability to run appropriate reports in both native and primary currencies.

Web Interface

The FactorSoft Web Interface gives your clients the ability to view their accounts on-line, in real-time (Enterprise Edition required).

Imaging

With this powerful add-on feature, invoices can be scanned into FactorSoft for retrieval at any time.

Flexible Management Controls

All critical aspects of portfolio management are controlled within FactorSoft, including Verification, Credit Checking, Make Buy decisions, Risk Analysis, Concentrations, Trend Analysis and Funds Employed reporting.

Customized Preferences

User and system preferences are used to customize the set up your system the way you want it, from choosing what to call your debtors to what color you want your invoice register to be.

Extensive Reports

There are numerous built-in reports including aging, transactions, statements, check distribution, trial balances, as well as custom reports you can create from the database.

Search Capabilities

With FactorSoft, you have the ability to search for invoices, checks, and debtors based on a partial check number, phone number, city, state, zip code or invoice number.

Multiple Client Terms

With FactorSoft, different terms can be set up for each and every client. You are in complete control of this important aspect of your business. These terms include; Recourse and Non Recourse, Fee Based, Daily Fee, A/R Finance, and Merchant/Statement Billing.

G/L Accounting Exports

This module allows you to export your accounting or check information directly from FactorSoft into a number of popular accounting systems.

Check Writing Features

Clients can be paid by wire service, bank transfer, via a check printer or by handwritten check. In a network environment, you can have a dedicated machine printing checks as you go, all day long.

Detailed Notes

There are many areas to enter notes throughout FactorSoft, which are used by the tickler file system to alert the user to various situations that may arise with clients and debtors.

Integrated Windows Features

FactorSoft has many Windows type features designed to enhance productivity. For example, click on the phone icon to dial a phone number. If you can print a report, you can fax it or email it (with appropriate hardware/software). Information 'bubbles' appear when the mouse rests on a contact, providing detailed information.

Preference Output

Based on client and debtor master settings, reports and statements can be faxed or emailed to clients and debtors automatically, without user intervention, saving time and money.

FactorSoft Product Information

Factoring in the Windows environment. It's about time! It's also about business. Covering all operation and collection aspects of invoice based factoring, this Windows based software application was developed after many years of experience creating custom software solutions for factoring.

FactorSoft is the most robust, complete, user-friendly software for the factoring industry available today. Its powerful features include:

The Windows Platform

The program is a full 32bit Microsoft solution. It requires Windows 98/NT/2000 or XP.

FactorSoft is written in Microsoft Visual Basic. You can use the Microsoft Office 2000 and XP products to access any of the data components of the system, giving you the ability to define your own special reports, or create mail merge letters using the best tools available.

The FactorSoft Enterprise Lite Edition runs on the Microsoft MSDE database engine. For the smaller user, this product provides a cost effective entry point to the FactorSoft platform.

The FactorSoft Enterprise Edition is meant for the larger organization with the need for the exceptionally robust Microsoft SQL Server database engine.

The FactorSoft Enterprise for Oracle Edition is meant for the larger organization who want to utilize the Oracle PL/SQL Server database engine.

Please visit our website for more detailed information about the necessary hardware and software infrastructure for all versions of FactorSoft.

Windows 98/NT/2000/XP and therefore this program run well on a minimum of a 124mb Pentium II computer with sufficient disk space.

We have run FactorSoft on Windows NT, Windows 2000 Server/Advanced Server, Novell NetWare 3.12 and Novell NetWare 4.10 networks.

Program Description

It is very difficult to describe a software program in words without pictures. So much of it is about look and feel, screens that make sense without needing to be a programmer to understand what is going on. This program is easy to use and works the way most factors run their businesses.

User and System Preferences

Some factors call their clients' customers "debtors" and some call them "customers." Some buy invoices on a "bill of sale," some on a "schedule". The product gives you the ability to setup preferences to call things what you want to, make things the color you want, even to have selected functions come up automatically when you log on.

In this document we will call them "debtor," "bill of sale" and "collection report." In the software you can call them anything you want.

Clients, Debtors, Contacts and Brokers

The software gives a kind of "Rolodex" of clients, debtors, contacts and brokers. We can look at them in any number of sequences and we can get to all the different kinds of information from those lists. With the right piece of inexpensive hardware, you will be able to dial any of these businesses with the click of a button.

The clients share debtors. You have access to all the data regarding what might be going on with the same debtor on all other clients. This gives the ability to set a credit limit for a specific debtor across all clients, allows discussion of multiple collection issues with the debtor at the same time, and allows viewing all notes against the debtor as a group.

Transactions

You buy invoices (bill of sale or schedule) and collect money (collection report) against a client's account. Each of these "batches" is called a "transaction." Money is paid to the client based on these transactions. The transactions will always balance to the accounts receivable.

When you first enter the data, the "batch" is "pending." When there are no errors and everything is as you want it, you may update the batch, making it a transaction. The accounts receivable and disbursement reports are immediately up to date.

Each transaction has an associated report that describes what invoices, deductions and calculations were made. These reports can be viewed and/or reprinted at any time.

Whenever you look at a transaction or are working on an "open" batch, you are able to view all the appropriate numbers you need to make relevant business decisions.

An updated transaction can then be faxed, e-mailed or printed and given to a client for their signature.

Client Terms

Each entry in the client terms table describes a relationship between the factor and one or more clients. In the client record, you select the arrangement for this client.

The client terms record gives the system information about what to deduct when the invoice is purchased, and what kinds of rebates will be given on payment, if any. Additional reserves can be automatically deducted before giving rebates.

Information is entered about recourse or non-recourse and how many days until an item is eligible.

Actual fees are normally based on how long it takes the invoice to pay. There can be as many days/rate combinations as necessary.

Purchasing Invoices

The bill of sale (or whatever you choose to call this document) is how we enter the new invoices. The form is designed for rapid data entry. The user enters an invoice, date, amount, and selects or adds a debtor. You are fully exposed to warnings, balances, notes and credit limit issues regarding debtors as the invoices are entered.

Expenses may be entered against the bill of sale. The program can automatically select the pre-determined rate for things like Federal Express delivery or you can enter the appropriate amount manually.

You are able to view recourse items if appropriate. The system shows you all items that are over the "programmed" days old, items that have been paid short and/or items that have been flagged for immediate recourse.

Click on a tab and you see the amounts for the check that will be written, current balances of all relevant accounts (accounts receivable, fee escrow, reserve escrow and cash reserves). On this screen you may decide to hold or supply additional funds to or from the cash reserve.

When the bill of sale "batch" balances, has no duplicate invoices or other errors you may update it. The report is printed and optionally, the check is written.

There is another much requested function whereby you can write the actual invoices for your client. They are then placed in a pending "batch" and you can then decide whether to purchase them or not.

Collections

The collection report is very similar to the bill of sale, except we post checks and apply them to invoices. You will have the same ability to post expenses and pay off recourse items as appropriate.

The calculation tab on this screen shows the projected fee and rebate calculation and again you can hold or supply funds from or to the reserve account.

Notes

Notes are reminders that are posted against debtors or against invoices. If notes are posted as requiring follow-up, they will appear in the tickler file for the relevant user on the appropriate day.

Users with appropriate security access can review notes posted to other users. Since notes are collected and viewed from newest to oldest, you have an excellent way to see the entire collection history for a specific client.

Notes can also be posted in such a way that they will pop up on a specific user's machine immediately. They are also available by email in the network version.

Search Capabilities

You have the ability to search for invoices based on invoice number or partial debtor information. Often, you receive a check without even knowing which clients' invoices are being paid.

These screens give you the ability to search based on a partial name key, phone number, city, state, zip or invoice number.

Checks and Payments

Clients are paid by wire service, bank transfer or check. There are a number of ways to handle check writing. In a network environment, you can have a dedicated machine printing checks as you go, all day long. You can bring up a list of checks that are required, write them by hand and key in the check number or you can bring up a function and write checks when you want to.

There is also an ability to indicate that a wire service or bank transfer was used to send the funds. In this case, a report is available to indicate what funds were sent from which bank account so that a check can be written at the end of the day and an appropriate transaction number can be added. This includes telephone transfers and intrabank transfers.

Accounting Reports

The system includes check distribution reports and trial balances based on the transactions with the clients.

With the ability to write general expense checks that may or may not be posted against a specific client, the system gives the profit and expense side of your general ledger.

Other Reports

There are a number of other built in reports including several aging reports, transaction reports, statements and a recourse report. Because this is a Windows solution, if you can print it, you can fax it or send it by e-mail with very little extra effort.

Any number of custom reports can be created using the Access database and queries. You can send a debtor a full statement of account with just the click of a button while you still have him on the phone or you can send the client a copy of a current or prior collection report while you are still discussing it.

Security

Users belong to groups and groups are allowed to perform certain functions. You develop the groups based on how you want to do business. Users that are not authorized to perform a certain function will not even see it on their screen.

Miscellaneous

There are a number of extra touches you will have to see to fully appreciate: the help screens, the optional training tips, the screen designs. For example, as an option, when you rest the mouse pointer on a client, debtor, contact or broker name for five seconds a balloon opens up to give you all of the relevant information.

©1997-2003 Bayside Business Solutions, Inc. All rights reserved. FactorSoft and its logo are registered trademarks of Bayside Business Solutions, Inc. All other names are trademarks or registered trademarks of their respective owners.

Win!Factor

Software and Vendor: Win!Factor 3.0 by Kingham Software, Inc., 196 Ave B NW, Winter Haven, FL 33881; tel 863 291-4268; fax 509 356-0855; E-mail: sales@winfactor.net. Web site www.winfactor.net

System requirements: Pentium computer with 32 Meg of RAM recommended; Windows 95/98/NT/2000 required.

Price: Win!Factor 3.0 leases for $525 per year for the single user version and $525 plus $105 per user per year for the network version. During the lease period the user gets access to free updates via WinFactor's web site.

A free trial of the software, which makes the full working version available for a specified number of uses, can be downloaded from the web site. If you decide to buy after the trial period, simply make the needed payment and your trial version becomes a leased version which you continue to use for the next year. At that the end of that time, you make an annual lease payment to continue using the program.

Kingham Software, Inc. is a software programming and consulting company who wrote its first factoring software for a client and realized this was valuable to an entire industry. Now after almost six years of fine-tuning, Win!Factor version 3.0 is an easy-to-learn, yet powerful, factoring software package for Windows users. Written in Microsoft Access, it features a wide range of financial, aging, and history reports that can be printed, faxed, exported to Microsoft Word and Excel or as HTML. The software also interfaces with QuickBooks®.

Features
- Unlimited Clients, Customers, Terms, Schedules and Receipts
- Automatic Fee Calculation
- QuickBooks® Ledger Interface
- Integrated To Do and Reminder system
- Invoice Verification system
- Invoice Collections system
- International Currency, Date and Address formats
- Co-Factor processing
- Broker Statements
- Purchase Order Funding/Conversion
- Portfolio Funding
- Cash Reserves
- Prints Checks

- Client / Customer Contact History
- Duplicate Invoice checking

Win!Factor Reports
- Aging Reports – Over 20 different Aging reports included
- Concentration reports
- Reserve Analysis
- Cash Standing
- Fees Accrued
- Purchases
- Receipts
- Broker Statements
- Co-Factor Statements
- Invoice History
- Client / Customer Listings
- Client / Customer Labels
- Return on Investment

The BluBeagle™ Suite
Web Based Solution for
Factors and Factoring Consultants

Software and Vendor: BluBeagle™ Suite by Factor Solutions, Inc. 18729 SE Lakeside Way, Tequesta, FL 33469.
Tel: (561) 741-7177 Fax (561) 658-6275.
Web Site: www.BluBeagle.com

System requirements: PC, Mac, Unix, and Linux compatible. MicroSoft Internet Explorer 6.0 Service Pack 1 or higher, or Netscape 7.1 or higher Internet browser required.

Overview

BluBeagle™ is an integrated solution that gives small factors and medium- to large-sized factoring companies all the tools they need to track their mission-critical data in one intuitive, comprehensive, and powerful product.

BluBeagle™ offers an instant, Web-based database solution for both factoring professionals and part-timers alike. Since it's hosted in a world-class data center, BluBeagle™ eliminates the high IT cost and complexity of maintaining and troubleshooting the software and hardware that other solutions require, while providing the highest level of security that technology can provide. And this is offered at a price that literally any size operation can easily afford.

What's more, you need only a dial-up, DSL, or cable Internet connection to access BluBeagle™. Thus you can run your factoring operation from virtually anywhere: your office, your home, a hotel room on the road, even a sandy, sunny beach. Your desktop computer, or even your PDA or laptop with a wireless internet connection, will connect you to literally all your data!

Companies using other high-priced, complicated, yet limited factoring software will be amazed at how Factor Solutions, Inc. has come up with such an affordable, complete, and easily mastered solution.

BluBeagle™ Features

BluBeagle™, the complete package from Factor Solutions Inc. is made up of four modules, which you can mix and match to your needs. Upgrading to additional modules is easy and can be done at any time at a very modest cost. In this way, you are paying for and using only features that you need.

The modules include:

1. **ConsultBlu** – The Consultant Module (business management and client/project tracking tool).

2. **FactorBlu** – The Factoring Module (includes ConsultBlu).

3. **AccountBlu** – The Accounting Module (direct and automatic accounting of all your transactions, and tailored to the factoring industry).

4. **SiteBlu** — The Web Site Module (custom prices available on request, when bought as stand-alone).

The first two modules are available separately or together. ConsultBlu provides an impressive array of tools and resources for independent factoring consultants. When purchasing FactorBlu, which includes the consultant module, both independent consultants and Factors as well as business development professionals of larger factoring companies will become highly effective with the many features provided.

1. ConsultBlu - The Consultant Module

ConsultBlu tracks all information about prospects and clients, along with interactions like phone calls and meetings, in a single record. With these records, you can see a full account of all interactions including history, status, activity, and more. You can also include files such as letters, contracts, or even photos. And because ConsultBlu, like the other modules, is web-based, these records can be accessed at the office or on the road. The Consultant can also track time and expenses related to each client, and bill for time and expenses if desired.

ConsultBlu gives you a more effective way to handle leads information. When a prospect completes and submits an optional web form, other site management systems send you this information by e-mail, requiring you to re-enter the data into your application. In contrast, ConsultBlu Web Forms create an instant, time-stamped online record containing all contact information and answers to custom questions, and store this record in a centralized database that can be accessed via ConsultBlu by development staff, management, and other departments as needed.

Because ConsultBlu uses e-mail addresses as unique identifiers, prospects can visit your site repeatedly without creating a duplicate record. If the same visitor submits another form, ConsultBlu simply adds the new information to the original contact record. System notes show you a history of the visitor's activities on your site.

To help you track leads, ConsultBlu lets you assign a probability of close status to each form so that you can run a pipeline forecast of the new business that will be closed in the month ahead.

Independent consultants will enjoy ConsultBlu 's ability to record the terms offered each client by factors contacted. What's more, once prospects become factoring clients, commissions earned from each client can be recorded and tracked. Consultants who opt to include ConsultBlu will have such income automatically entered into this built-in accounting program, which serves as their complete business bookkeeping solution.

If and when an independent consultant chooses to begin funding clients, the upgrade to ConsultBlu is easy and very cost effective for new and part-time factoring operations.

2. FactorBlu - The Factoring Module

FactorBlu includes ConsultBlu and is the heart of the BluBeagle™ software solution package for those who fund receivables. This module is far more affordable, much more user-friendly, and provides the desired features you need but often don't find in other factoring software products.

You, your clients, staff, consultants, co-factors, and lenders can connect to your FactorBlu records from within your web site. If you don't have a web site, you can inexpensively create one (see "4. SiteBlu – The Web Site Module" below) or simply log on to Factor Solutions' site to access your data.

Want to have an online form to instantly obtain prospects' application information? It's included as an option, can be modified as you wish, and is a great place to start. Need all of your set up documents to include a client's name and address information, and then be printed for signatures? Easy. Need to make changes to the wording in your contract documents?

Due diligence? There are several links in FactorBlu to credit reporting agencies and UCC services to make this step a streamlined part of your operation. And once you've approved an applicant and factoring begins, everything you and your clients need to routinely factor their invoices is right here.

What if a client doesn't have a computer or access to the web? He'll factor using your current practices of paper and fax. You simply receive the information and enter it for him. However, most clients will save themselves (and you!) an enormous amount of time by entering their invoice information online. After using this method just once, clients do not want to return to the "old" way of transacting their factoring business.

Everything they need for creating and submitting invoices for factoring is provided in simple, easy-to-follow mouse clicks. Once their invoices are submitted, you can email, fax, or snail mail the invoices your clients created (and you've verified and approved) to their customers. **This means much less time for both you and your client to complete routine transactions.**

FactorBlu stores all your business-critical data on one centralized MicroSoft SQL database so you can extract any information you want, whenever you want, and from wherever you want, knowing that it will always be up-to-date. That means clients can obtain online reports effortlessly, and without any expensive add-on software for you to buy. All the reports your clients want, and every report you'll need as well, are pre-loaded. Just click the link to the report you want, and there it is. No more time-consuming efforts to create and send a report, no more intrusive client phone calls asking if this or that invoice has paid. You both have 24/7 access to this information – again, at no extra cost to you.

But reporting convenience doesn't stop there. Thanks to FactorBlu's advanced sorting and filtering capabilities, you can customize the many reports that come pre-loaded so they meet your specific needs. What's more, FactorBlu can easily memorize frequently used reports. You can also allow others in your company to access reports by designating them as public.

Although reports come with top professional layout and contain all information needed, you can customize reports by both content and layout. You have the option of adding columns, filtering the data, and sorting the resulting information. You also have the option of adding an additional column for a running total and options for inserting grand totals and subtotals where you need them.

On all reports, you can drill down on summary information to the supporting detail, and on amounts to actual transactions. In short, the reporting features in FactorBlu are powerful, comprehensive, and impressive.

3. AccountBlu – The Accounting Module

Your accounting system is critical to your business. That's why Factor Solutions, Inc. offers powerful accounting tools to help you track every aspect of your finances, including:

- General Ledger and Chart of Accounts
- Accounts Receivable and Accounts Payable
- Banking and Online Bill Payment
- Employee Management and Payroll
- Financial Reports (P&L, Balance Sheet, Cash Flow Analysis, Aging Reports, and many more)
- Order Processing, Sales Orders and Purchase Orders
- Time & Billing

What does this mean? Simply put, you can track all your accounting needs within AccountBlu and never again have to export them to QuickBooks. Your factoring data is **automatically integrated** into AccountBlu, and you'll never again need to fuss with splitting customer payments into advances, rebates, fees, and so on. AccountBlu replaces QuickBooks (a $160 - $360 value right there, depending on which version of QuickBooks you buy) and eliminates the need to make double entries in your factoring and accounting programs, as well as the need for exporting data from one application to the other.

The Accounting Module has been carefully tried, tested, and reviewed by a CPA who owns and operates a factoring company. While the purchase of this module is optional, choosing to use this module will save the cost of yet another expensive piece of software and will keep everything you need to run your business neatly in one place, without having to export data or make duplicate entries into an accounting package.

However, if you are presently using accounting software and want to continue doing so manually, you need not include this module in your suite of BluBeagle™ software. Should you decide to upgrade to AccountBlu later, you can do so at any time.

4. SiteBlu – The Web Site Module

If you don't have a web site, BluBeagle™'s fourth module will provide a truly professional web presence at a very competitive price. Once you select your web site name (www.YourSite.com), Factor Solutions, Inc. will check to see if that name is available, register it, design your site as much as you want, and host it.

If you already have a web presence, you can transfer your hosting needs to Factor Solutions, Inc. for a very reasonable price ($10/month). If you have a web host and/or a web master you want to keep, no problem. Utilizing this module, like the accounting module, is strictly up to you. Regardless of whom you use for your web hosting and maintenance needs, links to your FactorBlu data can be easily added to your web site for instant access.

However, if you want to create a new site or "remodel" your existing site, with Factor Solutions, Inc. and the built-in MicroSoft SQL you can set your website apart with online site-building tools that allow you to choose from a variety of layout styles and designs. BluBeagle™ users can upload their own files to create a unique website look, and can customize site elements such as headers, footers, tab bars, sidebars and content wrappers. You can even display different looks and site elements on each tab.

Once your site is up, SiteBlu allows you to make changes immediately; there's no waiting for new information to post. You can upload or modify images, files, and text, and store items anytime. This ensures that visitors to your site always see the most current information. Web forms are integrated into SiteBlu, so making changes is as easy as cutting, pasting, and submitting.

With Factor Solutions, Inc.'s SiteBlu tools, you can build a variety of forms, from event sign-ups and contact-us requests to online order forms. You can optionally create custom questions and define how visitors respond: required or optional, multiple-choice or fill-in-the-blank. Text can be easily modified and re-arranged. Also optionally, you can define what kind of records should be created, depending on what online form visitors submit. For example, a visitor who submits a "Contact Us" form could become "Lead – Expressed Interest," while a visitor submitting an "Application Form" could be "Application Form Completed."

Most importantly, you can make changes yourself to the text of your web site, rather than relying on a Webmaster or designer.

Security and Performance

By adopting any one of BluBeagle™'s applications, you automatically enjoy the advantages of a world-class data center. Factor Solutions, Inc.'s team of IT professionals has years of experience managing a data center, ensuring the highest levels of data security (to Fortune 100 and government standards) as well as superior uptime and performance.

Security

Factor Solutions, Inc. organizes security efforts into two areas: physical access and Web-based access. To protect data from physical access, the data center employs 24-hour biometric admittance to keep anyone from entering without full security clearance.

For Web-based security, the system configuration employs these measures and more:

- **Internet firewalls**
  Firewalls block all attempts to access the data center other than from methods and points that are allowed

- **128-bit secure socket layer data encryption**
  When you or your employees access a BluBeagle™ application, your login, with a unique ID and password, starts a connection where all data is passed back and forth encrypted.

- **Application-only access**
  The system is divided into layers that separate data from the application. Everyone who logs in only has access to the application layer so no one can access your data to see or maliciously alter it.

- **Role-level access, idle disconnect and account lockout**
  Every user is assigned a specific role with specific permissions to only see and use the features related to their own jobs. The system also detects if your connection is idle and automatically disconnects to prevent someone else from sitting at your computer and using your access. Also, if anyone tries to access the application by guessing at a person's ID and password, the account will be locked out after 3 attempts.

As an added security measure, our IT team regularly backs up your data and stores the backups in a separate, secure location many miles away from the data center. In the event of a major natural disaster, we can restore your data within 48 hours. Compared to the standard security practices of in-house software, users typically experience significantly higher security measures after switching to a BluBeagle™ application.

Performance

Performance levels are addressed from a standpoint of both uptime and system speed. We understand how important uptime is for your business. In response, we have set our uptime objectives to surpass industry in-house and outsourced levels.

We have consistently exceeded those levels and strive to continue to do so.

We can achieve these uptime objectives because our data center configuration uses a three-tier architecture that separates the data delivery layer, the application layer and the database layer. Each layer uses multiple servers, and they employ fault-tolerant session failover. In other words, if one server fails, your connection is seamlessly handed over to another server, and you can continue to do your work without even noticing a change. We also have fully redundant hardware systems in place, including an independent power supply, so that if any hardware fails the backup hardware takes over and there is no interruption of service to you.

In addition to uptime, the data center configuration is also pivotal in ensuring the best system speed, which is achieved through load balancing, direct backbone connection and optimized page transmission. For load-balancing, we use the architecture's ability to shift connections among servers to spread the load evenly and assign each connection to the least busy server so that you always get the best speed.

Having a direct connection to the three major Internet backbone providers ensures that there are no data transmission bottlenecks to the data center. Depending on your location for each session, data is directed via the fastest route.

To maximize system speed, the data transfer is also optimized. BluBeagle™ application pages re-use standard page elements which they cache in your browser so that the data transferred is only those elements that are unique to the page requested. Having less data to transmit means your browser receives all the data it needs sooner and the page is displayed for you sooner.

By using Factor Solutions, Inc.'s hosted solution, you get a data center as sophisticated and secure as those used by Fortune 500 companies at no additional cost to you. The team of IT professionals takes care of all hardware and software upgrades, data storage, and backups. And most of these tasks can be done without any interruption of service to you. We achieve 99.9%

uptime, a performance level any other business application would be hard-pressed to beat.

Support & Training

The secret to a successful implementation of business software is making sure the users have all the documentation, tools, and support they need. BluBeagle™ is loaded with great resources and material, whether you decide to handle implementation and training yourself or choose assistance from any of Factor Solutions, Inc.'s experts. We have designed BluBeagle™ to be as easy to learn as possible, so there is no requirement that you must travel and spend several days to receive necessary training to use the software.

Most of the documentation is stored within the applications to ensure that you and your employees always have the most up-to-date information at all times. You can view this by going to the Support tab from within the application. The Support tab documentation includes:

- **User Guides**
  The user guides give you step-by-step instructions for implementing and using the main areas of BluBeagle™ applications.

- **Help**
  The online Help is a fully indexed and searchable database of information. You can access it from the Support tab or from any page within the application. If you click Help on a record, report or transaction page, topics directly related to the area where you are working appear. This context-sensitive help includes a "What Is?" section and a "How Do I?" section so you can quickly understand what you are looking at as well as how to use it. In addition, you can click each field on any page to get a complete description of what to enter in it.

- **Release Notes**
  Release notes give information about updates and new features that have recently been added. BluBeagle™ applications are Web-based, new features are continually

added, and improvements are provided without charging you a penny more.

- **User Groups**
  You can also tap into the extensive wealth of Factor Solutions, Inc.'s customers' knowledge. From the Support tab within the application, click the User Group link and sign up to participate in all the members' discussions. Members can create their own topics so they can ask questions specific to other people in their industry or pose more general questions. We strongly support our User Groups. A representative of the company is always participating in discussions to give assistance and to listen to suggestions for new features they should add or improvements they should make.

Introductory Price

BluBeagle™ provides many features, great ease of use, and excellent overall value, yet its price is affordable for even the smallest operation. If you have been using any other factoring software product, you will be pleasantly surprised. Introductory prices are below.

	Annual Subscription Prices		Prices per month (for cost evaluation purpose only)	
	1st user license	per add'l user lic.	1st user license	per add'l user lic.
FactorBlu				
for 1-5 clients	$360	$105	$30.00	$8.75
for 6-10 clients	$600	$175	$50.00	$14.58
for 11+ clients	$1200	$350	$100.00	$29.17
ConsultBlu	$120	$120	$10.00	$10.00
AccountBlu	$120	$30	$10.00	$2.50
SiteBlu	$250	N/A	N/A	N/A
Web site Hosting	$120	N/A	$10.00	N/A
Tech Support				
up to 5 hrs/year	$350	$350	$29.17	$29.17
up to 10 hrs/year	$600	$600	$50.00	$41.67
unlimited / year	$1000	$1000	$83.33	$83.33

Notes:
- FactorBlu includes ConsultBlu

- SiteBlu price is a one-time-only design fee for a basic professional site, if purchased in conjunction with subscription to other module(s). Rates for web site design for "special" sites and/or without subscription to other modules are available upon request. Web site hosting is available for $10/month.

- Technical Support refers to access to personal phone support. Online support, manual and help desk are included in each module price.

Pricing Options
- Sign up for 2 years at Introductory prices and get first 2 months free.
- Sign up for 3 years at Introductory prices and get first 3 months free.

Factoring Software Comparisons

Features	BluBeagle	WinFactor	Factor/SQL	FactorSoft
Web-based	Yes	No	No	No
Compatible Systems	PC, Mac, Unix, Linux	PC	PC	PC
Modular (Use only what you need)	Yes	No	No	No
Consultant Module available	Yes	No	No	No
Factoring Module available	Yes*	Yes	Yes	Yes
Integrated Accounting Module available	Yes	No	No	No
Web Site Creation &/or Hosting available	Yes	No	No	No
Online Client Invoice Creation	Yes	No	Extra	Extra
Online Client Invoice Submission	Yes	No	Extra	Extra
Online Reports Accessible by Clients	Yes	Extra	Extra	Extra
Online Reports Accessible by Consultants	Yes	No	Extra	Extra
Export to QuickBooks/other	No**	Yes	Yes	Yes
# of users per initial purchase	1	1	1	5

* Includes Consultant Module
** Not needed because of AccountBlu availability, but can be custom built if desired.

Costs	BluBeagle	WinFactor	Factor/SQL	FactorSoft
Purchase Price	--	--	$9,500 +	$12,575 +
Annual Lease / Subscription	$120 - $1320	$525	(see Annl. Tech Support)	(see Annl. Tech Support)
Additional Cost Per Extra User	Varies w/ module	$105 ea.	+ $2,400 for network version	$2,575 (5 user pack)
Financing Available for System?	No	No	$1,000 dn + $500 / ea. new client	No
Online Reports Extra Cost	$0	20%	Extra	$9,575 +
Training & Support	**BluBeagle**	**WinFactor**	**Factor/SQL**	**FactorSoft**
Training	Included	No	Included	$1200 + / day, Optional
Training Location	Optional	--	California (travel, food, lodging extra)	On Site (trainer expenses extra)
Software Upgrade Releases	Included in subscr.	Included in lease	In Tech Supp. charge	In Tech Supp. charge
Tech Support Availability	Optional	Included	Highly Recommended	Required
Annual Cost of Tech Support	$350 for 5 hrs/yr; or $600 for 10 hrs; or $1000 unlimited	Included	$1,900+	$4,575 +
Type of support provided	Email, Phone, online	Email, Phone	Email, Phone	Email, Phone

Analysis

The data tracked with any software is absolutely essential to the functioning of your business and whatever software you use must work well for you. If it doesn't your business will suffer and your headaches will be huge.

If everything else suggests "all systems go" don't let software costs be the only reason to keep you from entering the factoring arena. Very small factors who decide not to purchase one of the above programs when they start often begin with spreadsheets. Spreadsheets were used by factoring companies for quite some time before dedicated database programs became sophisticated enough to replace them. Now the databases are many, many times more powerful than spreadsheets.

Spreadsheets used in documents in the chapters "Record Keeping" and "A Sample Factoring Transaction" are available as Microsoft Excel templates from Dash Point Publishing. These spreadsheets are very basic (some might say "primitive"), don't include instructions nor is support offered, and you must know how to create and modify formulas. Formulas are included where necessary to get you started. If you can create and modify macros that will further enable their use.

These spreadsheets are not intended to, nor will they ever, compete with any of the databases described above which are in a far, far different league. Heck, they're in a different universe. But the spreadsheets do provide a starting point for just about anyone.

However, the entry level cost of the factoring module of BluBeagle^{TM} ($30 a month) is for people with only a few clients. The price, features and sophistication of this software make the many limitations and inconveniences of spreadsheets unnecessary.

If you start with dedicated database software, your record keeping will be far easier and new software will be one less thing to learn later. If you feel you must start with spreadsheets, making the move to higher end software can be a logical growth step and an indication that you are running your business successfully.

I have often been asked which software I recommend. Until the release of BluBeagle^{TM}, I would hesitate to make a recommendation because there were drawbacks to the others, and I had not extensively used the other software packages discussed in this chapter. However, a good deal of time was spent creating BluBeagle^{TM}'s design so it incorporates the factoring procedures in this book. If you closely follow the procedures and practices described in these pages, that software will look familiar and be suitable for a great many factoring operations.

Given the price and features of each product, the following suggestions make sense. If you intend to have only one or two clients at a time, none of whom will be quite active, simple spreadsheets will probably suffice. If your client load grows beyond that you'll definitely want to move up to something with more muscle.

For Mac and Linux users, the only game in town is the web-based BluBeagle^{TM} Suite. Likewise, if you are beginning as a broker consultant, the only software available for you is ConsultBlu within the BluBeagle^{TM} Suite.

If you decide to begin factoring a few small clients, the upgrade for consultants to FactorBlu is seamless and affordable. BluBeagle^{TM} was created for small factors who start as consultants, for those who begin as factors, and for factors who have been in operation for some time. And if you need a web site (no matter what size of operation you have) SiteBlu provides this option at very reasonable rates.

If you intend to get beyond a half dozen clients, you can comfortably continue with BluBeagle^{TM} and grow to nearly any size you desire. Its flexible pricing makes it affordable for any size operation, and even its upper end costs are considerably less than its two competitors at the high end – especially considering their extra cost of add-ons (which are included with BluBeagle^{TM}).

BluBeagle^{TM} and Factor/SQL offer the most features for growing small to mid-range factors, while prices of Factor/SQL and FactorSoft suggest their users will be large operations. With Factor/SQL's pricing of $1,000 down plus $500 per client, plus the highly recommended annual maintenance fee, Distinctive Solutions offers one way to start with a sophisticated software package. However, BluBeagle™ offers a far lower total cost, and its internet-based system provides forward-looking online capability for a price that anyone can afford. Further, BluBeagle™'s online invoicing system will save a lot of time for both you and your clients, and doesn't cost a penny more above its already very reasonable price. BluBeagle™ is the only package that gives multiple powerful features (many of which aren't even available in the other systems) without causing sticker shock for small factors.

Remember that you'll need a bookkeeping system to track your general income, expenses, and profitability. On this point BluBeagle™ has the others beat without a contest, since it is the only software that offers an optional integrated accounting module built in. Those who choose this module can say good-bye to exporting data to QuickBooks, and save a great deal of time with this feature alone.

All the other packages will export data to bookkeeping programs, but are not designed to replace them. Therefore you'll need either AccountBlu or some other bookkeeping software such as QuickBooks®. Bear in mind that AccountBlu is built specifically for the factoring industry, unlike QuickBooks® that is general for all industries. If you decide to use QuickBooks® in your factoring operation, the chapter "Bookkeeping with QuickBooks®" will show you how to set this up and make regular entries.

So what software is best for you? Readers of this book range from broker consultants to one-client part-time factors to million-dollar operations, and while one size of software may not fit all, it comes very close with the BluBeagle™ suite. BluBeagle™'s choices of optional modules for prices that any size operation can afford make it an easy decision for practically all consultants and new factors, especially those that are not large.

The next chart provides a definition of factoring operations, which is then used in the subsequent chart to indicate which software packages fit best with the types of factoring operations. While the Operation Type/Size may not precisely match in some cases, these distinctions give a general idea of which software is most appropriate.

Definitions of Factoring Operations

Operation Type/Size	Monthly Vol.	# Clients	# Staff
Consultant	Varies	Varies	Varies
Part-time Factor	Varies	1 - 10	1 - 2
Very Small Factor	< $50k	< 5	1
Small Factor	$50k - $2m	5 - 30	1 - 3
Medium Factor	$500k - $10m	15 - 100	4 - 30
Large Factor	> $10m	> 100	> 30

Software for Factoring Operations

Operation Type/Size	Spread-sheets	BluBeagle	WinFactor	Factor/SQL	FactorSoft
Consultant		X			
Part-time Factor	X	X	X	X	
Very Small Factor	X	X	X		
Small Factor		X	X	X	
Medium Factor		X		X	X
Large Factor				X	X

Now let's turn to Record Keeping and the forms you'll use prior to, and in conjunction with, the software you decide is best for you.

18
Record Keeping

As you can tell from the many forms in this manual, factoring involves a lot of record keeping. You have to enjoy this end of it (or work with someone who does), because it will consume much of your office time and energy.

What is offered here is what works for me. Decide what you will use based on your own judgment, and consult your attorney as to what might be best for you, especially in regards to any laws in your area which might affect your factoring practices. Ask your attorney about usury laws and licensing requirements in your state and be sure your practices are in compliance. If your attorney doesn't know the answers to these important matters, get a referral to one who does.

Preliminary Steps to Set Up a Client

Put together an information packet of documents and/or a web site, and include with it some articles on factoring or a copy of *Unlocking the Cash in Your Company*,[1] a brochure or summary of your company and what you do, your business card, an application form, and eventually a page with testimonials from satisfied clients.

To begin, have the prospect complete the application (preferably online). Then call the client to get acquainted, learn about his business experience, and get a feel for his need and suitability for factoring and whether you want to work with this person. If you do, run a BusinessCreditUSA report on a few customers as needed and an Accurint report on the client. If all

---

[1] This book is available with private labeling for your company. One of the book's chapters, "How to Find a Factor," can be omitted from private label editions.

looks positive, provide your setup documents and arrange a time to review them together. Then meet again by phone, or if he is local, meet for coffee or lunch and "help" fill out the documents then. The latter is much better, as you can review each document, explain its purpose, and answer questions. This also assures the prospect will get the paper work in...which most people find to be one of the biggest hurdles to closing a deal.

Once the prospective client has turned in your documents, do whatever due diligence you haven't yet done, and let him know you'll call very soon when your due diligence is complete. With the internet that won't take long and you may have already decided if you want this person as a client. If you do, approve him on the spot or at least get back to him quickly. Under promise and over perform every chance you get.

Documents You Need

The following documents are those I utilize to sign up a client. Samples are shown in the same order as described on the next several pages, followed by a more detailed description in some cases. The "Comments to the client" section includes the words I use when reviewing the documents with the client prior to funding.

- **Application Form** – with a signed approval for credit checks.

- **Factoring Checklist** – a step-by-step list of what needs to be turned in when they 1) apply, 2) turn in their first set of invoices, and 3) turn in each set of invoices thereafter.

- **Term Sheet** – a one-page summary of your factoring arrangements including discount fees, other charges, advances, recourse period, and anything else important to the factoring relationship.

- **Accounts Receivable Purchase Agreement** – this is the core of your business agreement, often referred to as the "contract."

- **Discount Schedule** – specifies the discount agreed and how it is calculated.

UCC-1 Form – must be filed in the state as described in the chapter "UCCs."

- **Certificate of Corporate Resolution** – if the company is incorporated, or Partnership Agreement if a partnership. This document can be skipped for Sole Proprietors.

- **Request** for Business & Personal Financials; an Aging Report is most helpful.

- **Personal Guaranty** – Occasionally a potential client will balk at this; it's your call as to whether you'll require it.

- **Notice of Assignment** – A letter to customers indicating assignment of Accounts Receivable and that payments are to be sent to your address.

- **Schedule of Accounts** – Clients must sign and turn in one of these with each set of invoices factored. Provide a sample as well as some blank ones to get them started.

- **IRS Form 8821** – Available from IRS's web site, have the client sign this form, then be sure you send it in. It instructs IRS to notify you of any notification from IRS to your client regarding a delinquency in their taxes and if IRS is planning to lien their assets. If they do, your UCC will fall into second position behind IRS. But you'll have 45 days to work out a program out to keep IRS happy and you in first position.

- **Delivery of Funds** – This gives you instructions as to how to transfer funds to the client, and who the client authorizes to sign the Schedule of Account form.

- **ACH Direct Deposit Request** – This provides needed bank account information if you offer ACH direct deposits, and the client desires this service.

- **Agreement for Factored Payments Received by Client** – This gives specific instructions to the client regarding what he is required do if he receives payment for a factored invoice.

- **Customer Contact Sheet** – Lists their customers, contact person, address, phone, fax, and notes. You may not need this if they've provided the information on their own customers list. It is very handy for verification and check-up calls.

Some will say this documentation isn't enough, while others will say only some of the above are needed. The forms you use are up to you: I've seen an Application that had nothing more than the owner's name, company name, address, phone number, and Social Security number on it, period. You're the boss and need to balance the security you gain from thorough due diligence, with the client's needs and inclination to not factor small receivables because of a mountain of paper work. But remember: the more a client needs cash, the more willing he will be to sign the documents you put in front of him.

Taking 30 to 60 minutes to verbally review these documents before signing is a well-spent investment of time. Doing so shows you care enough to take the time, and also will likely deflect potential problems later. By taking the time to explain each document, the client later can't say he "didn't understand" your terms. If the client decides not to factor after this review, you've only lost a few minutes – but not thousands of dollars.

The first two documents which follow are self-explanatory. Following the others are the explanations I give new clients of each document during this 30 to 60 minute review.

ABC Financial Services

(253) 555-5555	P.O. Box 9999
(253) 555-5554 Fax	ABC Town, WA 99999

Application Form

Date: _____

Name: _____ Title: _____

Company Name: _____ Phone: _____

Address: _____ Fax: _____

City, State, Zip: _____ Cell: _____

Referred by: _____ Email: _____

Describe your company _____
& the business you do: _____

☐ Sole Proprietor   ☐ Partnership   ☐ LLC   ☐ Corporation   FEIN # _____

How long in business/industry _____ Factored before? ☐ Yes ☐ No

Gross Revenue last 12 months _____ Other Factor Name: _____

Avg. volume to factor - Monthly: _____ Approx. # of customers: _____

Annually: _____ Approx. # to factor: _____

% Yearly Growth: _____ Range of Invoice Sizes: _____

Avg. Invoice Size: _____

Please explain need _____
in detail _____

Taxes due or past due: ☐ None ☐ Local $_____ ☐ State $_____ ☐ Federal $_____

Litigation/Judgments: ☐ Yes ☐ No   (If Yes, please describe on separate sheet)

UCC Filings: _____ Bank Loans: _____

_____ Collateral: _____

Principals of Company:

Officer Name	Title	Home Addr.	City, ST, Zip	SS. #	% Owned

(continues on back)

282 – Factoring Small Receivables

Customers you wish to factor:

Company Name Company Address City, State, Zip	Approx. Size of Co. ($ Sales/Yr)	Type of Business	Avg. Invoice Amt.	Avg. Mo. Amt. to Factor	Credit Terms You Give	Avg. Pmt. Time
1)						
2)						
3)						
4)						

3 Business References:

Name	Phone	Business/Company	Association with You
1)			
2)			
3)			

Other Information: _____

Banking Information

Name of Bank _____   Branch _____

Checking Acct # _____   Contact Person _____

Bank Routing # _____   Phone # _____

Professional References

Name of Attorney _____   Phone _____

Name of Accountant _____   Phone _____

The foregoing information is true and correct to the best of my knowledge and is given to induce ABC Financial Services to consider entering into a factoring agreement with this company. I hereby authorize ABC Financial Services or its agents to verify and investigate any or all of the foregoing statements, including but not limited to my/our credit worthiness and financial responsibility, in any way they may choose. I/We grant ABC Financial Services the right to procure any and all credit reports pertaining to any party listed in this application, including, but not limited to, all principals of the applicant company.

Agreed and consented to:

Signature _____   Print Name _____

Title _____   Date _____

The **Application** is used to obtain preliminary information about your prospective client, her customers, and her experience in the business, and potential deal killers. If you have a web site, this form should be made available to complete and submit online, saving both the prospect and you a good deal of time.

If after doing your due diligence you approve this client, the information on the Application is used to fill in needed information on the remaining setup documents, and also in your software used to track a client's transactions. While the information on this application may have some data you may not use, be sure to get at least the following:

- Demographic information (name, phones, address, etc.)
- Business type (Sole Proprietor, Corporation, etc.)
- Federal ID number
- Owner's business experience
- Existence of liens from loans, tax delinquencies, judgments, etc.
- Owner/officer information
- Customers to factor with at least their city & state (so you can find credit information)

Unless you have an SSL-secured web site, do not request a person's social security information, nor have them email it to you. The number can be "hacked" with these insecure transmissions and subject the person to identity theft.

Filling out an application is a very standard procedure an you should never have anyone question this document's purpose.

Comments to the client: "The application form tells me about your business and customers and helps me determine if we'll be able to work together. If we can, the information is used to prepare the documents that follow so that your company's name, address, and so on are written on them accurately."

Factoring Checklist

Step 1 - Preliminary Documents

	Need	Done	
a.	___	___	Completed and signed Client Application
b.	___	___	Due Diligence Fee
c.	___	___	Sample invoices and Aging Report if available

Step 2 - Due Diligence

Need   Done

Factor searches:

	Need	Done	
a.	___	___	Client Credit Report
b.	___	___	Customer Credit Standing
c.	___	___	UCC Liens, Tax Liens, Judgments, Litigation, Criminal Searches

Client-provided documents when requested:

	Need	Done	
d.	___	___	Business financial statements (P/L, Balance Sheet)
e.	___	___	Personal net worth statement
f.	___	___	Driver's License

Step 3 - Contract Documents

Need   Done

a.	___	___	Term Sheet
b.	___	___	Signed Accounts Receivable Purchase Agreement (keep 1 for your records)
c.	___	___	Signed "Exhibit A" Discount Schedule (keep 1 for your records)
d.	___	___	UCC-1 document (Factor will supply your copy)
e.	___	___	Signed Personal Guarantee (keep 1 for your records)
f.	___	___	Signed IRS Form 8821. (This is not an authorization to obtain confidential information; it requests IRS notify us about any correspondence to you that may impact our collateral).

Sole Proprietorships only:

g.	___	___	Copy of Business License, DBA Registration, Fictitious Name Filing, or other proof of business entity

Corporations only:

h.	___	___	Signed Certificate of Corporate Resolution
i.	___	___	Copy of first page of Articles of Incorporation

Partnerships only:

j.	___	___	Partnership Agreement

Step 4 - Include with first invoice/s

Need   Done

a.	___	___	Completed Schedule of Accts for first batch, numbered "xxx-1" (keep a copy of each Schedule for your records)
b.	___	___	Original invoice/s listed on Schedule of Accounts if to be mailed by Factor, or documents from which Factor will generate invoices
c.	___	___	Notice of Assignment letter with your signature (Your customers will sign and fax back prior to payment of first advance.)
d.	___	___	Customer Contact List for any customers whose address/phone number Factor does not have.
e.	___	___	If utilized, the Receiving Slip, bill of lading, signed work order, or other proof of customer acceptance of product/service (keep 1 copy for your records)

Step 5 - Include with subsequent invoice/s

Need   Done

a.	___	___	Completed Schedule of Accounts, numbered "xxx-2" etc.)
b.-e.	___	___	Same as Step 4 above, as needed

The **Factoring Checklist** is a summary of all the documents and steps involved in setting up a new account. As you review your documents with a prospect, use this as a point of reference which helps introduce and then cover the documents that follow.

This document will also help the client sign and return all the needed documents, making the setup process smoother for both of you. Be sure each needed document on the Checklist is signed and in your hands before proceeding to the client's first funding.

Comments to the client: "The Factoring Checklist will help us make sure all the documents are completed and turned in. Keep this handy as we go over the documents listed so we don't miss any. And when you sign and return the documents, double check that you're completing everything listed as needed on this checklist."

Term Sheet

from

ABC Financial Services

to

Client

ABC Financial Services proposes the following preliminary terms for factoring receivables:

- Initial credit line of $_____.

- No charge for electronic direct deposits, deposits to _____ Bank, or for checks sent by regular U.S. mail. Bank wires or next day Airborne Express $20 client cost (additional charges from your bank will be incurred to receive bank wires).

- Recourse period of _____ days.

- _____% Advance on all approved invoices to begin. Advance percentages may vary according to customer credit rating or other circumstances.

- Factoring Fee Rates:

Days out	Percent of gross invoice amount
0 - _____ days	_____%
Each _____ days thereafter	_____% additional
All invoices over _____ days add	_____% every _____ days

- Minimum fee of $_____ per invoice

- Reserve balance of _____% of credit limit.

These terms are offered provided account is established by ____/____/____.

Agreed and accepted:

_____   ABC Financial Services
Company Name

_____   John Q. Factor, President
by (print name)   by

_____   _____
Signature   Signature

The **Term Sheet** is a summary of all the important aspects of the factoring relationship you are establishing: the initial credit line, cost of funds transfers, factoring advances and fee rates, any charges you will have, recourse period if you have one, reserves information, and so on. Though they aren't stated on the sample Term Sheet, if you have due diligence fees, credit check charges, and/or term contracts, this information should be included as well. Reviewing this document after the Factoring Checklist makes the rest of the setup document review go more easily because you're covering the core of everything that follows right here.

Comments to the client: "This is a summary of the important elements of our relationship: the initial credit line is $_____, the charges (if there are any) for deposits, the recourse period of _____ days," etc.

Accounts Receivable Purchase Agreement

THIS AGREEMENT is made and entered into between the following parties:

ABC Financial Services
(**Factor**)
P.O. Box 99999
Anytown, WA 99999-9999
253 555-5555

(Client Company Name)
(**Company**)
__(Client Address)__

__(Client Phone)__

RECITALS

ABC Financial Services is in the business of providing short-term financing for business and professional enterprises by purchasing accounts receivable. Company is in the business of _____, and desires to obtain short-term financing from ABC Financial.

AGREEMENT

IN CONSIDERATION OF the representations, promises, conditions, and covenants contained herein, THE PARTIES HEREBY AGREE:

1. Assignment. Company, _____

(hereafter "Company") hereby agrees to sell, assign, transfer, convey and deliver Accounts Receivable exclusively to ABC Financial Services, (hereafter "Factor"). Factor hereby agrees to purchase and receive from Company all right, title, and interest in selected accounts receivable due to Company by its customers. Company acknowledges and agrees that the accounts receivable involved are commercial in nature, and not for Company's (or any employee's or owner's) personal or family purposes.

2. Account Submission. The right to select which accounts shall be purchased by Factor rests in the sole discretion of Factor. Company shall submit each Account to Factor for approval. When submitting Invoices on Acceptable Accounts for possible purchase by Factor, Company shall forward to Factor the original and/or

one copy of each such Invoice as mutually agreed, together with a copy of the bill of lading, proof of delivery, contract or purchase order, and other documents satisfactory to Factor and a properly executed Schedule of Accounts prepared on a form provided by Factor. The first such Schedule of Accounts form is attached as Exhibit B, incorporated by this reference.

3. Cancellation. Either party can cancel the application of this Agreement as to future accounts receivable, upon seven days written notice to the other party; however, all accounts receivable which have been sold or assigned will remain in the hands of Factor until collected or repurchased by Company.

4. Power of Attorney. Company irrevocably appoints Factor as its attorney in fact, which said appointment shall remain in full force and effect until all Accounts sold to Factor have been paid in full and all obligations of Company to Factor have been fully discharged, with full power to:

Factor Initials_____

Company Initials_____

A. Company Address. Strike or cover Company's address on all Invoices and statements of account mailed or to be mailed to customers and to substitute thereon Factor's name and address.

B. Mail. Receive and open all mail addressed to Company, or to Company's business or trade name at Factor's address.

C. Endorsements. Endorse the name of Company or Company's trade name on any checks or other evidences of payment that come into Factor's possession on Accounts sold to Factor by Company or on which Factor holds a security interest and on any Invoices or other documents relating to any of such accounts, and deposit same into any account of Factor.

5. Schedule of Accounts. The parties will continue to use Schedule of Accounts forms to list and identify all accounts receivable assigned and sold to Factor. The listing and use of this form shall constitute conclusive evidence of the sale, assignment, and receipt to Factor of such accounts receivable. If an invoice on a given Schedule of Accounts has been collected in full, Factor will refund to Company the difference between the amount collected, on one hand, and the initial payment and fee earned by Factor, on the other hand, as set forth in the Discount Schedule attached as Exhibit A and incorporated by this reference. This Discount Schedule shall be used in factoring all transactions with Company, unless Company's creditworthiness, or the creditworthyness of Customers of Company, substantially changes, as determined in Factor's sole discretion.

6. Fee and Reserve. The parties agree that for each purchase of accounts using the Schedule of Accounts form,

there shall be a fee paid to Factor equal to the sum of all the discounts for receivables based on their age, in accordance with Exhibit A. This fee is earned immediately upon receipt of the Schedule of Accounts form, in an amount calculated upon date of payment, which shall be at least $_____ per Invoice. There shall be a reserve account established of not less than the unpaid accounts receivable minus the fee due to Factor, plus _____% of the credit limit established. Factor shall have on hand, at all times, that reserve amount in collected funds, in addition to any initial payments, fees, interest or other charges due under this Agreement. No interest shall be due Company on the reserve account. If accounts receivable are uncollected for _____ days after the date purchased by Factor, Factor may in his sole discretion charge the reserve account, or in the alternative, require Company to repurchase accounts selected by Factor or to provide new invoices to Factor which compensate for such uncollected accounts. Such replenishment or repurchase or providing of new invoices shall occur within five (5) days of request by Factor.

7. Warrants. Company represents, warrants, and covenants to Factor that Company is the sole owner of the Accounts Receivable and they have not been previously assigned or encumbered in any way, and further represents, warrants and covenants that no customer or debtor listed on an accounts receivable has, or will have, any offsets, defenses, quality claims, or other matters which give rise to any dispute, except as are disclosed in writing in documents attached to the Schedule of Accounts. Company represents and warrants that all of the work, goods, services or other items required to make the accounts receivable presently due and owing

Factor Initials_____

Company Initials_____

have been provided, and there are no conditions or events required prior to the maturity of the full amount shown for each account on the Schedule of Accounts.

8. Factor Sole Owner. Upon delivery of a Schedule of Accounts or any account receivable by Company, Factor shall become the sole owner and holder of such accounts receivable, and all proceeds. Should Company receive payment for all or part of the assigned Accounts Receivable, Company shall so notify Factor immediately and deliver all checks and other instruments within two (2) business days. Company shall pay (or reimburse) any actual charges by a bank (or other party) to Factor, which arise because of bank account closure, NSF checks, the wiring of funds, and the like, together with a $25 fee per occasion to cover Factor's special handling costs.

9. Security Interest. Company hereby grants, as security for the timely performance of all of Company's obligations under this Agreement and the payments due Factor under this Agreement, a security interest in the following property of Company ("Collateral"):

"All accounts, accounts receivable, notes receivable, contract rights, claims, instruments, documents, chattel paper, inventory, equipment, money deposit accounts, insurance policies, reserves, reserve accounts, general intangibles, and the proceeds and products thereof; presently existing or hereafter acquired by debtor. All goods and inventory relating hereto in all stages of manufacture, process, and production. All books and records pertaining to accounts and proceeds of the foregoing property."

To perfect a lien in favor of Factor, Company authorizes Factor to file a UCC-1 Financing Statement and any other documents which Factor may deem necessary.

10. Taxes, Liens, Inspection. Except for amounts being contested in good faith, Company will pay, before delinquency, all taxes, license fees, and assessments relative to the Collateral or its use and shall pay any and all other taxes, liens, assessments, and charges relative to Company's business. Company will keep the Collateral free of all liens and encumbrances except the lien of Factor's security interest and except for those being contested in good faith. Factor or its agents shall have the right at all reasonable times during Company's business hours to inspect the Collateral and inspect, audit, and copy any books and records of Company relating to the Collateral.

11. General Provisions. The following general provisions apply:

A. Arbitration. The parties agree that any dispute between the parties concerning the execution, interpretation, performance or enforcement of this Agreement shall be determined by binding arbitration. The arbitration shall be held in accord with the rules of the American Arbitration Association, but not necessarily with their involvement. Judgment may be entered directly upon any award, in accordance with (Factor's) state law.

B. Costs, attorney fees. In the event of legal action or arbitration concerning the collection of fees or costs or interest owing to factor, the prevailing party shall be entitled to reimbursement by the other parties of all costs, including reasonable attorney fees and expert fees, incurred in enforcing this contract.

Factor Initials_____

Company Initials_____

The amount of attorney and expert fees awarded to the prevailing party shall be determined by the presiding officer of the forum finally deciding the controversy, and shall include fees for preparation, negotiation, trial, and any appeal from a trial, whether for collection of amounts due, enforcement of the contract, or enforcement of any rights or remedies created hereby.

C. Enforceability. If any provision(s) of this agreement is held to be invalid, illegal or unenforceable in any way, the remaining provisions shall nevertheless continue in full force and effect without any impairment or invalidation.

D. Final and complete agreement. This document is the entire, final and complete agreement of the parties, superseding or replacing all prior agreements, discussions and representations, written or oral, made or existing between the parties or their representatives concerning this transaction. There are not representations or agreements upon which either party has relied except those contained in this written document. No prior or subsequent correspondence, memoranda or the like shall modify the terms of this agreement.

E. Forum, Venue. (Factor's state) state law shall control this agreement, including but not limited to interpretation, amendment, all rights created hereunder, all remedies available to the parties, conflicts of laws, procedural questions, and the like. Venue for any proceedings shall be lodged in (Factor's county) County, state of (Factor's state).

F. Successor interests. This contract shall be binding upon the assigns, heirs, devisees and all other successors in interest to the parties thereto; however, Company shall not sell, subcontract, assign or in any manner transfer, voluntarily or involuntarily, any interest in this contract or any account assigned or sold to Factor, without first obtaining Factor's written consent

12 Authority. The signers represent and warrant their capacity and authority to act in executing this agreement in the capacity shown below, thereby binding themselves and their principals, if any are indicated.

13. Copies. A legible and complete copy of this document (including its signatures) shall for all purposes be equivalent to the executed original, whether reproduced by means of photocopy, carbon copy, fax transmission or by other means.

HAVING READ, UNDERSTOOD AND AGREED TO THIS DOCUMENT, AND IN WITNESS WHEREOF, the parties hereto have executed this Agreement.

Signed & Effective on _____, 200 _____

ABC Financial Services

(Factor)

By _____

Print Name: John Q. Factor

Title: President

_____

(Company)

By: _____

Print Name: _____

Title: _____

The **Accounts Receivable Purchase Agreement** is the heart of your factoring relationship, and also the longest of your documents. Don't gloss over or rush through the information here, but don't belabor it either. You must clearly understand everything in this contract before reviewing this document with your client; if you're not sure what a sentence or section means, clarify it with your attorney beforehand. If you have a client who desires to make significant changes, you may want to consult your attorney before doing so.

Take each section and summarize its key points in your own words, allowing your client the time and opportunity to ask any questions he may have. You will probably spend the most time on this document in your review with the client, so once you finish this the rest goes fairly quickly. If your client clearly understands what's here, the trust level from the client to you should increase, as the important aspects of the factoring relationship are laid bare here.

Comments to the client: "This is the contract between our companies so we'll spend most of our conversation on this document. Rather than going line by line as that will take too much time, I'm going to summarize each section in my own words. If you have any questions, please ask them as we go along. Now Section 1, Assignment, says...."

ABC Financial Services
Exhibit "A"
Discount Schedule

The discount earned by Factor for purchasing the Accounts Receivable shall be the following percentages of the face amount of the Account Receivable purchased.

1 ____ % if payment of an Account Receivable is collected up to ____ days;

2 ____ % if payment of an Account Receivable is collected between ____ and ____ days;

3 ____ % if payment of an Account Receivable is collected between ____ and ____ days;

4 ____ % if payment of an Account Receivable is collected between ____ and ____ days;

5 ____ % if payment of an Account Receivable is collected between ____ and ____ days;

6 ____ % if payment of an Account Receivable is collected between ____ and ____ days;

7 ____ % if payment of an Account Receivable is collected between ____ and ____ days;

8 ____ % if payment of an Account Receivable is collected between ____ and ____ days;

9 ____ % if payment of an Account Receivable is collected between ____ and ____ days;

10 ____ % if payment of an Account Receivable is collected between ____ and ____ days;

11 An additional ____% for every ____ days thereafter if payment of an Account Receivable is collected after ____ days.

Number of days out calculation is made from the date the advance is paid by factor to the date factor receives payment.

Seller (Company): _____

Signed by: _____

(Please Print Your Name): _____

Title: _____

Date: _____

Exhibit A, the **Discount Schedule,** is a simple yet detailed explanation of how your factoring fees are calculated on a day-by-day basis. This is quite self-explanatory and shouldn't take much time to review. If the client had any questions about how your fee is calculated, this should answer them.

Be sure to point out the sentence, "Number of days out calculation is made from the date the advance is paid by factor to the date factor receives payment." This clearly states that the clock fee does not start on the invoice date, but the date you gave the advance – and that it stops when *you* receive payment, not when the *client* receives payment, if that happens.

Comments to the client: "The Discount Schedule simply spells out how much the fees are for any given time until payment is received. If you want to know what the fee is, for example 15 days or 35 days after the advance, you can see the amount right here. Notice the fee clock starts on the date of advance and continues until I receive payment. So if you receive a check, the clock will continue to tick until you get it into my hands."

UCC-1 Form

UCC FINANCING STATEMENT
FOLLOW INSTRUCTIONS (front and back) CAREFULLY
A. NAME & PHONE OF CONTACT AT FILER [optional]   Phone

B. SEND ACKNOWLEDGMENT TO: (Name and Address)

Phone

Address   (Factor's Company Name and Address)

Address 2

City   State   Postal Code

THE ABOVE SPACE IS FOR FILING OFFICE USE ONLY

1. DEBTOR'S EXACT FULL LEGAL NAME - insert only one debtor name (1a or 1b) - do not abbreviate or combine names
1a. ORGANIZATION'S NAME
(Client's Company Name)
OR
1b. INDIVIDUAL'S LAST NAME | FIRST NAME | MIDDLE NAME | SUFFIX

1c. MAILING ADDRESS
(Client's Address) | CITY (Client's City, etc.) | STATE WA | POSTAL CODE | COUNTRY USA

1d. TAX ID #: SSN OR EIN | ADD'L INFO RE | 1e. TYPE OF ORGANIZATION | 1f. JURISDICTION OF ORGANIZATION [ck w/ Secty of State] | 1g. ORGANIZATIONAL ID #, if any
| ORGANIZATION DEBTOR | | | ☒ NONE

2. ADDITIONAL DEBTOR'S EXACT FULL LEGAL NAME - insert only one debtor name (2a or 2b) - do not abbreviate or combine names
2a. ORGANIZATION'S NAME
OR
2b. INDIVIDUAL'S LAST NAME | FIRST NAME | MIDDLE NAME | SUFFIX

2c. MAILING ADDRESS | CITY | STATE | POSTAL CODE | COUNTRY

2d. TAX ID #: SSN OR EIN | ADD'L INFO RE | 2e. TYPE OF ORGANIZATION | 2f. JURISDICTION OF ORGANIZATION | 2g. ORGANIZATIONAL ID #, if any
| ORGANIZATION DEBTOR | | | ☐ NONE

3. SECURED PARTY'S NAME (or NAME of TOTAL ASSIGNEE of ASSIGNOR S/P) - insert only one secured party name (3a or 3b)
3a. ORGANIZATION'S NAME
(Factor's Company Name)
OR
3b. INDIVIDUAL'S LAST NAME | FIRST NAME | MIDDLE NAME | SUFFIX

3c. MAILING ADDRESS
(Factor's Address) | CITY (Factor's City, etc.) | STATE | POSTAL CODE | COUNTRY

4. This FINANCING STATEMENT covers the following collateral:

All of debtor's accounts, accounts receivable, notes receivable, contract rights, claims, instruments, documents, chattel paper, inventory, equipment, money deposit accounts, insurance policies, reserves, reserve accounts, general intangibles, and the proceeds and products thereof; presently existing or hereafter acquired by debtor. All goods and inventory relating hereto in all stages of manufacture, process, and production. All books and records pertaining to accounts and proceeds of the foregoing property.

5. ALTERNATIVE DESIGNATION [if applicable]: | LESSEE/LESSOR | CONSIGNEE/CONSIGNOR | BAILEE/BAILOR | SELLER/BUYER | AG. LIEN | NON-UCC FILING
6. ☐ This FINANCING STATEMENT is to be filed [for record] (or recorded) in the REAL ESTATE RECORDS. Attach Addendum [if applicable] | 7. Check to REQUEST SEARCH REPORT(S) on Debtor(s) [ADDITIONAL FEE] [optional] | All Debtors | Debtor 1 | Debtor 2
8. OPTIONAL FILER REFERENCE DATA

FILING OFFICE COPY — NATIONAL UCC FINANCING STATEMENT (FORM UCC1) (REV. 07/29/98)   WASHINGTON FILLABLE (REV. 09/13/2001)

Note: wording in #4 above should be identical to wording in the Accounts Receivable Purchase Agreement, Section 9: Security Interest. Also, some states require an entry in the box "Jurisdiction of Organization" in #1. Contact the Secretary of State's office to learn what this is for your client (usually a city). Many states also require you to either include the client's Organizational ID or check "None" in #1. Again, ask the Secretary of State what to enter here.

The **UCC-1** form is important for securing your investment and protecting you should your client go bankrupt or his debtors garnish his assets. Now that the national form is used nearly everywhere, completing this form has become more standardized and therefore easier. However, a few states will have unique requirements, so be sure you follow the instructions provided so you don't omit any required box's information. If you do omit something, your filing will likely be returned and you'll probably have to re-file, and perhaps be required to pay the filing fee again.

Notice that the client does not need to sign this document. As a courtesy you should provide her a copy of the filing once you receive it from the Secretary of State, but this is not required. Therefore when reviewing setup documents with a client, you need not show them the UCC-1 form. If you do – and it's not a bad idea to show them a sample – this is a good time to explain why you're filing the UCC-1 and why you want to be in first position.

Comments to the client: "Here's a sample of the UCC-1 filing I submit to the state for each client I have, just like banks and all factors routinely do. If the worst were to happen with your company and you declare bankruptcy, this filing will enable me to recover money I'm owed by putting me first in line to collect on the assets listed in #4. Also, we will both be protected if someone obtains a judgment against you and garnishes the assets listed here, if I've filed this before their action. However, tax garnishments and tax liens will supercede my UCC-1 after a 45-day notification from IRS, so I want to be informed if IRS is going to take action against you. That's what the 8821 form is for."

Form **8821**	**Tax Information Authorization**	OMB No. 1545-1165
(Rev. January 2000)		For IRS Use Only
Department of the Treasury Internal Revenue Service	► IF THIS AUTHORIZATION IS NOT SIGNED AND DATED, IT WILL BE RETURNED.	Received by / Name / Telephone / Function / Date

1 Taxpayer information.

Taxpayer name(s) and address (please type or print)	Social security number(s)	Employer identification number
Client Company Name	000:00-0000	00: 0000000
Client Address	Daytime telephone number	Plan number (if applicable)
Client City, State, Zip	(000) 000-0000	

2 Appointee.

Name and address (please type or print)	
ABC Finacial Services	CAF No. 00000000 (assigned by IRS to you)
PO Box 9999	Telephone No. (253) 555-5555
Any Town, USA 99999-9999	Fax No. (253) 555-5554
	Check if new: Address ☐ Telephone No. ☐

3 Tax matters. The appointee is authorized to inspect and/or receive confidential tax information in any office of the IRS for the tax matters listed on this line.

(a) Type of Tax (Income, Employment, Excise, etc.)	(b) Tax Form Number (1040, 941, 720, etc.)	(c) Year(s) or Period(s)	(d) Specific Tax Matters (see instr.)
Income	1040	1996-2006	Collections
Employment	940	1996-2006	Collections
Employment	941	1996-2006	Collections

4 Specific use not recorded on Centralized Authorization File (CAF). If the tax information authorization is for a specific use not recorded on CAF, check this box. (See the instructions on page 2.) . . . . ► ☐
If you checked this box, skip lines 5 and 6.

5 Disclosure of tax information (you **must** check the box on line 5a or b unless the box on line 4 is checked):
  a If you want copies of tax information, notices, and other written communications sent to the appointee on an ongoing basis, check this box . . . . ► ☑
  b If you do not want any copies of notices or communications sent to your appointee, check this box . . . . . . ► ☐

6 Retention/revocation of tax information authorizations. This tax information authorization automatically revokes all prior authorizations for the same tax matters you listed above on line 3 unless you checked the box on line 4. If you do not want to revoke a prior tax information authorization, you MUST attach a copy of any authorizations you want to remain in effect AND check this box . . . . ► ☐
To revoke this tax information authorization, see the instructions on page 2.

7 Signature of taxpayer(s). If a tax matter applies to a joint return, **either** husband or wife must sign. If signed by a corporate officer, partner, guardian, executor, receiver, administrator, trustee, or party other than the taxpayer, I certify that I have the authority to execute this form with respect to the tax matters/periods covered.

Signature	Date	Signature	Date
Print Name	Title (if applicable)	Print Name	Title (if applicable)

General Instructions

Section references are to the Internal Revenue Code unless otherwise noted.

Purpose of form. Form 8821 authorizes any individual, corporation, firm, organization, or partnership you designate to inspect and/or receive your confidential information in any office of the IRS for the type of tax and the years or periods you list on this form. You may file your own tax information authorization without using Form 8821, but it must include all the information that is requested on the form.

Form 8821 does not authorize your appointee to advocate your position with respect to the Federal tax laws; to execute waivers, consents, or closing agreements; or to otherwise represent you before the IRS. If you want to authorize an individual to represent you, use **Form 2848**, Power of Attorney and Declaration of Representative.

Use **Form 56**, Notice Concerning Fiduciary Relationship, to notify the IRS of the existence of a fiduciary relationship. A fiduciary (trustee, executor, administrator, receiver, or guardian) stands in the position of a taxpayer and acts as the taxpayer. Therefore, a fiduciary does not act as an appointee and should not file Form 8821. If a fiduciary wishes to authorize an appointee to inspect and/or receive confidential tax information on behalf of the fiduciary, Form 8821 must be filed and signed by the fiduciary acting in the position of the taxpayer.

Taxpayer identification numbers (TINs). TINs are used to identify taxpayer information with corresponding tax returns. It is important that you furnish correct names, social security numbers (SSNs), individual taxpayer identification numbers (ITINs), or employer identification numbers (EINs) so that the IRS can respond to your request.

For Privacy Act and Paperwork Reduction Act Notice, see page 2.   Cat. No. 11596P   Form **8821** (Rev. 1-2000)

The **IRS 8821 Form** gives instructions to the IRS to inform you of any activity or communication from the IRS to your client. To download it in PDF format go to the IRS web site at
http://www.irs.ustreas.gov/formspubs/index.html and type

"8821" in the "Search Forms and Publications for" field. If the client is behind in her taxes, this is an early warning system so the receivables you've purchased aren't garnished by the IRS.

A few notes about completing this form.

1. If your client **is a Sole Proprietor**:
    a. Section 1
        - Put their personal name in #1 followed by "DBA 'Business Name.'"
        - Include their Social Security Number
        - Include their FEIN number if different from their Social Security Number
    b. Section 3
        - Put 1040 as the type of tax in the first line, and make the "Year(s) or Period(s) box a 10-year spread.
2. If your client **is not a Sole Proprietor**:
    a. Section 1
        - Put their business name and address here. Be sure to include their FEIN number.
    b. Section 3
        - Put "1120 S" as the type of tax in the first if the business is an S-corporation.
        - Put "1120" as the type of tax in the first box if the business is not an S-corporation.
3. **Regardless** of your client's business type:
    a. Section 4
        - *Be sure* to check box 5a.
    b. Section 7
        - Be sure the client signs and dates the form. It is worthless without both the signature *and* date.

Comments to client: "Here's the form I just mentioned that instructs the IRS to notify me of any communication to you regarding taxes they say you owe. This information is strictly a notification to me – I do not notify them of the amount of business that you do or anything like that. This simply advises me of a potential problem so we can proactively take care of it early."

Certificate of Corporate Resolution

We, _____, President, and _____,
Secretary, a corporation, do hereby certify that said corporation is duly
organized and existing under the laws of the State of _____,
that all franchise and other taxes required to maintain its corporate existence
have been paid, and will be paid, when due and that no such taxes are
delinquent; that no proceedings are pending for the forfeiture of its Certificate
of Incorporation or for its dissolution, voluntarily or involuntarily; that it is
duly qualified to do business in the State of _____, and is in
good standing in such State; that there is no provision of the Articles of
Incorporation or by-laws of said corporation limiting the power of the Board of
Directors to pass the resolution set out below and that the same is in conformity
with the provisions of said Articles of Incorporation and by-laws; that the
Secretary is the keeper of the records and minutes of the proceedings of the
Board of Directors of said corporation and on the _____ day of
_____, 200___, there was held a meeting of the Board of Directors
of said corporation, which was duly called and held in accordance with the
applicable law and the by-laws of the corporation, at which meeting all the
Directors were present; and that at said meeting the following resolution was
duly and legally passed and adopted and that the same has not been altered
amended, rescinded or repealed and is now in full force and effect:

The President of this corporation has been and hereby is authorized and
directed to execute on behalf of this corporation on such terms as shall be
acceptable to the President and agreement for the sale of this corporation's
current and future accounts to ABC Financial Services, a (Factor's state)
(corporation/partnership/sole proprietorship/limited liability company),
together with such other documents and instruments as may be necessary to
accomplish such sale.

President	Director
Vice President	Director
Secretary	Director
Treasurer	Director

*IN WITNESS WHEREOF, we have hereunto set our hands as President and
Secretary, respectively, of said corporation, and have attached hereto the
official seal of said corporation, this _____ day of _____, 200___.*

President	Secretary
President (Please Print or Type Name)	Secretary (Please Print or Type Name)

The **Certificate of Corporate Resolution** is needed if the client's business is incorporated. Its purpose is to show that the corporation's board of directors has given the person signing your factoring documents the authority to do so.

For many small companies that are incorporated, the board often consists of the president and no one else, making this document a snap. If a business is a sole proprietor, this document is unnecessary. If the business is a partnership, the Certificate of Corporate Resolution is unnecessary but all partners need to sign all the other documents. If the business is an LLC, the members of the LLC should sign everything as well.

Comments to client: "This document needs to be signed by your Board of Directors; it simply says your corporation is in good standing and you have the Board's authorization to sign these documents. If you're the only person on the Board, you need to sign as the member for each Board position you hold."

Personal Guaranty

The undersigned Guarantor represents that he or she has read and understands the Accounts Receivable Purchase Agreement, with Exhibits A and B, between _____ (hereafter "Company") and _____ (hereafter "Factor"). In consideration of Factor's agreeing to factor accounts receivable for Company, the undersigned Guarantor(s) do hereby separately and jointly agree:

Guarantee. The undersigned hereby jointly and severally and unconditionally guaranty and promise to pay Factor, its successors or assigns, on demand, in lawful money of the United States of America, any and all indebtedness of Company to Factor in the matters set out in the agreement referred to above.

Extent of Liability. Guarantor agrees that Guarantor's liability under this agreement will be open and continuous for as long as this guaranty remains in force. Guarantor intends to guaranty at all times the performance of all obligations of Company to Factor. No payments upon Company's indebtedness to Factor shall be held to discharge or diminish the liability of Guarantor for any and all remaining and succeeding indebtedness of Company to Factor. The liability of Guarantor under this agreement shall be enforceable against both the separate and community property of Guarantor existing at the date of execution hereof or hereafter acquired.

Effective date, termination. This guaranty takes effect when received by Factor, without the necessity of any acceptance by Factor and shall continue in full force until such time as Guarantor shall notify Factor in writing of Guarantor's election to terminate this guaranty. Any such election to terminate the guaranty will be effective only as to fees earned after the date Factor receives Guarantor's notice.

Action upon default. Upon any default by Company in payment to Factor, Factor may, at its option, demand and be entitled to payment from Guarantor of the full amount of any of Company's indebtedness to Factor. If Guarantor does not pay the amounts demanded, Factor may proceed at once against Guarantor to collect such sum without first proceeding against Company's customer(s). The failure of Factor to demand payment at the time of any default by Company shall not constitute a waiver of Factor's right to proceed against Guarantor in the future, nor shall such failure to proceed against Guarantor relieve Guarantor of its obligations hereunder.

Attorney fees. In any action or suit against Guarantor to enforce this guaranty, Factor shall be entitled to recover, in addition to costs and disbursements allowed by law, a reasonable amount for Factor's attorney fees in such action or suit, or appeal therefrom.

Waiver. Guarantor hereby expressly waives presentment, protest, demand, or notice of any kind, including notice of nonpayment of any of Company's indebtedness and notice of any action or nonaction on the part of Company, Factor, or any surety, endorser, or other Guarantor. Guarantor further expressly consents to jurisdiction in the Superior Court of the State of _____ *[factor's state]* for the County of _____ *[factor's county]* for enforcement of any action relating to this guaranty.

IN WITNESS WHEREOF Guarantor has executed this agreement this _____ day of _____ , 200 ____ .

_____   _____
(Guarantor)   (Guarantor)

_____   _____
(Street Address)   (Street Address)

_____   _____
(City, State, Zip)   (City, State, Zip)

The **Personal Guaranty** is a document which commits the person signing to pay you back from his personal assets if the business is unable to do so. As such this document carries some punch in your favor in case an account goes sideways. If you must turn over an account to collections, this is often the first document the collections people will ask if you have.

Occasionally you'll find a client who is unwilling to sign a personal guaranty. You will need to decide if this will kill the deal or you can live without it. However, if the person signing the guarantee has little or no personal assets, this document won't be worth much. Be careful if a business owner will not sign this document but obtains the signature of another person for the personal guaranty; that individual may have no net worth. Doing this protects the business owner's personal assets at your, and perhaps this other person's, expense.

If the person signing has personal assets but does not want to take the personal risk of signing this document, you might want to satisfy yourself as to his perception of his risk. If he doesn't have enough confidence in his company to guarantee his personal assets, this might give you pause as to working with him in the first place. However, many attorneys discourage their clients from signing personal guarantees of any kind, and the person may be acting on his attorney's advice.

If your client is married and lives in a community property state, the client's spouse should sign this personal guaranty as well.

Be sure the client does *not* write his title at the company by the signature line, as doing so makes this a *corporate* guarantee and defeats the purpose of a *personal* guarantee.

Comments to client: "This is a personal guaranty which states if my company is owed money by your company which your company cannot pay back, you will make good on this debt from your own personal assets."

(Factor's letterhead here)

date

Customer
Address

Attention: Accounts Payable

Notice of Assignment and Change of Payee

We are pleased to inform you we have established a working relationship that provides *Client* with a working capital line of credit. These funds will enable further growth and expansion from which *Client* and their customers will benefit both now and in the future. Accordingly, *Client* has assigned all present and future Accounts Receivable with your company to *Factor.*

This letter hereby authorizes and instructs you to remit your payment of all invoices from *Client* directly to *Factor*, and to continue to do so until notified otherwise by *Factor.* Payments made to any party except *Factor* will not relieve your obligation for Accounts Payables due *Client*, and this notice may not be revoked except in writing by an officer of *Factor.*

Please make your checks payable to, and send them to:

> *Factor* FBO [For Benefit Of] *Client*
> *Factor Address*

Your cooperation is appreciated. While your signature is not required to validate this assignment, we ask that you sign and return this letter so we know you have made the needed changes in your Accounts Payable system. Therefore please sign below and return via fax to *Factor's fax* at your earliest convenience. Please keep a copy of this letter for your records.

Should you have any questions concerning this letter, please call *Factor* at *Factor's phone* or *Client* at *Client's phone.*

Sincerely,

Factor's Name   *Client's Name*
Title   *Title*

Received and Acknowledged:

Signature: _____

Print Name: _____

Title: _____

Date: _____

The **Notice of Assignment and Change of Payee** is the strongest notification to your client's customer of the factoring relationship and assignment of receivables. This letter also gives you the greatest protection from a client receiving payment for factored invoices.

Here the customer is given notice that the client's receivables have been assigned to you and the customer must now pay you in lieu of the client. Further, the client is not allowed to redirect funds or inform the customer of the termination of the assignment; only an officer from your company can rescind this letter, which must be done in writing. Requiring that rescision letter to be notarized protects you even further, making it quite difficult for a dishonest client to attempt such a redirection.

This letter makes clear that payments to the client do not relieve the customer of the obligation to you. That means a customer will have to pay you, even if he has already (yet erroneously) paid the client for a factored invoice.

Some factors omit the customer's signature lines from this document and simply send the letter to the customer. This is done so the customer doesn't think he can pay anyone he wants if he refuses to sign the letter. Other factors want this signature on file so they know the customer has received the letter, made the address change, and is aware of his responsibility to pay the factor directly.

Comments to client: "This letter notifies your customer of your stronger financial position as a result of factoring, and that you are assigning the payment rights of your factored invoices to my company. Your customer's obligation of payment is not met unless my company is paid for factored invoices, and the assignment continues until my company notifies them otherwise. It also informs them of the new remittance name and address.

"By having your name after FBO, your customer will clearly understand that they are still paying your invoices." *(If you require a signature:)* "We need to receive this letter signed by your customer before I can advance your first funds, so be sure they take care of this promptly. I'll fax the letter to them once I have your signature on a template of this letter."

Notification Letter to Customers (Weaker)

(Client's letterhead here)

date

Customer
Address

Attention: Accounts Payable

In order to accommodate the growth we are experiencing in our business, we have retained the firm of *Factor* to manage our receivables. The availability of this service will allow us to serve our customers in a more efficient and timely manner. Accordingly, *Factor* will be collecting your payment on all future invoices.

This letter hereby authorizes and instructs you to remit payment of all open and future invoices from *(customer company)* directly to *Factor*, and continue to do so until notified otherwise by *Factor*. Please make sure your checks for these invoices (indicating for which invoice payment is made) are made payable to:

> *CLIENT'S COMPANY NAME*
> c/o *Factor*

and mail them to:

> *Factor*
> *Factor Address*

Your cooperation is greatly appreciated. Please acknowledge receipt of this letter by signing below and returning to *Factor* via fax to *Factor's fax* at your earliest convenience.

Should you have any questions concerning this letter or your billing, please call *Factor* at *Factor's phone*.

Sincerely,

YOUR NAME
President

Received and Acknowledged:

Signature: _____

Print Name: _____

Title: _____

Date: _____

306 – Factoring Small Receivables

This **Notification Letter to Customers** gives your client's customer notice that the customer must now send payment you in lieu of the client. This letter is weaker than the previous one because the checks are made out to the client, even though they are to be mailed to you. If a client receives such a check, he could deposit or cash it because the check is made out to him. If this happens, you have no recourse to the customer, as you do with the first letter, because the customer was not instructed to make the check out to you.

Comments to client: "This letter notifies your customer of your stronger financial position as a result of factoring, and notifies your customer they must send payments to your new remittance address." *(If you require a signature:)* "We need to receive this letter signed by your customer before I can advance your first funds, so be sure they take care of this promptly."

Notification Letter to Customers (Weakest)

(Client's letterhead here)

date

Customer
Address

Attention: Accounts Payable

This letter hereby authorizes and instructs you to remit payment of all open and future invoices from (your company) to our new remittance address:

CLIENT'S COMPANY NAME
Factor Address
Factor City, State, Zip

Your cooperation is greatly appreciated. Please acknowledge receipt of this letter by signing below and returning by fax to *Factor's fax number.*

Name: _____

Title: _____

Sincerely,

YOUR NAME
President

This **Notification Letter to Customers** simply notifies the customer of a change of address for remittance payments, and is used in non-notification factoring relationships. If the customer pays a client directly for factored invoices, you have no protection whatsoever here and are dependent on your client's honesty. For that reason, attorneys strongly advise against using this type of notification and remittance procedure.

However, for clients who are jittery about what their customers will think about payments going to a finance company, this letter puts their concerns at ease. You must determine if a client's comfort level, and the resulting ease of closing a deal, is worth the less secure position in which you will be as a result.

If you use this document you'll want to make an initial verification call to customers to make sure the product or service for the first invoice has been received properly. Have your client create this document and put it in the customer's hands, who then signs it and faxes it to you.

If you choose to use this letter, it's a good idea to not advance funds the first time until you have received the letter back from the customer with her signature. The same is true with the other letters also if you require a signature on those.

Comments to client: "This letter notifies your customer of the change of remittance address so their payments are sent directly to me. I need to receive this letter signed by your customer before I can advance your first funds, so be sure they take care of this promptly."

Schedule of Accounts

ABC Financial Services

555-5555 tel   555-5554 fax

Schedule Number: -   Exhibit B

	Customer	Invoice #	Ref. / P.O. #	Inv Date	Invoice Amt
1					
2					
3					
4					
5					
6					
7					
8					
9					
10					
11					
12					
13					
14					
15					

Total _____

The undersigned hereby sells, assigns and transfers all of its right, title and interest in above listed accounts receivable ("invoices") to ABC Financial Services, Inc., pursuant to that certain Accounts Receivable Purchase Agreement between the undersigned and ABC Financial Services, Inc.

Date: _____

Company: _____

Signature: _____

Factor use	**Total** _____
	Adv. _____
	Less Adj. _____
Date Funded _____	Total Adv. _____

The **Schedule of Accounts** must be completed and signed by your client each time she has invoices to factor. This document is referred to in the Accounts Receivable Purchase Agreement (sections 2 and 5) and is an extension of that contract ("Exhibit B").

By completing this form, the client provides a record of which invoices are factored, and by signing the Schedule, makes the assignment of the receivables to you. If this document isn't signed, the receivables aren't assigned and they are not your property. Therefore don't advance funds until the client signs this form. Clients will occasionally forget to sign this, so be sure to check for the signature on every Schedule from every client.

Comments to client: "You need to complete and sign this form each time you want to receive an advance. It's pretty simple; just follow the sample Schedule I've provided. For each invoice put your customer's name, the invoice number, P.O. or other Reference number if needed, the invoice date, and amount. Once the form's filled in, be sure to sign this or the assignment is not made and I can't advance funds. If you forget to sign it, which everyone does occasionally, I'll let you know and wait for your signature before advancing the money."

Delivery of Funds

Select from the following options for delivery of funds.

___ 1. ACH electronic direct deposit (no charge; 2-3 business days to appear in your account). **Please complete the ACH Direct Deposit Sign-up Form if choosing this option.**

___ 2. Bank wire ($*** charge deducted from amount wired; additional costs to receive; appears same day in your account)

        Name of Bank: _____

        Bank routing #: _____

        Account #: _____

        Name on Acct: _____

        Bank address _____

        Bank phone # _____

___ 3. Customer pick up

___ 4. Regular first class mail (no charge)

___ 5. Priority mail ($*** or actual charge)

___ 6. Airborne Express or FedEx next afternoon delivery ($*** charge)

___ 7. Local branch deposit *(bank branches near factor)*

        _____

        _____

        _____

        _____

        Account #: _____

- -

Please complete the following in addition to the above
Person/s authorized to sign Schedule of Accounts form

        _____

        _____

Company Name   _____

By   _____

Date   _____

The **Delivery of Funds** form simply gives you instructions as to how your client wishes to receive advances and rebates. Put your preference of these methods first on this form to encourage your client to receive funds this way. Likewise, if you are charging for any of these transfer methods, make the charges fair and at least cover your costs.

If you are willing to make deposits at the local branch of your client, list those banks that are in easy driving distance of your office. Putting those too far away will mean you'll spend a lot of time driving around town, which isn't the best use of your time. You may decide to charge a nominal fee for this service, especially if you can make ACH direct deposits. Do not include the option for ACH direct deposits until you have been approved for this by your bank.

Comments to client: "On this form you're telling me how to transfer funds to you. These are in the order of my preferred methods; those at the top save me time and are most convenient. Other methods will take more time or have costs involved. Be sure to include, on the lines under the dotted line, the names of people who are authorized to sign Schedules for your company."

Agreement for Factored Payments
Received by Client

If you receive a customer payment for any factored invoice, <u>do not deposit the funds into your bank account nor cash the check</u>. Handle the payment the following way:

1. Immediately fax the check and its stub to *factor* (fax # 000 000-0000). Include a note indicating how you are delivering the payment to us (regular mail, Priority Mail, overnight, or hand deliver).

2. Deliver the check as indicated on your note. Your account will be credited for the payment as being received the business day we receive it, not when you fax it. If the check is large you may find it cost effective to send it via overnight delivery or Priority Mail. According to your delivery method, send it to:

   Mail and Priority Mail: Overnight Delivery:
   Factor's Mailing address   *Factor's Office location*

3. To avoid improperly routed payments in the future, contact your customer's Accounts Payable department or bookkeeper to thank them for payment and remind them to send future checks to your Accounts Receivable remittance address:

   Factor's address

I agree to immediately forward all payments for factored invoices to *factor* as directed above. I understand that by depositing or cashing such payments I am committing a breach of contract that may result in termination of the factoring agreement and carry severe penalties.

Signature: _____

Print Name: _____

Date: _____

The **Agreement for Factored Payments Received by Client** gives specific instructions to the client regarding what he is required do if he receives payment for a factored invoice.

Sooner or later a client will receive a factored customer payment, and if the check is made out to him, he may be inclined to deposit the check and "pay you back" from his own bank account. This is not something you want to occur. In my experience, even honest clients sometimes see nothing wrong with doing this. However, that is a practice you never want to allow as it can lead to multiple problems.

This document gives explicit directions for the client to follow when he receives a factored customer payment. The form also reminds him that converting checks is a breach of contract with potentially serious repercussions. By signing this form, he has no excuse that he "didn't know" he couldn't deposit or cash such checks, and in fact has clear steps to follow when he receives them.

Comments to client: "This form reiterates what is mentioned in the Accounts Receivable Purchase Agreement as to what you must do with factored checks if you ever receive any. Here are the simple steps to follow so you know exactly what to do. As you can see, cashing or depositing factored payments is a breach of our contract so be sure that never happens."

Customer Contact Sheet
ABC Financial Services
555-5555 tel   555-5554 fax

Client: _____

Customer Co. Name and Address	Store # (if used)	Contact Person	Title/ Dept.	Phone	Fax	Notes

The **Customer Contact Sheet** is not a legal document but simply a form to help you keep track of a client's customers, and whom to contact there if necessary. Once a client is under way and this information entered into your computer, you probably won't use this form too much.

Comments to client: "This form helps me know who to contact at your customers' businesses, if and when that's necessary. If I need to make a follow-up call on a slow payer, this helps me get to the right person quickly and therefore helps us get paid faster."

Once Under Way

Keeping careful and accurate paperwork is absolutely critical. Organization helps you stay on top of things, protects you if the client disagrees with some invoice, fee, or other item, and is your paper trail if you need it. The more complete, accurate and systematically filed your paperwork is, the better for everybody.

Customer Payments

One issue that sees some variation among factors is the question as to whom customer payment checks should be made: the factor or the client?

Having a limited power of attorney clause (Section 4 in the sample contract in this chapter) will make depositing checks made out to your clients very simple. In fact, you may wish to have all checks made out to your clients instead of you. But make sure your bank will allow you to deposit checks made out to clients (many will not) and that the bank has on file a copy of your contract with each client.

Why would you want checks made out to your client instead of you? Two reasons.

1. New clients are frequently concerned about the "appearance" factoring will have to customers. Anxiety is produced wondering, "Will my customer think I'm in financial trouble if checks are made out to a financial company?" If you can present factoring as simply outsourcing of receivables management in which checks will continue to be made out to the client, red flags are avoided. There is also less confusion for the customer if the only change he has to make is the remittance address.

2. If checks are made out to your company, most customers will think they need to have you fill out a W-9 form. This form is used to report to IRS payments they make to you. However, the amount they report to IRS will be the full amount of what you have been paid for all invoices, which does not accurately reflect the actual income (your fee) received. Thus IRS gets the picture that you've received quite a bit more than you have in fact earned. Trying to

explain all this to customers can leave them bewildered and perhaps thinking you're doing something shady.

You can save yourself a lot of explaining (to customers and IRS) by simply having the check *made out to the client* and *sent to you*. As long as your contract has a properly worded power of attorney, your bank approves, and the bank has a copy of your contract with each client including the power of attorney, having checks made out to the client will save a lot of headaches.

On the other hand, there are strong arguments in favor of having checks made out to your company rather than your client. Many say the best way to have a check made out is like this:

"Pay to the Order of ABC Factoring Company, FBO Client Company" [FBO stands for "For Benefit Of"].

Why do many factors prefer the check *not* be made to the client? First, if your client obtains a check, he can't deposit it if it's made out to you. Second, you are in a stronger legal position if you make it clear that because factored invoices are assigned to you, any payment made to your client does not constitute payment; see the comments following the Notification Letter to Customer (A).

These concerns often affect larger factors with larger sums of money at stake, and are grist for lawsuits which result when a factor is not made whole when substantial payments are involved. For very small factors whose factoring volume is too small to take to court when such problems arise, these technicalities may be more trouble than they're worth. Going to court to collect $100,000 is worth the time and legal expense; going to court to collect $10,000 is not. (See the *FactorTips* article, "A Small Factor's Thoughts about Big Factors' Concerns" in the Appendix.)

Be aware that factoring attorneys strongly recommend factors use the FBO method. You need to decide if this will be your practice.

Invoices

Invoices are about as diverse as the businesses who create them, but generally include a date, number, company name and address, bill to name and address, terms, quantity of product or hours of service rendered, description of product or service, subtotal, tax, and freight and/or miscellaneous charges. What you want to pay most attention to with invoices is that YOUR company's address is on them, conspicuously evident under words that say something like "Remit to" or "Pay to." You can have your name and address put on with a sticker or inked stamp as many factors do (though some clients think this looks tacky...I tend to agree).

If your client is generating invoices on a computer, it's usually not hard to add your "remit to" address. If you're creating the invoices for your client (and some will want you to...another reason to have software which does this well) you can make the invoice look like and say anything you want. Ideally, yours would be the only address on the invoice, with the client's phone number listed for "service" and yours for "billing." (See sample invoice in the next chapter.) I prefer having only one address on the invoice since customers often pay to the client's address if there are two addresses on the invoice. It's best to have only your address and print "please remit to this address."

I've seen various ways of getting invoices out the door. Many factors say if the client generates them, you should have the client mail both the originals and copies to you. Then you put your sticker on the originals, keep copies for your records, verify them, and mail them as you pay the advance. That works well but is time consuming and you're paying the postage. I've seen one factor supply an inked stamp that says "payable to" the factor's name and address, and give a stamp to each client. The client then faxes to the factor a copy of each invoice with the Schedule of Accounts, from which the factor makes the verification calls (including verification about the proper "remit to" address), and the client mails the invoices (using the client's time and expense). Once the factor verifies the invoices, the advance is given.

A variation is to have the client print your "remit to" address on their invoices which are created by their computer so it looks professional, and then wait for their fax. Alternatively, have the client just drop it by your office or go get it on your next bank run...another reason to stick with local clients. This works well, though receiving faxes or copies does leave you open to fraud, as you don't know for certain the client sent the invoice, changed the amount on it after faxing it to you, and/or sent it with your address on it. For this reason many factors require the client to supply the factor with the original invoice plus a copy. The factor then mails the original. However, if you feel safe letting the client mail the originals, it will save time stuffing envelopes and the cost of postage stamps.

If you're going to be printing and mailing or faxing the client's invoices – the safest method of all – calculate that into your fee or add a billing fee and charge accordingly. If done for more than a few customers you should be compensated if the time involved is more than minimal or if you're producing all or most of a client's invoices. On the other hand, especially with your larger or best clients who generate more revenue for you, you may choose to include such invoicing as part of your service – as long as it doesn't cost you too much time, and therefore money.

Invoice Verifications

Ordinarily, the more you verify invoices the safer you'll be. The next book in this series, *Factoring Case Studies,* includes many stories of factors who didn't verify invoices properly or at all. Some factors say that being "consistent in your inconsistency" is a good practice for verifications. That is, if you have an unpredictable pattern to your verification practices, a dishonest client will have a harder time getting away with fraudulent invoices and phony customer approvals.

Some types of business lend themselves well to verifications signed by the customer, indicating payment is approved. A good example is time cards signed by the customer for employees hired through a temporary agency. Temp agencies often make great factoring clients, and verifications can be a snap if time cards are agreed by all as a promise to pay. Simply have the signed time cards faxed or mailed to you with the invoices. A document signed by the customer will protect you better in any dispute than a note you make from a verification made by phone. However, when you must make phone verifications, the following form can be used to make sure the important questions are asked and you have a written record. The information here can be condensed into a simple "Notes" field in any of several software contact managers. If using one of these programs, be sure the entry is dated and the name of the person who made the call is included.

Verification Form

Client: _____
Customer: _____
Phone: _____
Contact Person: _____

Invoice #	Inv. Date	Item	Amount
_____	_____	_____	$_____
_____	_____	_____	$_____
_____	_____	_____	$_____
_____	_____	_____	$_____
_____	_____	_____	$_____

If a service
Was the service performed?   ___ Yes ___ No
Are you satisfied with the service?   ___ Yes ___ No
Comments: _____
_____
_____

If a product
Did you order the goods?   ___ Yes ___ No
Have you received and inspected the goods?   Received
                                             ___ Yes ___ No
                                             Inspected
                                             ___ Yes ___ No
Are the goods satisfactory?   ___ Yes ___ No

Comments: _____
_____
_____

Signed: _____
Date: _____

Unfactored Invoices

If a client factors some but not all invoices with a given customer, tell him to have **all** payments sent to you to save confusion on the part of the customer. (This is done with the Notice of Assignment and Change of Payee letter shown earlier.) When you receive a payment for an invoice which you can't find on any Schedule of Accounts using your factoring software, you'll know you didn't factor that invoice. You then rebate 100% of unfactored invoices upon receipt of payment. The client must trust you with this, since it's the best way for you to handle a client's customer with some invoices factored, and some not factored.

Attorneys who specialize in factoring suggest you be careful when handling unfactored invoices. Some say than when you receive a check made to your factoring company for unfactored invoices, you should return them to the customer rather than bank them and repay the client. Why? In the future the customer may claim you owe him money because he paid you money you shouldn't have received, even if you properly paid the unfactored funds to the client. Therefore the argument is made you should return unfactored payments to the customer.

However, this can create a huge nuisance for both you and the customer if such payments are a frequent occurrence. Therefore another recommendation is that you just bury the receipt of unfactored payments into a miscellaneous income account. This seems like somewhat irregular bookkeeping to me, however.

On the other hand, if your practice is to have customer checks made out to the client and sent to you, a customer later coming to you for unfactored payments can't happen because the check was never made to you in the first place. This seems to be the simplest solution to the issue of payments for unfactored invoice. The other, if you have customer checks made out to your company FBO the client's company (the recommended practice), is to simply keep your factoring limited to fairly small transactions so the resolution of such issues will not be worth a court battle…which is one of the underlying precepts of this book in the first place.

Factoring Record

The name and format for this document are my creation, but every software package and factor uses his or her own variation. You don't need to copy mine exactly, as I've seen factors get by with less information than this. However, I like this form for its completeness and so do my clients.

When you receive a Schedule of Accounts you'll transfer the information from it onto the Factoring Record/computer program. Check to make sure all invoice information is written accurately on the Schedule – invoice number, date, amount and customer name. As customers make payments, you enter them into the Factoring record/computer program and the rebates and factoring fees due will be calculated.

If your reports are not available to your clients online, routinely provide them. How often? Preferably every week if she's actively factoring, or at least every time she gives you a new Schedule or when you pay a rebate (see chapter entitled "A Sample Factoring Transaction"). Clients whose factors use web-enabled software can obtain these reports online, saving the factor the time and trouble of providing them.

Rebates

These can be done numerous ways, and the client needs to be clear about which you're going to do when she signs the application papers. Rebate methods are designed to provide the factor with security, but can easily lead to misunderstanding (and with it, distrust) in you from your client.

One method is to pay back rebates due from a given Schedule when all the invoices on the Schedule have been paid. This may sound a bit unfair, but when you have advanced money and are waiting to be paid, you're vulnerable and this protects you by creating a temporary reserve. Again, explain this clearly when you review how to do the Schedule, and your client will understand why you're doing it (your security, not to rip her off). It will keep her paying attention to particular invoices that are slow, and encourage her to contact the slow paying customer. Believe me, clients want their rebates! On the other hand, a client may be resentful if all but one invoice on a Schedule with eight invoices isn't paid. Always find creative ways to keep yourself safe and the client happy with your service.

A second method of rebates gives you better security but is more complicated, and is the method many larger factors use. It's more complicated because you utilize a specific factoring fee...the most you can charge per your Agreement...and then rebate part of that fee based on when the invoice is paid, in addition to rebating the security deposit when the security deposit reaches a certain percentage of total invoices. If that sounds confusing, the following example should clarify.

Suppose you want to charge 5% for the first 30 days, and 2% for each 15 days thereafter, up to 90 days. It looks like this:

5%	30 days
7%	45 days
9%	60 days
11%	75 days
13%	90 days

The highest fee you'll collect is 13% at 90 days. The contract is so worded that your fee is 13%, and you give rebates on the fee when the invoice is paid before 90 days: if paid in 30 days, the fee rebate is 8%, thereby making the fee 5% (13% - 8% = 5%); if paid in 45 days, the fee rebate is 6%, making the fee 7% (13% - 6% = 7%), and so on. In addition, you are also holding a security deposit reserve. If you advance 70% and your total fee is 13%, your security deposit is 17% (30% - 13% = 17%).

With this method of calculating rebates, you don't pay rebates according to any Schedule of Accounts, but on a calculated percentage of the total outstanding balance of invoices due, which accrues from this 17% security deposit plus fee rebates. This calculated percentage is usually 50%.

Getting lost? Okay, say you factor a $5,000 invoice; with a 70% advance, $850 (17%) is kept as security deposit. Then you factor another invoice with the same client, again for $5,000; another $850 is kept. $1,700 is now in reserve ($850 + $850 =

$1,700). Even if the first invoice is on a Schedule by itself and is paid, you do not pay the rebate because only $1,700 is in reserve (not yet 50%, or $2,500). The reserve continues to build up on unpaid invoices until you go over 50% of the unpaid balance of total invoices factored, at which point you begin paying rebates and only pay enough to keep the reserve at 50%. Confusing?

Yes, and somewhat different from how I (and most clients) first understood how rebates are paid: "You're paid your advance immediately, and when your customer pays the factor, you get what was withheld, less the factor's fee." With this method, getting paid a rebate is not that simple and if a factor were to do this to me as a client without explaining this extremely carefully before I signed my life away, I'd think he was trying to pull a fast one when I expect a rebate and it doesn't come. The first and third (see below) methods make the contract language much simpler, are easier for the client to understand, and are easier to track by both the factor and the client. The disadvantage is that you, the factor, are not as well covered by the reserve.

A third method is to simply pay rebates on a regular weekly, biweekly, or monthly basis. If done weekly, on Monday you total all rebates due from invoices paid the previous week (which usually gives them time to clear), fax each client an updated Factoring Record, and deposit or mail their rebates on Tuesday. While you are least protected with this method, clients are happier as there is almost no wait for rebates. Further, you don't end up paying large sums that have accumulated from payments on a single schedule, which may be difficult to cover if your available cash is low. If your client has some invoices nearing recourse, draw her attention to the fact and indicate you intend to withhold all or part of the upcoming rebate to cover the charge back. This way, you won't need to take charge backs out of her next advance or require her to pay you directly...both of which can wreak havoc with the client's cash flow. If you've clearly explained that you're a recourse factor and she understands her responsibility for unpaid invoices, she will grasp what you're doing.

If you go with the first method, it's a good idea to suggest to your client that she group invoices on Schedules according to how long the invoices will take to pay. In other words, when it's feasible, put all the invoices that will probably pay in 15 days on one Schedule, and those that will take 45 days to pay on another. Don't mix 15 day pays with 45 day pays on the same Schedule, because she'll have to wait several more weeks to get her rebates for the quicker pays that way. Your client will figure this out sooner or later on her own, and if you tell her this strategy right up front, she'll appreciate your honesty and realize you really do want to help her...not just make an extra buck at her expense.

Regardless of how you pay rebates, make sure you understand the various methods yourself, describe the one you use and then explain carefully to the client how the rebate is calculated. If you don't, you may have an understandably grumpy (or worse) client who expects a rebate that may not be as quickly forthcoming as she expected.

Separate Reserve Account

Creating a separate reserve account was discussed in the chapter "Reducing Your Risk," and bears repeating here. I have found this tool to be exceptionally helpful and an excellent means of protecting both you as a recourse factor, and the client when customers short pay invoices or don't pay at all. Here's how I do it.

First, when I review my setup documents with a prospect, I explain that I will create a "rainy day" fund that will help if and when a customer doesn't pay in full or at all. This reserve money will come from rebates, yet the client will still receive rebate payments when a customer checks arrives.

The reserve fund will gradually build up to equal 10% of the client's credit limit. Since I start my new clients with a $10,000 credit line, their reserve has a $1,000 cap to start. How is money put into this reserve? Each time an invoice is paid, 5% of that invoice is placed into the reserve.

Here's an example. Let's say a client receives a 75% advance and pays 5% in fees at 30 days. When a $1,000 invoice pays at 30 days, $750 or 75% pays for the advance and $50 or 5% pays for the factoring fee. The remaining $200 or 20% is due the client as her rebate.

However, instead of paying the full 20%, I will pay her a $150 or 15% rebate, and place the remaining $50 or 5% into the reserve. Each time a customer payment is received, another 5% will go into the reserve until the reserve cap is reached. From that point, the client receives the full rebate – 20% in the above example.

Structured this way, the client continues to receive rebates in addition to advances, while concurrently setting aside reserve money for potential problems. Over time, the client will build up to $1,000 in her reserve account. Then, if a customer pays, for example, only $600 for a $1,000 invoice, the money owed from that short payment can be taken from the reserve fund, and not from the client's next advance or rebate. This can be a great help to a client's cash flow. To replenish the amount used, future payments then refill this reserve fund (as was done before the draw on the reserve) until its cap is again reached.

When a client's business grows, her factoring volume increases, and her credit limit is increased; the reserve fund grows with it simply by remaining at 10% of the credit limit. So if you increase the credit limit from $10,000 to $15,000, the reserve fund cap increases from $1,000 to $1,500 (thereby remaining at 10% of the credit limit).

Because this reserve fund accumulates from money that would have been paid the client as rebates, this is the client's money. Therefore the funds remaining in the reserve when the client stops factoring are paid in full to the client.

When explained carefully to new clients and the rationale made clear, most prospects see the prudence of setting aside funds in this reserve and willingly agree. The client's cash flow remains steady even with short or non-payment, your funds are at less risk, and everyone feels better.

Office Files

Everyone has his own filing system and yours will evolve. For what it's worth, this is how mine is organized.

Client Files

I have folders grouped and color-coded by the following categories in this order (each client has one folder of each color):

1. Date-stamped check stubs, other payment records from customers – a green folder.

2. Schedules of Accounts – an orange folder.

3. Bank Documents (ACH form, Delivery of Funds form, bank deposit slips) – a yellow folder.

4. Introductory Documents (application, signed setup documents, customer lists, etc.) – a blue folder.

5. Verification Documents (signed Notification Letters from customers, registered UCCs, completed 8821 forms, and the like) – a red folder.

You'll be into the green and orange folders constantly, so keep these in front. Alphabetize each color of folders by client. Each folder has documents placed chronologically with new documents in front. Do these *have* to be color-coded? No; but I find I don't have to think about what I'm looking for when the information is sorted by color.

Prospect Files

Hot Prospects. In this file put applications or other documentation you have on prospects which appeal to you and/or are interested in factoring with you. Follow up on these at least once or twice a week, and you'll close more deals than if you wait for them to call you.

Cooler Prospects. These are prospects that have cooled. Every month or so, go through this file and update their status to Hot or relegate them to the file called…

Duds. Those who have lost interest in factoring with you or whom you have declined. You may want to keep them on file for a year or so, then toss their papers to free up filing space.

Other Files

Customer Credit Reports. I keep a separate file for credit reports I've run on customers, and use alphabetical tabs to separate and organize these. At the top of each credit report I write the client's name for whom this credit report was run. By keeping all the credit reports together, I can quickly see if a report has been run on any customer, without remembering which client the customer belongs to.

Bank Records. I keep the following bank records separate from client files.

1. Bank Statements
2. Cancelled Checks (filed by number so they're easier to find)
3. Voided Checks (likewise sorted by number)
4. Deposit Slips (see below).

Each time you make a deposit in your bank account, you receive a deposit slip. These are very important to keep because the bank (and you) will make errors from time to time. Once my bank erroneously recorded a $7,000 deposit as a withdrawal, which threw my account balance off by $14,000. Having the deposit slip with the transaction number made tracking the error easy, and proved not only the money was there, but that the bank made the mistake, not I.

You can track a mistake quickly if your deposit slips are organized. Here's my method. Checks received daily from all customers go into one deposit. On the deposit slip given to the teller, the name of each customer is written to the left of their check amount, and a duplicate slip is made using carbon paper. When the bank's deposit slip is brought back to the office, I staple my carbon copy to the bank deposit slip (which is dated).

I save each deposit slip and at the end of the month place that month's bunch in a separate file. When it comes time to balance the checkbook from the bank statement and a recording error was made unknowingly during the month, referring to the correct deposit slip usually pinpoints the error easily.

I strongly suggest you use online banking, which allows you to check deposits, withdrawals, and balances on a 24/7 basis. Use this daily to make sure your records match the bank's, and balancing your checkbook when the monthly statements arrive is a snap.

Filing and keeping complete records of everything you do is important in factoring. Having everything in a place where you can find it quickly is not only handy, but can protect you if a question or dispute arises, if you or the bank make a mistake, if you make a computer entry error, or if your computer crashes and you haven't backed up well. Leave a paper trail anyone can follow, and you'll be glad you did.

Document Stamps

There are certain document stamps you'll find helpful as your factoring business progresses. They include:

- **A stamp** (or stickers) **with your "remit-to" address** to place on invoices as needed.

- **A dated "Received" stamp** to stamp every check stub from customers. If a customer's check doesn't include a stub, make a copy of the check and date-stamp "Received" on the copy, and file this in the green check stub folder.

- **A dated "Paid" stamp** to stamp all paid bills, with your check number written for easy tracking.

- **A dated multiple-message stamp** which includes the messages **"Entered," "Delivered,"** and others. You can date-stamp the top of each Schedule of Accounts with "Entered" once the advance is given, so you know visually that's been done. You can also date-stamp "Delivered" on the bottom of invoice copies, once you've mailed, faxed, or emailed the original to the customer. Again, this serves as a reminder (and proof in the future) of what has and what hasn't been taken care of. If someone claims they never received an invoice you've marked as "Delivered," you know it was sent. If it's not stamped, it wasn't mailed.

- **A dated "Faxed" stamp** to mark all pertinent faxed documents. When a deposit is made into a client's account directly, I'll fax him the deposit slip or an updated Factoring Record so he knows the money's been transferred. Stamping it tells me I've faxed them the notification. If I fax an invoice instead of mailing it, stamping it gives a record of what's been faxed and what's been overlooked. If you send a fax from your computer, maintain your fax logs for several months before purging them.

   If there is more than one person who sends checks or faxes or mails invoices or other documents, it's not a bad idea to initial each document stamped "paid," "faxed," or "delivered" so there's accountability in your office for who did (or didn't) perform a needed task.

- **A "For Deposit Only" stamp** is useful for checks you write to clients and then deposit directly into their accounts. Write their company name or account number under the stamped words, "For Deposit Only" on the back of the check.

- **A "Void" stamp** to mark your misprinted or otherwise uncashed checks.

- **A check endorsing stamp**. If checks are made out to your company, the following information is usually satisfactory for endorsement:

Pay to the Order of
My Friendly Bank
000000000 *(Bank's ABA number)*
For Deposit Only
ABC Financial Services
Acct. # 000-000-000

As mentioned elsewhere, you may have checks made out to the client and mailed to your address. When I receive checks made out to the client, I use a stamp that says the following (using my company name and bank account number of course), above which I sign the Client company's name:

Client's Company Name *(hand written)*
Pay to the Order of
My Friendly Bank
000000000 *(Bank's ABA number)*
For Deposit Only
ABC Financial Services
Per Power of Attorney on File
Acct. # 000-000-000

Be sure you have a power of attorney in your contract that allows you to endorse your client's checks, and also be sure your bank will accept them for deposit. Ask the bank manager or person setting up your account how the bank wants your endorsement stamp worded *before* you have an endorsement stamp made. Otherwise you may waste time and money having worthless stamps made.

19

A Sample Factoring Transaction

Jones Computer Peripherals

Let's walk through a sample factoring transaction, from start to finish, using all the due diligence, setup documents, and factoring records now at our disposal. We'll use a sample client of Jones Computer Peripherals, Inc., a fictional company that distributes hardware in the computer industry. Mr. Jones hears about you from an associate, Ms. Jackson, who recommended you because you are factoring her and she is happy with the service you provide. (You spent $2,000 in advertising to find Ms. Jackson, and that is finally beginning to pay off! She'll also enjoy the finder's fee you pay.)

You talk with Mr. Jones on the phone and learn he sells computer peripherals to three nearby school districts, some small computer retail stores, and takes direct orders over the phone from customers who saw his product reviewed in a magazine. His phone has been ringing off the hook since the review, and he is having trouble finding enough money to buy inventory to keep up with the orders. Because he has been in business for only a year, the banks won't help him and there's a note of concern in his voice that his success may swamp his young company.

He has become familiar with your company from your web site, and he completed your online application. His customers look good, you have found no red flags on your public records search of him, and you agree to meet him for lunch at a restaurant central to both of you. After pleasantries are exchanged and you get to know one another, you pull out the setup documents and carefully review each one. You ask if he is clear about what each means before going on to the next, and allow plenty of room for questions and clarification.

You've both allowed enough time in your schedules to discuss the documents there, and you've provided two complete sets so you'll each have a signed original set.

Once the documents are reviewed and signed, follow these steps over the next few days and weeks, as outlined on the Transaction Flowchart below.

1. Receive the Schedule of Accounts (see below), invoice(s) (or create the invoice(s) for your client, see below), and client's notification letter(s) to customers (see below).

2. Make sure the customer/s, invoice number/s, and invoice amount/s are accurately written on the Schedule.

3. If errors or omissions are found, notify the client.

4. a) Enter the data from the Schedule onto the client's Factoring Record. Enter the Schedule number, Customer Names, Store Number(s) if needed, Invoice Number(s), Invoice Date(s), Invoice Amount(s), Advance Amount(s) (the computer will calculate this), and Date of Advance for each invoice.

   b) Be sure your company name and address are on the invoices before they are mailed, then mail.

5. Verify the invoices with the customers, using a signed invoice or other appropriate form (see below), or making a phone call.

6. If there is a problem with the goods/services, notify the client.

7. Advance funds for the Schedule (see sample check below). Reference the Schedule number. (E.g., JON-1 refers to Schedule of Accounts #1 for Jones. Likewise, JON-1.3 refers to Jones' Schedule #1, invoice #3 on that Schedule). Put this reference number on the check. Give or mail the check to the client, deposit it in the client's bank account, or send the ACH or wire. This starts the clock for calculating your fee.

8. Stamp the date the advance is given on the Schedule, and enter any other needed information into the Factoring Record and your checking account program.

9. Now you simply wait to receive payment on the invoices.

10.-11. If a problem surfaces or recourse is imminent, notify the client. If the customer is slower paying than usual make a check-up call saying your manage the receivables for this client and "want to be sure they received the invoice" or that you are "checking on payment status." Log the date, time, person's name, and what they said.

12-13. When payment arrives (see sample customer payment check below), verify its accuracy and notify the client if the amount received is significantly different from the invoice amount. If acceptable, the clock stops for your fee calculation.

14. Endorse and deposit the check (see example below) and enter the payment information in your checking account program and the Factoring Record (see below). Put in the Date Received, Number of Days (= Date Payment Received – Date Advance Sent; the computer will calculate this), Amount Received, and Customer's check number. The Factor's Fee and Rebate Due for each invoice will be calculated automatically.

   If you're using a spreadsheet, the formula for calculating your fee is:

   Factor's Fee = Invoice Amount x % Rate.

   The formula for calculating the rebate is:

   Rebate = Amount Received – Advance Amount – Factor's Fee – Other Fees & Adjustments.

   Stamp the date received on the stub or copy of the check, and reference the Schedule number(s) (see example below). Transfer the payment splits (advance, rebate, factor fee, broker fee) onto your bookkeeping program File the stub or check copy in the client's green folder.

15.-17. If a rebate is due, pay the client. Clients are always glad to get this! Give the client an updated copy of the Factoring Record with it. If this client was introduced to you by a broker, client, or other person, calculate finder's fees due and pay according to your agreement.

18. Thank your client for the business and ask if she knows when and about how much the next Schedule will be. Keep her thinking ahead...with you in mind. Every so often, remind her you give finder's fees when she refers you to someone who becomes your client.

Remember, the first couple of Schedules will be the slowest with each client, so be somewhat flexible yet clear as to what you need to make everything go smoothly. After a client has done a few Schedules, you'll both get into a groove and factoring will become an easy, and hopefully pleasant, relationship for everyone involved.

Transaction Flowchart

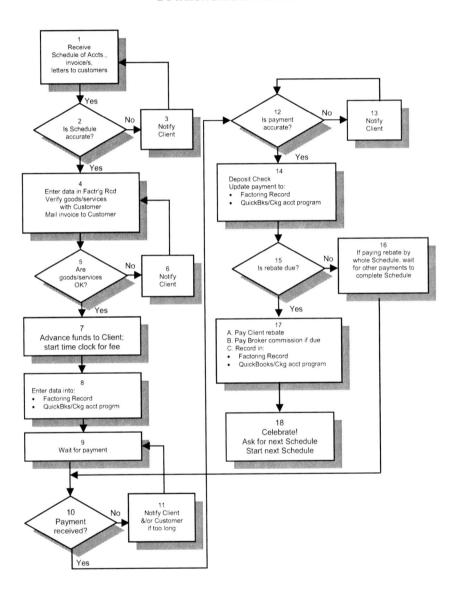

Schedule of Accounts

ABC Financial Services

555-5555 tel   555-5554 fax

Schedule Number: JON -   1   Exhibit B

	Customer	Invoice #	Ref. / P.O. #	Inv Date	Invoice Amt
1	Boeing	1051		7/15	$2,105.00
2	Customer Service	1052		7/16	$539.50
3	WalMart	1053	2691	7/17	$1,276.21
4	Seattle Schools	1054		7/18	$4,023.00
5					
6					
7					
8					
9					
10					
11					
12					
13					
14					
15					

Total $7,943.71

The undersigned hereby sells, assigns and transfers all of its right, title and interest in above listed accounts receivable ("invoices") to ABC Financial Services, Inc., pursuant to that certain Accounts Receivable Purchase Agreement between the undersigned and ABC Financial Services, Inc.

Date: 7/18

Company: Jones Computer Peripherals

Signature: *John Jones*

Factor use		Total	$7,943.71
	70%	Adv.	$5,560.60
		Less Adj.	
Date Funded 7/18		Total Adv.	$5,560.60

Jones Computer Peripherals

Invoice

Remit to:
P.O. Box 9999
ABC Town, USA 99999-9999

Telephone:
Service: 253 555-0001
Billing: 253 555-5555
Telephone: 253 555-5554 fax

Customer Service Co.
Attn: Tom
1432 28th Ave. N.
Seattle, WA 98200
555-3133 Fax 555-3114

7/17	1052
Invoice Date	**Invoice #**
Net 30	
Terms	**PO #**
JON 1.2	
Code	

QTY	DESCRIPTION	RATE	AMOUNT
2	Computer Gizmos	250.00	$500.00

Subtotal:	$500.00
Tax:	39.50
TOTAL:	$539.50
Amount Paid:	
Balance:	

Thank you for your business.

ABC Financial Services
P.O. Box 9999
ABC Town, USA 99999-9999
253 555-5555 * 253 555-5554 Fax

July 27

Customer Service Company
1432 28th Ave. N.
Seattle, WA 98200

Attention: Accounts Payable Manager

Notice of Assignment and Change of Payee

We are pleased to inform you we have established a working relationship that provides Jones Computer Peripherals with a working capital line of credit. These funds will enable further growth and expansion from which Jones and their customers will benefit both now and in the future. Accordingly, Jones Computer Peripherals has assigned all present and future Accounts Receivable with your company to ABC Financial Services.

This letter hereby authorizes and instructs you to remit your payment of all invoices from Jones Computer Peripherals directly to ABC Financial Services, and to continue to do so until notified otherwise by ABC Financial. Payments made to any party except ABC Financial will not relieve your obligation for Accounts Payables due Jones Computer Peripherals, and this notice may not be revoked except in writing by an officer of ABC Financial.

Please make your checks payable to, and send them to:

ABC Financial Services FBO [For Benefit Of] Jones Computer Peripherals
P.O. Box 9999
ABC Town, USA 99999-9999

Your cooperation is appreciated. While your signature is not required to validate this assignment, we ask that you sign and return this letter so we know you have made the needed changes in your Accounts Payable system. Therefore please sign below and return via fax to 253 555-5554 at your earliest convenience. Please keep a copy of this letter for your records.

Should you have any questions concerning this letter, please call ABC Financial Services at 253 555-5555 or Jones Computer Peripherals at 253 555-0001.

Sincerely,

John Q. Factor

John Q. Factor
Operations Manager
ABC Financial Services

John Jones

John Jones
President
Jones Computer Peripherals

Signature: _____

Print Name: _____

Title: _____

Date: _____

ABC Financial Services
P.O. Box 9999
ABC Town, USA 99999-9999
(253) 555-5555 * (253) 555-5554 Fax

Factoring Record

Jones Computer Peripherals
7/18

Schedule	Inv#	Inv. Date	Inv. Amt	Adv Amt	Date Adv Pd	Adv Adj	Date Recd	# of days from Date of Inv	Adv	Fee %	Amt Recd	Factr Fee	Adj	Reserve or Rebate	Rebate Pd	Date Rebate Pd
Totals			$ 7,943.71	$ 5,560.60												
JON 1			7,943.71	5,560.60												
1 Boeing	1051	7/15	2,105.00	1,473.50	7/18			3	0							
2 Customer Svc.	1052	7/15	539.50	377.65	7/18			3	0							
3 WalMart	1053	7/15	1,276.21	893.35	7/18			3	0							
4 Seattle Schls	1054	7/15	4,023.00	2,816.10	7/18			3	0							

===

Jones Computer Peripherals

P.O. Box 9999
ABC Town USA 99999-9999
Service: (253) 555-0001 * (253) 555-0002 Fax
Billing: (555) 555-5555 * (555) 555-5554 Fax

[Factor's Address]
[Factor's City, State, Zip]
[Client's phone #s]
[Factor's phone #s]

Letter of Acceptance

Customer Service Company
1432 28th Ave. N.
Seattle, WA 98200

Attn: Tom S.
Fax: 555-3114

RE: Verification of Invoice/s

To maintain a high standard of quality control and customer satisfaction, please certify that the products and/or services have been received and accepted for the following invoice/s.

Invoice Date	Invoice #	Amount	Notes	Ref. #
7/15	1052	$539.50	Computer Gizmos	JON 1.2

All materials and/or services have been properly rendered for this/these invoice/s: there are no off-sets or defenses, the amounts are correct, and the invoice/s will be paid to the above address according to the terms and conditions set forth.

Please sign and fax back to: _____
(253) 555-5554 *[Factor's fax]*   Date

_____
Authorized Signature

_____
Print Name and Title

Factor's Advance Check to Client

ABC FINANCIAL SERVICES   1035
P.O. Box 9999
ABC Town, USA 99999-9999   July 18

Pay to the
Order of   Jones Computer Peripherals $ 5,560.60

_____ Five thousand, five hundred sixty and 60/100 **********   Dollars

For ___ JON – 1 advance ___   *John Q. Factor*

                                                NON-negotiable

Customer's Payment Check to Factor

Customer Service Company   2084
1432 28ᵗʰ Ave. N.
Seattle, WA 98200   August 8

Pay to the
Order of ABC Financial FBO Jones Computer Peripherals $ 539.50

_____ Five hundred thirty-nine and 50/100 *****************   Dollars

For   Computer Gizmos   *Thomas P. Scott*

                                                NON-negotiable

Factor's Endorsement
of Customer's Payment Check

Check made out to Client: Check made out to Factor:

Jones Computer Peripherals Pay to the Order of My Friendly Bank 000000000 For Deposit Only ABC Financial Services Per Power of Attorney on File Acct. # 000-000-000	Pay to the Order of My Friendly Bank 000000000 For Deposit Only ABC Financial Services Acct. # 000-000-000

Copy of Customer's Payment Check for File

		2084
Customer Service Company 1432 28th Ave. N. Seattle, WA 98200	COPY	August 8
Pay to the Order of ABC Financial FBO Jones Computer Peripherals		$ 539.50
Five hundred thirty-nine and 50/100 ****************		Dollars
For Computer Gizmos	*Thomas P. Scott* NON-negotiable	

	Advance	Rebate	Fee	Broker Fee	Reserve
JON 1.2	377.65	107.89	22.93	4.05	26.98

ABC Financial Services
P.O. Box 9999
ABC Town, USA 99999-9999
(253) 555-5555 * (253)555-5554 Fax

Factoring Record

Jones Computer Peripherals
9/27

Schedule	Inv #	Inv Date	Inv Amt	Adv Amt	Date Adv Pd	Adv Adj	Date Recd	# of days from Date of Inv	Adv	Fee %	Amt Recd	Factr Fee	Adj	Reserve or Rebate	Rebate Pd	Date Rebate Pd
Totals			$ 7,943.71	$ 5,560.60							7,943.71	$ 653.12				
JON 1			7,943.71	5,560.60							7,943.71	653.12		1,729.99	1,729.99	
1 Boeing	1051	7/15	2,105.00	1,473.50	7/18		9/12	59	56	9.0%	2,105.00	189.45		442.05	442.05	9/17
2 Customer Svc.	1052	7/15	539.50	377.65	7/18		8/12	28	25	5.0%	539.50	26.98		134.88	134.88	8/20
3 WalMart	1053	7/15	1,276.21	893.35	7/18		9/10	57	54	9.0%	1,276.21	114.86		268.00	268.00	9/24
4 Seattle Schls.	1054	7/15	4,023.00	2,816.10	7/18		9/3	50	47	8.0%	4,023.00	321.84		885.06	885.06	9/10
JON 2			6,859.28	4,801.50							4,375.28	147.46		1,946.33	1,946.33	
1. Customer Svc.	1055	8/22	775.28	542.70	8/28		9/6	15	9	3.0%	775.28	23.26		209.33	209.33	9/24
2. Kent Schools	1058	8/24	3,600.00	2,520.00	8/28			34	30	5.0%						
3. Jim's Computer	1060	8/24	2,484.00	1,738.80	8/28		9/20	27	23	5.0%	3,600.00	124.20		1,737.00	1,737.00	9/24
JON 3			9,777.85	6,844.50												
1. Customer Svc.	1065	9/20	900.00	630.00	9/27			7	0							
2. Boeing	1071	9/20	452.35	316.65	9/27			7	0							
3. Jim's Computer	1084	9/20	875.50	612.85	9/27			7	0							
4. Clark Schools	1085	9/25	5,000.00	3,500.00	9/27			2	0							
5. Clark Schools	1087	9/26	2,550.00	1,785.00	9/27			1	0							

Factor's Rebate Check to Client

ABC FINANCIAL SERVICES
P.O. Box 9999
ABC Town, USA 99999-9999

1050

August 20

Pay to the Order of   Jones Computer Peripherals

$ 107.89

One hundred seven and 89/100   **********   Dollars

For   JON – 1.2 rebate

John Q. Factor

NON-negotiable

20

Bookkeeping with QuickBooks®

Like any business, to properly track your company's income, expenses, and profits you need some kind of bookkeeping software separate from the factoring software reviewed earlier. There are various products on the market – QuickBooks®, PeachTree, Simply Accounting, and others. Personal finance software like Quicken and MS Money may be adequate for very small operations but lack many of the features of the more robust products such as QuickBooks®.

Because QuickBooks® has the largest number of users and is the software I use, this chapter will describe the bookkeeping system I have established and used for the past several years using QuickBooks®. This will follow with an alternative outline of data entry steps used by another small factor, Kari and Kevin Clark of Premier Funding of Lebanon, Oregon. The Clarks, as I did, developed their system on their own and I present both to show that there are more ways than one to keep your bookkeeping records.

While the terms that follow will be those of QuickBooks®, the general procedures will be similar with other systems even though implementation of procedures and terminology might be somewhat different. I am using QuickBooks® Pro 2003. The Clarks' version is somewhat older so some of their menu references will vary from this version.

This chapter assumes you have a working knowledge of QuickBooks® and how to set up a new company. If you have never used QuickBooks® before, please become familiar with its operation by studying the owner's manual and tutorials. Intuit has several versions of this product. If you have an older version, you should have no trouble following along but might find slightly different menu selections in your version.

Setting Up a Chart of Accounts

The Chart of Accounts includes 15 types of accounts which are, in order:

- Bank
- Accounts Receivables
- Other Current Asset
- Fixed Asset
- Other Asset
- Accounts Payable
- Credit Card
- Other Current Liability
- Long Term Liability
- Equity
- Income
- Cost of Goods Sold
- Expense
- Other Income
- Other Expense

The first task is to create the accounts you will be using, and assign each the proper "type" in the Chart of Accounts. As long as you haven't entered data into these accounts you usually can change their type later if you find another makes more sense.

Account Names

Below are the name of accounts I've established, and the type each account needs to be.

Name	Type
Checking	Bank
Savings	Bank
Advances	Other Current Asset
Rebates	Other Current Liability
Unfactored Invoices	Other Current Liability

Client Reserves	Long Term Liability
Loans	Long Term Liability
(Name of Credit Card/s)	Credit Card
Fees	Income
Broker Fees Income	Income
Bank Charges	Expense
Broker Fees Expense	Expense
Interest Income	Other Income
Other Income	Other Income
Other Expenses	Other Expense

You also need to include the various expense categories you have and name them whatever you choose, such as:

Auto	Expense
Bad Debts	Expense
Charitable Donations	Expense
Computer Expenses	Expense
Conventions & Conferences	Expense
Due Diligence	Expense
Dues & Subscriptions	Expense
Furniture	Expense
Insurance	Expense
Internet	Expense
Licenses & Permits	Expense
Loan Interest	Expense
Marketing	Expense
Memberships	Expense
Office Equipment	Expense
Office Supplies	Expense
Overnight & Wire Charges	Expense
Payroll Expenses	Expense
Postage	Expense
Professional Fees	Expense
Rent	Expense
Taxes	Expense
Telephone	Expense
Travel	Expense
Utilities	Expense

To create each of the above accounts, do the following:

1. Click in the Chart of Accounts icon at the top.
2. Click the Account button and select New (Ctrl-N).
3. Select the type of account you want to create (such as Bank, Income, Expense, etc.).
4. Enter a name in the Name field (such as Checking, Fees, Telephone, etc.).
5. Click OK, or click Next if you're creating another new account.

Subaccounts

Once these accounts have been set up, you will add subaccounts to several of them. I have organized my accounts that contain subaccounts as follows:

Name Subaccount	Type
Checking	Bank
Savings	Bank
Bad Debt Account	Bank
General Savings	Bank
Advances	Other Current Asset
BAC	Other Current Asset
JER	Other Current Asset
WER	Other Current Asset
VAR	Other Current Asset
Rebates	Other Current Liability
BAC	Other Current Liability
JER	Other Current Liability
WER	Other Current Liability
VAR	Other Current Liability
Unfactored Invoices	Other Current Liability
Visa	Credit Card
MasterCard	Credit Card
Client Reserves	Long Term Liability
BAC	Long Term Liability
JER	Long Term Liability
WER	Long Term Liability
VAR	Long Term Liability

Loans	Long Term Liability
Owner Loan	Long Term Liability
Roberts Loan	Long Term Liability
Smith Loan	Long Term Liability
Broker Fees Income	Income
Broker A	Income
Broker B	Income
Broker C	Income
Fees	Income
Billing Fees	Income
Factoring Fees	Income
Broker Fees Expense	Expense
Broker A	Expense
Broker B	Expense
Broker C	Expense

To create a subaccount, do the following:

1. Click in the Chart of Accounts window.
2. Click the Account button and select New (Ctrl-N).
3. Select the type of account you want (Expense, Income, Other Current Asset, Other Current Liability, etc.).
4. Enter a name in the Name field.
5. Click the Subaccount check box and select the account under which this will be a subaccount.
6. Give a description to this subaccount if you choose.
7. Click OK, or click Next if you're creating another new account.

In the Chart of Accounts, these subaccounts will show current balances, and the total balance will be reflected in the account which is the "parent" of its subaccounts. These running totals are provided for most account categories, but not for the following:

- Income
- Cost of Goods Sold
- Expense
- Other Income
- Other Expense

Explanation of Accounts and Subaccounts

Let's look at these accounts and subaccounts.

Checking. You should only need one checking account, as keeping one checking account for expenses and another for client transactions will involve a lot of funds transfers back and forth, as either account runs low. This checking account will see a lot of activity, and you'll be in it constantly.

Savings. I have one savings account, and split it into two subaccounts to track 1) a general savings fund, and 2) a Bad Debt Reserve fund. Both are kept in the same savings account as far as deposits, withdrawals, and bank statements are concerned (the "parent" savings account), yet I can distinguish between the two on paper by using the distinct subaccounts.

To establish and build up the Bad Debt Reserve, at the end of each month I take a percentage of total factoring fees earned (usually 10 to 20%) and transfer that amount from checking into the Bad Debt Reserve savings account. That account builds up over time, and if a client's factoring account goes bad, I can replenish the money lost in the bad debt from this savings subaccount back into checking, for future invoices. I'm also earning a little interest when nothing is taken from it and money remains in the account. More on recording a bad debt in a minute.

Advances. Notice that under Advances, Rebates, and Client Reserves, there's a subacccount for each client, using the client codes (the first three letters of the company name – BAC, JER, etc.). Each time an advance is made, the check is made out to the client and the Account entry is, for example, "Advances:BAC." Once this check is entered, the balance for the client's Advance account appears in the Chart of Accounts window, and the total of all client advances is shown in the balance of the Advances account.

The type of account for Advances is Other Current Asset because you are owed for the advances you've paid for client invoices. While it would make sense to make the type of this account Accounts Receivable (which in turn would provide nice aging reports in QuickBooks®), only one A/R entry is allowed per transaction. So when you make a deposit of multiple checks from various customers, you would need to make multiple entries of Advances, one for each payment. Since QuickBooks® doesn't allow more than one A/R or A/P entry per transaction, Advances need to be tracked as Other Current Asset, which can be entered multiple times in a transaction. Though you lose the benefit of aging reports this way, the factoring database software products described earlier each provide various aging reports. Therefore you really don't need this feature in QuickBooks®.

Rebates. Like Advances, there's a subaccount for each client. As we'll see below, when a customer check is received, part of that payment is posted to the client's rebate account, e.g. "Rebates:BAC." If a rebate check is not created immediately, there will be a balance in the client's subaccount and "parent" Rebates account, showing rebate money is owed since I have not as yet prepared a rebate check.

The type of account for Rebates is Other Current Liabilities because you owe your client money for rebates once a customer pays a factored invoice. The reason the type is not Accounts Payable is the same as described for Advances above: you can't have more than one A/P entry per transaction, and you need to be able to enter multiple rebates on deposits of checks from customers.

Unfactored Invoices. Occasionally you will receive customer payments for invoices that weren't factored. These funds are not your money and you owe the client for the amount of unfactored invoices you receive. That makes these Other Current Liabilities because you will be paying the amount back soon. Like rebates, this is an account you should keep at a zero balance because money placed in this account is money you owe a client and need to pay back, usually promptly. If you routinely keep it at zero, and find there is a balance in the account, you're alerted to the need to prepare a check to pay back the unfactored invoice.

Credit Cards. Keep a separate account for each business credit card you have, and don't charge personal expenses on a business credit card. Don't co-mingle personal credit cards with your business account; in other words, use a distinct credit card for your business expenses that you don't use for personal expenses. This makes tracking business expenses a lot easier.

Client Reserves. As described in the chapter "Reducing Your Risk," I keep a separate reserve account for each client. This reserve amount is a portion of each rebate, so a separate entry for this Client Reserve from each customer payment is needed until the client's Reserve cap is attained. Each client has a Client Reserve subaccount, e.g. "Client Reserves:BAC." The type of account for Client Reserves is Long Term Liability because the reserves are held indefinitely, until either they are needed to cover an unpaid or short paid invoice, or the client stops factoring and the reserve amount is given back to him.

Loans. If you have borrowed money from more than one person or organization, you need a separate subaccount for each loan. For example, keep an Owner Loan subaccount for money that comes from your own resources, plus another for money loaned by Sam Roberts, and another for funds loaned by Julia Smith. These subaccounts would be named Loan:Owner, Loan:Roberts, and Loan:Smith. These loans are Long Term Liabilities because you owe this money for the long term; you will not pay it back soon after you receive it.

Broker Fees Income. This Income account is separate from Factoring Fees, and represents the portion of each fee you make that is paid the broker. You can make Broker Fees a subaccount of Fees, but since you'll have a separate subaccount for each Broker, data entry is easier if Broker Fees is its own account.

You must claim Broker Fees Income as income to IRS, because it is a portion of the total fee you earn. You're separating it here for the sake of bookkeeping and tracking, but it is part of the fee income you make from factored invoices, and as such it's taxable.

Fees. Fees are an Income account split into two subcategories, Billing Fees and Factoring Fees, because you probably will want to track these two sources of income.

Billing fees are extra fees you may charge for preparing and sending invoices for clients, if that is your arrangement. Factoring Fees are those you earn from each factored invoice (e.g. 5% of the invoice's face value when paid in 30 days), and will probably be the bulk of your income. You could create a sub-subaccount for Factoring Fees from each client, but that's not really necessary and may slow down data entry you make routinely in QuickBooks®.

Broker Fees Expense. Like Broker Fees Income, you'll want to maintain a separate subaccount for each broker. When you pay them each month, the broker's Expense subaccount is charged.

Due Diligence. Costs of credit reports, UCC searches and filings, and anything to check out prospective clients and customers is posted as a Due Diligence expense.

Loan Interest. Each month, quarter, or whenever you make payments to your lenders, you charge the interest portion of the payment to Loan Interest expense.

Interest Income. Any income you make from savings accounts or other invested money that earns interest is posted to this Income account. Do not put your income from Factoring Fees here because that is not Interest Income.

Other Income and Other Expenses. Miscellaneous income and expenses which don't fit into other categories go here.

Sample Bookkeeping Transactions

Using the sample factoring transactions from the previous chapter, let's make the corresponding entries in QuickBooks® using the Accounts and subaccounts we've established. If you use one of the Factoring Software applications described earlier, the bookkeeping entries and how funds are split between accounts can be exported to QuickBooks®. This will save you an enormous amount of data entry time, once you get both QuickBooks® and your database program configured.

If you use spreadsheets, the spreadsheet will calculate your splits (advances, rebates, fees, etc.) and then you must manually enter these into QuickBooks®. This isn't too bad if you have only a couple clients, but can become more and more time-consuming as your portfolio grows. This is yet another reason to use a good dedicated factoring database program. Learn how each handles this import/export function because a program that does this efficiently will save you countless hours.

What follows are the steps to take for manual entry of the QuickBooks® information for advances, rebates, fees, and so on.

Advances. When you receive a new Schedule with factored invoices you are going to buy, use your client's Schedule and/or your factoring software to determine the amount of the advance. When you are satisfied the invoices on the Schedule are ready to purchase – for our example, the invoices on Schedule JON-1 in the last chapter, enter the following into the QuickBooks® check entry screen (or Checking Account register):

Pay to the Order of: Jones Computer Peripherals

Account	Amount	Memo	Customer:Job
Advances:JON	$5,560.60	JON 1	(empty)

The check is cut and payment deposited into the client's account via customer pickup, bank branch deposit, mail, overnight, ACH, or wire. The client's Advance subaccount (Advances:JON) now has a balance of $5,560.60, and the "parent" Advances account increases by the same amount.

Payments. A month later, the first payment for an invoice on this Schedule is received: $539.50 from Customer Service Company for invoice #1052 (referred to as JON 1.2 – the second invoice on Jones' first Schedule). You endorse the check and on the check stub (or on a copy of the check if no stub in provided) enter the splits which are assigned to this payment: Advance, Rebate, Fee, Broker Fee, and Reserve. This entry with the corresponding dollar amounts has been made on the sample in the previous chapter.

To enter this payment in QuickBooks®, create a new deposit and enter the total of the check in the Deposit column for this entry. Next, click the Splits button and make the following entries:

Account	Amount	Memo	Customer:Job
Advances:JON	$377.65	JON 1.2	Customer Svc. Co.
Rebates:JON	$107.89	JON 1.2	Customer Svc. Co.
Fees:Factoring Fees	$22.93	JON 1.2	Customer Svc. Co.
Broker Fees Income:Bkr A	$4.05	JON 1.2	Customer Svc. Co.
Client Reserves:JON	$26.98	JON 1.2	Customer Svc. Co.

If there are other checks with factored payments to be added to this deposit, include them after these entries in the same way. Be sure the total showing in the register's Deposit column equals the same amount the check/s add up to on your deposit slip.

When the above entries are made, you'll notice a change in the Chart of Accounts balances for the Advances, Rebates, and Client Reserves. The Advances ("parent" account and Advances:JON subaccount) will decrease by $377.65 each; the Rebates ("parent" account and Rebates:JON subaccount) will increase by $107.89 each; and the Client Reserves ("parent" account and Client Reserves:JON) will increase by $26.98 each.

You'll leave the Reserves account alone unless Jones has exceeded his Reserve account cap. For my clients, this cap is 10% of a client's credit limit. Thus a client with a $10,000 credit limit has a Reserve cap of $1,000. If his reserve cap is not yet met, you have just added to the reserve. This reserve will help pay back this client's customers' unpaid or short paid invoices. If this entry takes them over the cap, prepare to give them a refund of the difference between the Reserve cap and the amount now in their Reserve.

You'll do nothing more with the Advances account and Advances:JON subaccount. This payment simply decreases the amount of advances you have on the street.

Unfactored invoices. If payment is received for an unfactored invoice, enter it this way:

Account	Amount	Memo	Customer:Job
Unfactored Invoices	$500.00	Inv #751	XYZ Mfg. Co.

Paying a client for an unfactored check is simple: make a new entry to pay your client (or add it to another check you've already prepared for the client) and post it to Unfactored Invoices like this:

Pay to the Order of: Jones Computer Peripherals

Account	Amount	Memo	Customer:Job
Unfactored Invoices	$500.00	Inv #751	XYZ Mfg. Co.

Rebates. Since you've received a payment for the factored invoice from Customer Service Company, the Rebates account and Rebates:JON subaccount will both no longer be 0, but $107.89. This means you have a rebate that is now payable. Therefore, prepare a check to Jones Computer Peripherals and date it for the day you plan to pay the rebate due. Here's what the rebate check entry will look like:

Pay to the Order of: Jones Computer Peripherals

Account	Amount	Memo	Customer:Job
Rebates:JON	$107.89	JON 1.2	Customer Svc. Co.

If you pay rebates once a week or once a month, add future rebates to this check in the same way, and pay the check on the date the rebate is due.

You can also add the client's next advance to the rebate check if desired. A check with this rebate and the next advance would look like this:

Pay to the Order of: Jones Computer Peripherals

Account	Amount	Memo	Customer:Job
Rebates:JON	$107.89	JON 1.2	Customer Svc. Co.
Advances:JON	$4,801.60	JON 2	(empty)

You can also add the unfactored invoice payment to a rebate and/or advance check in the same way. A check with all three of these – a rebate, an unfactored payment, and the next advance – would look like this:

Pay to the Order of: Jones Computer Peripherals

Account	Amount	Memo	Customer:Job
Rebates:JON	$107.89	JON 1.2	Customer Svc. Co.
Unfactored Invoices	$500.00	Inv #751	XYZ Mfg. Co.
Advances:JON	$4,801.60	JON 2	(empty)

Broker Fee Payments. If there is a broker, you need to put the broker fee due into a check for the broker, which will be paid on the first of the following month. Here's what that check entry will look like:

Pay to the Order of: Factoring Brokers Inc.

Account	Amount	Memo	Customer:Job
Broker Fees Expense: Broker A	$4.05	JON 1.2	Customer Svc. Co.

Loan Interest Payments. To keep regular monthly payments simple, I pay brokers and lenders at the same time (the first of each month). Many factors do so on the 10th, in order to give a little time for accounts to settle at the end of the month. While it helps to keep a running tab of what you owe brokers, the amount paid lenders will usually be the same from month to month, unless a lender increases the amount of money loaned. When you prepare the interest check to a lender, include with your check a Lender Report as described in the chapter "Money, Money, Money." Here's how the check will be entered:

Pay to the Order of: Sam Roberts

Account	Amount	Memo	Customer:Job
Loan Interest	$100.00	June	(empty)

Charge Backs. If you are a recourse factor and a customer doesn't pay (or short pays a significant amount) – or if you're a non-recourse factor and a customer disputes an invoice, refusing to pay – you are in a situation where the client owes you money. To account for this condition, you need to create charge backs to cover what you are owed for your advance, fee, and broker fee. Here's what you do.

Create a simple form called a Charge back Record. Mine looks like this:

Charge Back Record

Date	Schedule	Customer	Total	Adv.	Fee	Bkr Fee

Now let's suppose a $1,000 invoice is not paid and you are owed money. With the 80% advance you gave and a 15% fee at 90 days, and a broker fee of 15% of your fee, the breakdown of the debt looks like this:

Advance:	$800.00
Fee:	127.50
Broker Fee:	22.50
Total Charge back:	$950.00

To document your charge back, fill in the Charge Back Record this way:

Charge Back Record

Date	Schedule	Customer	Total	Adv.	Fee	Bkr Fee
6/22	JON 5.3	Nopay Corp.	$950.00	$800.00	$127.50	$22.50

If there is at least $950.00 in the client's Reserve account, you can make a separate QuickBooks® entry that will zero out. That is, the total payment for the entry will equal zero – you neither owe nor or are owed any money. The transaction looks like this:

Account	Amount	Memo	Customer:Job
Advances:JON	-$800.00	JON 5.3 adv chgbk	Nopay Co.
Fees:Factoring Fees	-$127.50	JON 5.3 fee chgbk	Nopay Co.
Broker Fees Income: Broker A	-$22.50	JON 5.3 bfee chgbk	Nopay Co.
Client Reserves:JON	$950.00		

Net payment: $0.00

If the client has less than $950 in his Reserve account, the shortfall will have to be made up from other rebates, future advances, and/or cash from the client. Suppose the client has zero in his Reserve account, but you owe him $200 in rebates and he's factoring a new invoice for $2,000 with an 80% advance. Here's how the entry looks:

Pay to the Order of: Jones Computer Peripherals

Account	Amount	Memo	Customer:Job
Advances:JON	-$800.00	JON 5.3 adv chgbk	Nopay Co.
Fees:Factoring Fees	-$127.50	JON 5.3 fee chgbk	Nopay Co.
Broker Fees Income: Broker A	-$22.50	JON 5.3 bfee chgbk	Nopay Co.
Rebates:JON	$200.00	JON 4.4 rebate	Kent Schools
Advances:JON	$1,600.00	JON 7 advance	(empty)

Net payment: $850.00

In this transaction, you write a check for $850.00 ($1,600 + $200.00 – ($800.00 + $127.50 + $22.50), while still receiving the money owed you in charge backs.

If a client has no further rebates due and his business is too slow to provide enough new invoices to cover the charge backs, you can see how his Reserve account can be very helpful: the client keeps his account out of the red, and you are assured of payment for charge backs that are due. If you build up and maintain a Reserve for most if not all of your clients, sooner or later some of these accounts will be used...count on it. If you never keep a Reserve account for any client, sooner or later you'll wish you had.

Bad Debts. What do you do when a customer never pays an invoice, the client goes out of business and cannot pay it back, and you must charge it off to bad debt? First of all, as mentioned earlier you have already established a Bad Debt Reserve subaccount of your savings account. Second, establish a Bad Debt account whose type is Expense.

When you charge off the bad debt, open the client's Advance subaccount (Other Current Assets) and in the Decrease column, type the amount of the advance/s you're writing off. Post this to the Bad Debt account (Expenses) to remove it from this client's Advances subaccount. That decreases client's Advance subaccount (Other Current Assets) to zero, and creates an entry that shows up on your P & L report as an expense.

If you have plenty of factoring funds available, that's all you have to do. However, if you need to replenish funds lost to bad debt to have more factoring capital available, make one more entry. Go into your Bad Debt Reserve savings subaccount and transfer the amount of the write off (add the fee you've lost if you choose and post that amount as Fees:Factoring Fees); charge this against your checking account. Then transfer funds from savings to checking. That will diminish your Bad Debt Reserve funds, and increase your funds available for buying new invoices. Then continue to add money to the Bad Debt Reserve savings subaccount every month to build it back up.

Reports

Two Reports you will probably refer to frequently are the Profit & Loss Report (also known as an Income Statement) and Balance Sheet.

Profit & Loss. This report provides the total of all your company's income accounts, the total of all your expenses, and the difference between them for a given period – a day, a week, a month, a quarter, a year. In short, this shows if your company is profitable or not. If you're spending less than your making (as mentioned in the chapter "Break-Even Analysis") you're profitable for that period of time.

When you run a Profit & Loss report you will first see a list of your Income accounts and subaccounts, and the amount of income each account and subaccount has generated for the time period. Below this is a list of your Expense accounts and subaccounts that had activity for that period of time. The difference, as net income or loss, is at the bottom. Here is a sample monthly Profit & Loss Statement.

ABC Financial Services
Profit & Loss
June

	Jun	
Ordinary Income/Expense		
Income		
Broker Fees Income		
Broker A	105.50	
Broker B	48.54	
Broker C	127.56	
Total Broker Fees Income		281.60
Fees		
Billing Fees	250.00	
Factoring Fees	5,654.10	
Total Fees		5,904.10
Total Income		6,185.70
Expense		
Bank Service Charges	15.00	
Broker Fees Expense		
Broker A	87.25	
Broker B	75.64	
Broker C	155.28	
Total Broker Fees Expense		318.17
Charitable Donations	150.00	
Due Diligence	75.00	
Interest Expense		
Loan Interest	500.00	
Total Interest Expense		500.00
Internet Expenses		
Cable Modem	50.71	
Web Site expenses	19.95	
Total Internet Expenses		70.66
Office Supplies	160.34	
Overnight Delivery & Wires	40.00	

Payroll Expenses		
Officer Salary	3,000.00	
Total Payroll Expenses		3,000.00
Telephone		
Cell Phone	57.27	
Office Phone & LD	86.74	
Total Telephone		144.01
Uncategorized Expenses	0.00	
Total Expense		4,084.35
Net Ordinary Income		2,101.35
Other Income/Expense		
Other Income		
Interest Income	8.94	
Total Other Income		8.94
Net Other Income	8.94	
Net Income		2,110.29

Balance Sheet

A Balance Sheet is a snapshot on a given day of your company's assets and liabilities; the difference between them is your equity. The larger your equity, the more stable is your company.

ABC Financial Services
Balance Sheet
As of June 7

ASSETS		June 7
Current Assets		
Checking/Savings		
Ckg	24,675.33	
Savings		
Bad Debt Reserve	5,244.99	
General	15,185.29	
Total Savings		20,430.28
Total Checking/Savings		45,105.61
Other Current Assets		
Advances		
BAC	14,652.20	
JAC	17,826.45	
WER	15,622.80	
VAR	10,800.00	
Total Advances		58,901.45
Total Other Current Assets		58,901.45
Total Current Assets		104,007.06
TOTAL ASSETS		104,007.06
LIABILITIES & EQUITY		
Liabilities		
Current Liabilities		
Credit Cards		
Visa	1,224.51	
Total Credit Cards	1,224.51	

Other Current Liabilities		
Rebates		
BAC	30.22	
JAC	15.63	
WER	225.00	
VAR	120.00	
Total Rebates	390.85	
Unfactored invoices	742.83	
Total Other Current Liabilities		1,133.68
Total Current Liabilities		2,358.19
Long Term Liabilities		
Client Reserves		
BAC	763.67	
JAC	1,000.01	
WER	449.10	
VAR	128.85	
Total Client Reserves		2,341.63
Loans		
Owner Loan	60,000.00	
Roberts Loan	10,000.00	
Smith Loan	10,000.00	
Total Loans		80,000.00
Total Long Term Liabilities		82,341.63
Total Liabilities		84,699.82
Equity		
Retained Earnings	2,670.24	
Net Income	2,841.16	
Total Equity		19,307.24
TOTAL LIABILITIES & EQUITY		104,007.06

QuickBooks® provides a huge array of other reports; spending a few minutes with an accountant or bookkeeper will help you learn the value of some of these reports and how to use them in determining the overall health of your company. But for the sake of this book, the above information should be enough to get you started.

Other Bookkeeping Methods

Other factors have developed their own system of bookkeeping with QuickBooks® or other accounting software. What's been presented works for me, but I quickly acknowledge alternative ways of tracking your business income and expenses. Kari and Kevin Clark of Premier Funding in Lebanon, Oregon, who are contributors of one of the case studies in the book *Factoring Case Studies,* provide one such alternative. Here is a simple outline of the QuickBooks® entries Kari makes when making advances and rebates.

I. Advances
When purchasing invoices from a client

A) Create Bills
   1. On tool bar click picture of Bill
   2. Select Vendor (client)
   3. Set terms to 30 days
   4. Date = date of advance
   5. Ref. Number = Invoice Number
   6. Amount Due = amount of actual invoice
   7. Bill due is already entered the same date as the date of invoice
   8. Account: Your business checking account name
   9. Memo = Location of job (Optional) or Schedule reference (e.g. JON 1.2)
   10. Customer = name of your client's customer
   11. Click Next (do not click ok until all bills are entered
   12. When complete, click ok

B) Create Invoices
    1. Activities, Create invoices
    2. In drop down box, select customer
    3. Date = date of advance
    4. Invoice Number
    5. Terms
    6. Item – Drop down box, and select invoice
    7. Description = Invoice number
    8. Quantity = number of dollars, i.e. actual invoice amount (100 = $100)
    9. Rate (is already entered in) & Amount (Automatically entered)

C) Pay Bills (80% Advance)
    1. Activities
    2. Pay Bills
    3. In Amount paid column, enter actual advance (80%)
    4. When finished, click OK

D) Print Check
    1. Click on picture of check
    2. In memo section, type ADVANCE (optional)
    3. Click OK
    4. File
    5. Print Forms
    6. Print Checks

If there are more invoices than what fits on the voucher part of the check, click on the picture of the check, then, with the check still on the screen, click on the Tool Bar REPORTS, then OTHER REPORTS, then CHECK DETAIL. Make sure the date is correct (or it will show all checks you've written for the month). Print out the report and attach it to the check voucher for your client. Use this also for the REBATE, if necessary.

II) Rebates
When a Customer pays

A) Receive Payments
1. Activities, Receive Payments
2. Customer Job, drop down box select customer (or type the first couple letters of the Customer's name and it will appear automatically)
3. Date Payment Received
4. Amount of check
5. Check Number
6. Click Deposit to proper account (Should automatically show your business acct. name)
7. Click Clear Payments
8. Click next to invoices to be paid with this check. If the amount paid for a particular invoice is less than what is owed, you will have to enter that amount manually.
9. Click either NEXT if there are more checks to record, or OK if that is all

B) Pay Bills
1. Activities, Pay Bills
2. Click "Show All Bills"
3. Mark bills paid one at a time
4. Click Discount info. and apply proper discount. (4%, 6%, etc.)
5. Click OK to complete

Print checks
1. On Menu bar, click on picture of check
2. In memo section of check, type "Rebate"
3. File, forms, print checks

Part 4

Enrichment

21
Factoring Resources

There are numerous resources available to help a small factor get started and then continue the business over time. Some of those listed below, such as products and services provided by the author, are targeted for people just starting out. Others provide information or services for those who have been factoring for some time.

Becoming familiar with all of these early on will help not only as you start factoring, but as your business matures and you find the need for more sophisticated resources or expertise.

Resources for New Small Factors

SmallFactor.com

www.SmallFactor.com is hosted by the author and offers the following features:

- A portal site with links and resources related to many services and products needed by small factors. These include links to:
  - marketing
  - due diligence
  - factoring exchanges
  - software
  - office needs
  - publications
  - related services
  - and much more.
- Lists of screened small factors in North America who purchase receivables too small for larger factors (sorted by state)
- FAQs

FactorTips

"What Small Factors Need to Know," *FactorTips* is published monthly and emailed free to subscribers. Each issue includes a featured article, free giveaways, announcements, classified ads, a featured reader's web site, and more.

Dash Point Publishing, Inc.

Dash Point Publishing, Inc. produces numerous resources for new small factors which can be purchased from its web site as well as by phone, fax, mail, or email.

Web Site

www.DashPointPublishing.com provides an online catalog with a shopping cart for ordering the following items.

Software
Record Keeping Templates
Files in MS Word & Excel format for PC
Download from www.DashPointPublishing.com
Buy and download these files to save hours of typing or scanning. All Record Keeping documents used in this book are available and spreadsheet calculation formulas are included. Available from web site, via email, or included in The Small Factor Resource Collection (see below). $39.95

Names of the documents are:

ACH Direct Deposit Form	Factoring Record
Agreement for Factored Pmts	Lender Agreement
Application Form	Lender Report
AR Purchase Agreement	Notice of Assignment
Charge Back Record	Personal Guaranty
Client's Letters to Customers	Projected Budgets
Corporate Resolution	Promissory Notes A and B
Customer Contact Sheet	Proposed Budget
Customer's Letter of Acceptance	Schedule of Accounts
Delivery of Funds	Telephone Log
Discount Schedule	Term Sheet
Factoring Checklist	UCC1 Wording
Factoring Profitability Calculator	Verification Form

APR & Income Calculator

The returns you can make factoring small receivables are consistent and high. Want to see immediately not only your APR returns, but what can be made monthly, yearly, and over 5 years? These calculators will show you in seconds.

The two Excel spreadsheets are available in one file and instantly calculate your:

- Annual Percentage Rate (APR) Returns on factored funds, plus
- Projected Income based on the volume you factor and your advances, fees, etc.

©2002 Download $5.95

Factor Consultation Form

This easy-to-follow form helps prospective factoring clients determine if a factor provides the services he needs. In a simple Word document, this form walks the business owner through the discussion, providing the important questions to ask and space to write the answers.

©2003 Download $3.95

Books
The Small Factor Series
Includes:

1. *Factoring Fundamentals*
   How You Can Make Large Returns Investing in Small Receivables
   ©2003   Paperback $14.95   eBook $9.95

2. *Factoring Small Receivables*
   How to Make Money in Little Deals the Big Guys Brush Off
   ©1995, 1996, 1998, 2001, 2002, 2003 (6th edition)
   Paperback $49.95   eBook $39.95

3. *Factoring Case Studies*
   Learn and Profit from Experienced Small Factors
   ©2003   Paperback $14.95   eBook $9.95

4. *Unlocking the Cash in Your Company*
How to Get Unlimited Funds without a Loan
©2003   Paperback $12.95   eBook $8.95
Quantity discounts and private labeling are available for the paperback version. Factors and brokers ordering in quantity can have their logo on the cover and a customized first page.

Booklet
Growing Your Company without Debt:
How Today's Small Business Can Get Cash by Tomorrow
A brief introduction to factoring for prospective clients
©1996, 1998 $3.25 ea.
                        Quantity discounts available
        eBook $1.95

Bundles
DashPointPublishing.com bundles many of its products that save money and answer specific factoring needs. For a current listing go to the web site's Catalog and click on Bundles.

More Resources

Associations
International Factoring Association
The goal of the International Factoring Association (IFA) is to provide "information, training, purchasing power and a resource for the Factoring community." It highlights developments and changes in the industry and provides a forum for educational meetings and seminars.

Membership is open to all banks and finance companies that, regardless of size, perform financing through the purchase of invoices of other types of accounts receivable. Their membership directory includes company information, specialties, and links to their web sites and allows you to search for factors in a specific industry or areas of the country.

Member services include a quarterly newsletter, a web site forum, an annual convention (see below for each of these), links to factoring-related sites from IFA's web site, plus a list of vendors with products or services of benefit to the factoring industry. These vendors include attorneys, UCC search firms, funding sources, and many more. In addition to Qualified Vendors there are also IFA Endorsed Vendors who will offer discounts or preferred services to IFA members. The scope and number of vendors in their database, and the services they provide, are truly vast and cover every conceivable facet of factoring you can think of and will ever need.

The IFA's web home page is www.factoring.org. Membership is $200 per year to companies that fund transactions; people who are strictly brokers may not participate as members. The resources the IFA provides are extremely helpful to factors of any size. Browsing their web site before becoming a member doesn't really give you a feel for the scope of what they offer. But once you join and open the door to their vendor lists, forums and newsletter, you'll feel a bit like Dorothy as she opened the door to the Land of Oz…suddenly everything is in vivid color and you realize you're not in Kansas any more.

To join, submit your company information via email to info@factoring.org. You'll need to confirm that you are a funding source and not just brokering transactions.

American Cash Flow Association

The American Cash Flow Association® (ACFA) started in the late 1980's as an organization to train brokers in the discounted mortgage and factoring fields. It has evolved to cover a broad range of cash flow instruments and funding sources, and now trains people to be cash flow consultants in over 60 identified cash flow streams.

Their literature says, "The cash flow industry helps individuals and businesses convert payments they receive over time–from privately held mortgages or other installment contracts, business notes, invoices, structured settlements…or a variety of other debt instruments–into a lump sum of cash today."

It describes itself as "a national member organization serving the cash flow industry which fosters growth, pioneers advancement of the industry and supports its membership with products and services. The Association promotes professional standards and provides a forum for communication, including the exchanges of ideas and transaction of business, leading to success in the cash flow industry."

Those who attend their training seminars automatically gain membership while others may join at a cost of $149 to $599 per year. It has numerous local chapters scattered across North America, produces a monthly journal and sponsors an annual convention (see below for both). Begin surfing their extensive web site at www.acfa-cashflow.com/about/about.htm.

Training

Dash Point Publishing

In addition to the numerous books and other resources provided, the author provides e-course offerings in factoring. Utilizing *The Small Factor Series* as reference texts, these lessons are sent via email to participants for in-home study. Further information about this training can be found at www.DashPointPublishing.com.

Distinctive Solutions

Distinctive Solutions offers an on-site course in California for those interested in further study in the factoring industry. Designed to give you the information needed to begin financing receivables, participants are also provided the legal forms and documents, prepared specifically to their needs.

Topics are:

1. OVERVIEW
   - Credit Philosophy
   - Factoring
   - Market Place
   - Competition
   - Personnel

2. UNDERWRITING
   - Qualifying Clients
   - Rating Account Debtors
   - Account Maintenance
3. MARKETING
   - Existing Bank Customers
   - Prospect Lists
   - Advertising
   - Referrals
   - Cross Selling
4. PRICING
   - Risk Pricing
   - Competitive Pricing
   - Service
   - Pricing Models
5. LEGAL AND OTHER DOCUMENTATION
6. ACCOUNTING

To learn more, go to Distinctive Solutions' web site at www.dissol.com and click the Products link. From there you can submit a form requesting further information.

FactorHelp, Inc.

FactorHelp, Inc. provides manuals, handbooks, and legal/audit forms specifically for people having very significant funds with which to factor. Each resource comes with a CD and is described at www.FactorHelp.com, where you can order. This material is not intended for the casual, part-time, or small factor; rather, their audience is factors with operating capital well into seven-figures. Below is a summary of their products and prices.

Factoring Operations Manual provides step-by-step details on how to operate your factoring business: from underwriting new business, to portfolio monitoring, to workouts, and everything in between. Price: $5,750.00.

Factoring Employee Handbook is ready for your employees and management personnel. This handbook was written by a lawyer and HR expert, covers all important policies, and complies with EEOC and FMLA requirements. Price: $99.95.

Factoring Accounting Manual details the proper accounting methods for accounts receivable that are being factored. This manual includes a sample chart of accounts, different methodology for tracking reserves, how to guide your clients on the proper accounting methods for booking factoring transactions, and much more. Price: $395.00.

Factoring A/R Audit Forms help you effectively evaluate new clients and mitigate risks. These forms are Excel spreadsheets with automatic calculations included. Enter your client's raw data into the spreadsheets and print the results. Price: $99.95.

Factoring Business Plan Template offers a template specifically written for the factoring industry. This professional Business Plan includes sections on start-up budgeting, financial projections and industry data. Price: $695.00.

Lenders' Podium

Lenders' Podium is an independent, attorney-run organization which promotes continuing education in the organization, operation, and administration of commercial lending and factoring businesses. It regularly sponsors conferences across the country covering all aspects of secured lending and factoring. These conferences feature up-to-date information about legal and business developments in the commercial lending industry.

Lenders' Podium's factoring conference is entitled *The Law and Business of Factoring* and is usually offered a couple times each year. Taught by attorney Robert A. Zadek, this 2-day course includes a full set of legal forms he developed which are designed to help novices and seasoned factoring professionals, attorneys, and accountants build and strengthen their factoring know-how. His unique program devotes considerable time to revenue enhancing techniques and will increase your awareness of the factoring industry's challenges and opportunities.

This information is most beneficial for those who intend to factor at a serious level. While the information will help factors of any size, the material generally assumes those in attendance run full-time factoring operations. Registration and further information can be obtained at www.lenderspodium.com.

Mr. Zadek's legal documents are remarkably extensive and protect his clients who are factors quite completely. People who read them for the first time are often overwhelmed with their sheer length. However, as he points out, to be completely protected, factors with significant amounts of capital at risk need what's there. If you intend to invest significant funds in your factoring business, Mr. Zadek's material is extremely valuable and well worth the expense. I wholeheartedly recommend his products and services to those who have serious money invested in factoring.

His material is created from the perspective that factors with significant funds will need to go to court to collect from a problem client. These documents protect you in court, and are necessary if tens or hundreds of thousands of dollars or more are at stake. In such situations, the legal process is usually the only way to recoup such funds, and spending many thousands of dollars in legal expenses is necessary and worth the cost.

However, for those who intend to start and remain small, going to court to recover $5,000 or $10,000 will probably not justify the expense such cases require. While large factors protect themselves by going to court, small factors protect themselves by keeping their exposures low. When a (relatively small) loss occurs, they simply turn the problem over to collections, write off those which are uncollectible, and move on. Once again we come face to face with the Cardinal Rule of Money.

SubFactors.com

Readers of *Factoring Fundamentals,* Book 1 in this series, will recall six types of receivables I suggest small factors avoid. One of these six is construction because of the higher risks involved in this industry.

However, Ken Earnhardt of KLT&J, Inc., has created a program called SubFactors.com. This franchise provides a complete training program for factoring small construction subcontractors, and is based on Ken's considerable experience in factoring these particular receivables.

If you have little exposure to the construction industry and do not have a SubFactors.com franchise, I still recommend you avoid these receivables. However, if you enroll as a franchisee in Ken's program and follow this program very carefully, you will benefit from his wealth of expertise and can make very impressive returns in this particular factoring niche.

Ken has been a small factor since 1984 and is one of the contributors to Book 3 in this series, *Factoring Case Studies.* I have had the pleasure of knowing and working with him and can vouch for both his expertise and his sincere interest in helping people.

SubFactors.com was borne out of a desire to assist small subcontractors convert their accounts receivable into cash through a network of small factors. This is a comprehensive franchise program that provides all the necessary tools, information, and know-how to:

- Minimize your risk through strategic alliances and transaction limits
- Track and monitor each transaction using BluBeagle™ factoring software
- Set up necessary accounting procedures
- Market your services
- Complete necessary documentation
- Protect your investment in each transaction.

If you are interested in becoming a SubFactors.com franchisee you may request further information from their website at www.SubFactors.com or by calling toll free 877-971-3883.

Broker Training

Some small factors find brokers are a good source of new business, and that brokering larger deals themselves leads to additional income. Below are two organizations which provide either a place to locate brokers, and/or training resources for becoming a broker.

American Cash Flow Association

As mentioned above, the ACFA is an organization which trains brokers in numerous cash flows instruments, one of which is factoring. Training courses are 3-day classes offered throughout the country on a regular basis. While this organization does not provide instruction to students to become funding sources, many go on to be financial participants in these investments.

The ACFA provides various levels of broker training and as described elsewhere, and resources to help both their graduates and funding sources. These resources including post-training support, a large annual convention, a monthly journal, and more.

The Commercial Finance Institute

This organization provides a comprehensive manual which prepares finance consultants to be brokers in factoring and equipment leasing. Written by practicing factoring and equipment leasing professionals, the manual provides concise and detailed industry-specific information in these two fields.

The manual's factoring section provides details on the general practice of factoring, an extensive marketing section, and a business section. Those who wish to gain further brokering and marketing information will find this manual helpful.

The manual is available for $139 plus $6.99 shipping from The Commercial Finance Institute, PO Box 25992, Greenville, SC 29616. Tel 864-963-7800.

Periodicals

The Commercial Factor

IFA's quarterly newsletter, *The Commercial Factor,* is emailed to IFA members with e-mail addresses. Timely articles, factoring industry news, and vendor ads are instructive and include links to appropriate sites, email addresses, and anything else you would expect. Current and back issues are posted on their web site. To receive this free newsletter and email of upcoming events, send email to listserver@factoring.org and in the subject line type "Subscribe IFA."

American Cash Flow Journal®

With more than 25,000 readers the *American Cash Flow Journal®* reaches more people than any other publication of its kind. Published monthly by the American Cash Flow Association it includes articles and news pertaining to the cash flow industry in general, including factoring. This is a good place to see what's "out there" in the cash flow industry and the part factoring plays in it. This is also a place for display ads to invite brokers to bring you deals. ACFA members receive the *Journal* as part of their membership; nonmembers may subscribe for $99 per year. It is printed in newspaper tabloid format and sent U.S. Mail. Individual articles can be read from the web site at the link below. I write a regular column for small factors in this journal. Go to www.americancashflow.com/acfj or call 407-843-2032 for copies or subscription information.

Annual Conferences and Conventions

Annual Factoring Conference

The Annual Factoring Conference is put on by Distinctive Solutions and the IFA each spring in a different city yearly. Dedicated strictly to factoring issues, there are distinguished speakers and workshops covering a variety of topics of interest to factoring companies large and small. Many presenters are attorneys specializing in factoring issues. This conference is a must for those involved in factoring full-time with significant funds invested. You need not be a customer of Distinctive Solutions software to attend. For more information or to register call 800-563-1895 or log on at www.factoringconference.com.

Cash Flow Convention

The Cash Flow Convention of the American Cash Flow Association is held in a different city each year prior to and during Memorial Day weekend. This large convention (2000-3000 people) covers the entire cash flow industry with a host of speakers and workshops, as well as a large Exhibit Hall full of booths of numerous factoring firms, companies offering support services, and other funding companies. The other funding firms buy paper instruments such as real estate notes, business notes, tax lien certificates, structured settlements, annuities, judgments, etc. City attractions and "name" entertainment are part of each year's event. Get more information by calling 800-253-1294 or log on to www.americancashflow.com and click the link to the Cash Flow Convention.

Both Distinctive Solutions and the ACFA sell CDs and cassette tapes of presentations from previous conventions.

Factoring Exchanges

The web has several sites which are either financial "matchmaking" services that pair companies seeking funding with companies providing funding, or are run by brokers which do the matchmaking themselves. Some deal only with factoring while others include factoring as just one of many arrows in their financial quiver.

A few of the sites befitting small factors are reviewed below; there are many more out there. The reasons for their omission is either 1) they target larger funding companies, 2) are brokers whose sites don't provide a means for factors to become a part of their network, or 3) I'm just not aware of them. As with factoring software, the information changes frequently over time so don't be surprised if their services and/or rates you find differ from the time of this printing.

Factor Search
The IFA has a section of its web site called Factor Search which is accessible to members and businesses looking for a factor. The prospective client is asked to provide:
- General data (company name, address, etc.)
- Area of business specialty (choose from a list of 19 general industries)
- If their customers are domestic, import, or export
- Continent where customers are located
- Average monthly invoicing in U.S. dollars
- If receivables are currently used as collateral

- Names of three top customers (not to be contacted now)
- A brief description of the company seeking factoring

Factors also provide parameters they seek in clients and Factor Search does the matching. When a prospective client completes his information, a list of matching factoring companies and a contact name for each is presented. Factors that meet the business search criteria are notified by email of matches and may then contact the prospect. To view the form go to the IFA's home page at www.factoring.org and click on Factor Search.

American Capital Exchange

The American Cash Flow Association sponsors the American Capital Exchange. This provides anyone with sellable paper (accounts receivables, real estate notes, settlements, judgments, annuities, etc.) a means to find a buyer to cash them out. Also, enrolled broker consultants submit deals to enrolled funding sources here. Learn more about how the Exchange works at www.americancapitalexchange.com.

CFOL.com

CFOL.com stands for Commercial Finance Online and was started in 1993. CFOL.com bills itself as a "global finance engine." When you go to www.cfol.com and the home page opens, you'll see the left of the screen is intended for those seeking money, while the right is for those investing money.

If you click the left-side link called Funding for your Business you will be taken to a page that explains their EasyApply process. This says that after a prospective client completes the online form, EasyApply matches her information to its extensive membership of financial institutions and professionals. These include factors in addition to a host of other types of financiers, such as private investors, investment bankers, mortgage banks and brokers, asset-based lenders, commercial banks, financial consultants and money brokers, leasing companies, and many more.

Those using this service to find a funding source pay a one-time membership fee of $25. These are the steps for those seeking funds to use CFOL.com's database:

1. Fill out the membership application.
2. Login to your account.
3. Fill out the financial application.
4. Submit it to the entire CFOL.com database.
5. Search all you desire in the search engine.
6. Return as often as you like to submit again or redo your request.

After someone has become a member she may log into the system and fill out the request for funding. This request is then sent to every financial provider active in CFOL's system, of which there is a huge number.

What is unique about CFOL is the ability of registered funding seekers to enter a special members-only search engine. Once a funding seeker finds a good prospective funding source that she feels would have an interest in her financing, she can submit directly to that organization or individual the application she filled out.

A funding seeker can return as often as she likes, login to her member area and totally reconfigure her request. This means that if she have no success attracting a financial institute or individual, she just change any of her information and re-submit.

Funding sources begin participating in much the same way as those seeking funds, following these steps:

1. Fill out the membership application.
2. Login to your account.
3. Configure all your company information.
4. Configure all your employee accounts if you need them.
5. Search all you want in the search engine.

As a matching service rather than a broker, funding sources pay a flat fee to access the data base and no commissions are due once a factoring relationship has been established. Their fees are as follows:

12 Months Full Membership: Includes access to financial opportunities.	$999
3 Months Full Membership: Includes access to financial opportunities.	$399
1 Month Full Membership: Includes access to financial opportunities.	$199
1 Week Trial Membership: Sample the system.	$49

When filling out your membership registration form, you'll come to a section where you indicate the type of funding you provide. Include "Financing – Accounts Receivable" as well as the appropriate types of "Factoring," of which eight are specified.

Lenders Interactive Service

This is a handsome site with good ease of use and is somewhat similar to CFOL.com in its approach. As their name suggests, terminology and emphasis are on loans (consumer and business). However there are a number of factoring companies in their database and their search engine includes the categories "Factoring" and "Accounts Receivable Financing" when funding seekers select the kind of financing they want.

Searches are free for people looking for funding and they are not even required to register. They – or you – simply go to the home page, click on the big Search for a Business (Commercial) Loan button which takes you to a simple registration form. Fill in the form (or skip it) and go to the next page. There you fill in a simpler form indicating geographical area, type of financing sought, dollar amount, purpose of the "loan," and credit status. Click the Start Search button and poof! You get an instant list of funders with name, address, contact name, telephone, fax, email and web site with links, and a one-liner saying what they do. Very nicely done.

Funding sources can't browse the funding requests, but like most of the others you are emailed when a match is made. Clients are also likely to call you directly if they like your one-liner summary compared to what competitors say.

Here is text from the site's page describing LIS's services:

"What We Offer Our Members:

- Immediate e-mail of applicants that match your choices in four areas: location, dollar amount, type of financing, and industry. Plus, credit rating, property value/owing, annual gross/net, loan purpose and other information. Leads are always fresh – never recycled!

- Screened applicants, from our millions of hits, instantly Hyper-Linked to Your Website – Free!

- Free web page for annual members.

- Limited total membership to enable you to compete with only a few others – NOT the "feeding frenzy" of other programs.

- More effective advertising than banners or paid click-through programs that can cost many thousands per year – all click-throughs from LIS have been pre-screened to your exact lending profile!

- All loan types: Commercial, Consumer, Mortgages, etc.

- No Points! No Per-Lead Charges! No Click-Through Charges!

- LIS does not receive commissions – your only cost is your membership fee. (Prices listed below.) We accept check, Visa, Discover, or MC."

Out of curiosity, I ran a few searches as if I were a small manufacturing company in Washington state looking for factoring. With the dollar amount of $50,000 or higher, several factoring companies were found. However, when searching for $10,000, only one came up, and none appeared for $5,000. This reinforces the underlying premise of this book – most larger factors don't want small deals.

Like cfol.com, LIS is paid by membership fees charged the funding sources. Rates are based on length of time and number of states from which to receive prospective deals, as shown below.

	2 Months	6 Months	Yearly
1 state	$110	$235	$395
2-20 states	$210	$435	$730
21-50 states	$325	$650	$1070
Any/all foreign countries combined	$120	$245	$425

I like the tone and sense of dignity of Lenders Interactive Service. See for yourself at www.lendersinteractive.com.

Factors.com

This site does a good job of providing value for all three parties involved in factoring: clients, brokers, and factors. Here you will find listings of its factor members, plus a service called Factor Match, described below.

To assist clients and brokers, Factors.com has four indexes (lists) which sort the included factors by company name, state, industry, and volume. Each of these is nicely implemented and factors fitting the needs of any client can be found quickly. Just as clients can look for a factor here, brokers can use this site to quickly find a match for their clients, as well.

Clients wanting to learn more about factoring will find several articles on factoring from the Article Archive. A Glossary defines many factoring terms that might be unclear to newcomers. Ask the Experts provides a forum for posting any question you might have about factoring, and someone from their "Panel of Experts" will provide an answer. Previous questions and answers are listed for your perusal.

There is a Broker Index in addition to the four Factor Indexes. To be included, a broker must meet two criteria: 1) she must have been in business at least one year, and 2) the broker must have verifiable, proven brokering record with factors. On the registration form, a broker must list three factors with whom the broker has done business.

To find a broker using the Broker Index, click on its link and a list of states appears, and states in which brokers are listed stand out. Click on a state with a broker, and a list of the broker companies appears. Click on a broker company and you'll see his address, phone, web site, and email.

Factors pay to be listed on Factors.com. Here are their fees:

Membership Options:

Annual Charter Membership	$1,495
Annual Charter Membership excluding Factor Match Leads	$995
Monthly Charter Membership (3 mo. minimum)	$150
Monthly Charter Membership excluding Factor Match Leads (3 mo. minimum)	$100

Sponsorship Options:

Annual Basic Membership	$199
Featured Sponsorship - 6 months*	$1,495
Index Sponsorship - 6 months*	$695
Each Additional State - 6 months*	$150

*Annual membership required

There is also a Factor Resources page which lists businesses that provide services factors use, such as Consultants, Credit and Collections, Software, and others.

As its name suggests, Factor Match introduces prospective clients seeking funding with factors. This service works much the same as that of other sites, and is another good matchmaking service.

To access all these resources, go to www.factors.com. In the left margin of each page there are links to all the pages mentioned. While there is so much on the home page you might feel a bit cramped, navigation couldn't be easier and this is a truly valuable site.

expressFactor

This site is maintained by a company that is compensated by a 10% broker commission, rather than by membership fees like the others reviewed thus far. Because you pay a commission based on a percentage of your factoring fees (as you would to a broker) you pay no up-front costs to use this service. Unlike others that charge by the month or quarter to look for leads, you don't pay until you are making money from the factoring match they provide. They are a true online factoring broker with a well-conceived and well-executed process.

Funding seekers and funding sources fill in a registration form which indicates what each is looking for in a match. Once registered you gain access to a page called My Account. Here funders download the Broker Agreement to ensure payment of commissions and noncircumvention (normal paperwork) which you sign and fax back.

At that point you're entered in the database and expressFactor emails you when "a prospect lists invoices that match your investment criteria." Factors who receive such matches then login to a specific page on the site to bid on the business of prospects matched. Once the client has accepted a factor's bid and formed a factoring relationship other factors cannot bid on future invoices with this client.

If yours is the chosen bid the next step is to get your set-up documents in your new client's hands. When you first register you can send your forms to expressFactor via email and they'll put them in your account so all future clients can download them after accepting your bid. If you prefer, you can just send the forms directly to each new client as they come on board. As factoring starts expressFactor allows you to continue to use their site for invoice submission if desired.

expressFactor is managed by a team of three people with very impressive credentials in finance and law. In addition to the web site's brokering offerings they provide advisory services to business clients in financial forecasting, strategic planning, restructuring, and product pricing.

Response time to email is excellent and they want to provide top service, which is evident in the look and details of this nicely done site. Take a tour and also look at the instructive graphic of their process (found through the Instructions link) at www.expressfactor.com. You can also find this site from the author's web site, www.SmallFactor.com. Just click the links to Factoring Exchanges and then expressFactor.

Other Web Resources

Forums

The IFA hosts a forum available only to IFA members – another reason to join IFA if you're serious about your factoring business. The forum is located in a Yahoo! Group at www.groups.yahoo.com/group/Factoring_Assoc. Here you can share information with others in some very helpful areas such as the following:

- *Fraud forum* is an area to warn other factors about fraudulent deals going around. If you are considering taking on a new client, check here first to see if others have had experience with this company or individual.
- *Operational Issues* forum allows you share operational ideas or post questions to other factors.
- *Credit Forum* is designed to allow credit managers to post or gather credit information on businesses.
- *Looking for Participants* is where to find factors looking to co-factor deals (called participation).
- *Looking to Buy/Sell Portfolios* lists factors who would like to...well, buy or sell portfolios. Have a client or clients who have become too large for you to handle? Here's the place to find a larger factor to take over.
- *Job Listings* forum allows you to search for potential employees with experience in the factoring industry. This can also be a place to find a job if that's what you're looking for.

Marketing Databases

If you are looking for mailing lists to send information about seminars or direct mail, or use for cold calling or telemarketing, database services can deliver extremely pinpointed prospects. Consider using infoUSA who provides such lists quite easily online at a reasonable price. Go to www.SmallFactor.com and click on the Marketing Resources link. Scroll down a bit and you will find a link to infoUSA's database service where you can narrow down prospective clients using clear and simple selections.

Other companies mentioned in the chapter "Credit Reports" (in particular Experían and Dun & Bradstreet) also provide marketing databases. Go to their respective sites and you'll easily find their offerings.

Opt-in Email Databases

If you wish to run a marketing campaign using email, many companies provide opt-in email lists with thousands, if not millions, of email addresses for numerous different categories. These email addresses all belong to people who have requested information products so sending large numbers of email using these databases is not spamming.

Most companies have minimum charges usually starting from around $400 to $1,000 per order. A query to any search engine looking up "opt-in email" will find more than you'll ever use. If you're an internet whiz this can be a good way to find clients; but you do need some internet savvy and a pretty well laid out plan to make the best use of this method. Used well it can be quite powerful.

Credit Reporting Sites

In addition to the sites reviewed in the chapter "Credit Reports," another site to note is CreditWorthy, which provides links to an array of resources surrounding the credit reporting industry. The link most interesting to small factors is a listing of Credit Providers. Click on it and you go to a page listing the following links:

Attorney - Collection
Attorney Association
Collection Agencies - Foreign
Collection Agency Associations
Consultants
Credit Associations
Credit Insurance
Credit Reporting Agencies
Credit Scoring
Education & Training
Financial Services
Financial Statements
Industry Research & Reports
Lien Services
NACM & Affiliates
Public Records
Skip Trace & Search
Stock Exchanges

Attorney - Creditor Rights
Bankruptcy
Collection Agencies - U.S.
Company Directories
Country Risk
Credit Cards
Credit Management
Credit Research
Deduction Management
Electronic Commerce
Financial Statement Analysis
Industry Credit Groups
Letters of Credit
Miscellaneous Services
Newsletters & Publications
Receivables Mgmt Services
Software & Programs
UCC Services

Many of these will take you to services that can be helpful. If you click on the Credit Reporting Agencies link you'll find several agencies including some of those reviewed earlier in the chapter "Credit Reports": D&B, Experían, and BusinessCreditUSA. Also included are dozens more firms with similar credit services for specific industries such as transportation, specialty foods, wood products, international credit reports, and others. Further, as you can see above, NACM has its own section in this list. See what you can find at www.creditworthy.com.

Conclusion

This book and the others in this series give you the tools to begin factoring small transactions, and helpful resources to further expand your knowledge and thus your business. Following the Cardinal Rule of Money, factoring can be an enjoyable, good, and profitable business, with the satisfaction of knowing you are providing a valuable service your clients need and appreciate.

Best wishes in your factoring adventures!

Appendix

The Small Factor Series

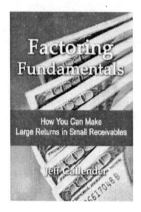

Book 1
Factoring
Fundamentals

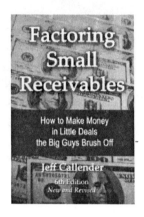

Book 2
Factoring
Small Receivables

Book 3
Factoring
Case Studies

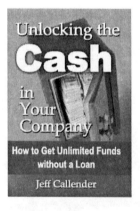

Book 4
Unlocking the Cash
in Your Company

About This Series

The Small Factor Series is designed to:

1. Introduce readers to the investment of factoring small business receivables.

2. Provide a step-by-step manual with complete instructions for small factors.

3. Provide numerous real-life examples of factoring clients from the files of people who have been investing in small receivables for some time.

4. Introduce factoring to small business owners and provide answers to numerous questions these potential factoring clients have.

Each book in the series is written to address the above points:

- Book 1, *Factoring Fundamentals: How You Can Make Large Returns Investing in Small Receivables,* provides the introduction.

- Book 2, *Factoring Small Receivables: How to Make Money in Little Deals the Big Guys Brush Off,* is the step-by-step manual.

- Book 3, *Factoring Case Studies: Learn and Profit from Experienced Small Factors,* describes real client experiences of small factors which illustrate the many lessons and suggestions made in the first two volumes.

- Book 4, *Unlocking the Cash in Your Company: How to Get Unlimited Funds without a Loan,* introduces small business owners to factoring and how it can help their cash flow.

Two Articles
from *FactorTips*

The following article was published in Issue #9 (October 4, 2002) of *FactorTips*, a free, twice monthly e-zine produced by the author. To subscribe, go to www.Factor-Tips.com and sign up at the bottom of any page.

+ + +

A Small Factor's Thoughts about Big Factors' Concerns

As mentioned in the previous issue of *FactorTips*, last week I attended Bob Zadek's Lenders' Podium conference on "The Law & Business of Factoring" in San Francisco. As usual, it's taken nearly a week to catch up from the two days absence; hence the later than usual publication of this issue.

This was my first experience in person with Mr. Zadek, who, true to form, is entertaining, witty, and extremely knowledgeable about factoring law. He is also full of very helpful and practical suggestions about how to run a factoring operation. One of his suggestions is this issue's QuickTip on factoring temp agencies.

It was nice to meet a couple of you who subscribe to *FactorTips,* but for the most part those in attendance were from banks and larger factoring companies. This is Mr. Zadek's audience, and understanding that helped me appreciate even more the value of being a small factor. Compared to factors who fund larger companies with bigger volumes (and with them, much higher stakes), I factor especially small companies with very low volume.

Being an attorney, much of Mr. Zadek's presentation focused on the legal documents and procedures larger factoring operations need to utilize to minimize their risk. He told many stories of factors having problems collecting, and how the documents he provides stand up in court and protect his clients, the factors. When factors have tens or hundreds of thousands of dollars at stake in a single client, litigation is usually the only means of recouping lost money. However, such factors can easily end up paying $50,000 in legal fees to recover a $500,000 debt they are owed. That kind of expense is not only within their means, but worth spending to recover such a large potential loss.

As I sat there considering transactions with so many zeros, I realized how my operation is in a whole different league than those of the folks sitting around me. If this were baseball, I'd be playing in a B League, while they're in AAA or the Majors. Like most medium-sized and larger factors, these people have no interest in clients factoring $10k per month. They commonly factor $50,000 to $500,000 each month per client. And at that level, they'd certainly *better* have good legal documents and representation.

I currently factor about a dozen active clients, the two largest of which factor around $15-20k per month; the rest are all under $10k. Considering my comparatively humble portfolio, I felt a sense of relief throughout the conference. I was relieved that my business model demands that once my clients need to factor more than $25k-$30k per month, I pass them on to a larger factor.

By limiting my exposure in this way, I will never go to court to try to recover $500,000 from any client. I will never need to spend $50,000 to *try* to recover an amount of money that would devastate my company if it were uncollectible. In fact, as long as most of my clients remain near or under $10k per month, I'll probably never go to court in the first place.

If I'm owed $5,000 or $10,000 and need to spend that much in attorney fees to collect, there's no sense in going to court at all. It's far wiser to simply hand an account over to collections and if necessary take the bad debt write off, then move on. I won't like it, but my business will easily survive and I won't waste an inordinate amount of time, energy, stress, and money trying to collect.

The only unpleasant aspect of factoring, to my thinking, is trying to collect. If you run your operation properly and efficiently, the time you spend doing that will be minimal. Therefore, like larger factors, we small factors cannot be sloppy with our setup documents or lackadaisical in our due diligence. Either is a surefire blueprint for losing money. Our clients need to understand there can be legal implications and unpleasant results if they intentionally try to defraud us. However, if we small factors are minding the store and don't take on more clients than we can efficiently manage, or dollar volumes than we can't afford, the war stories Mr. Zadek tells will not be ours.

Small factors with aspirations of dealing with larger clients and larger volumes need to realize the headaches and dangers that go with that territory. As for me, I'm happy not going anywhere near there. For example, one story Bob told was of an attempted intentional fraud.

This client was phony from the get-go and tried to factor seven customers on his first funding. This guy actually set up seven fax machines with seven different phone numbers, one for each of his "customers" who were very large corporations like Coca-Cola. When the factor faxed the Notice of Assignment letters to these customers, the crook made a very simple but

stupid mistake. Upon receiving the letters, he signed and immediately faxed them right back to the factor. Apparently he figured by doing this he would get his advance – over $200,000 – that much faster.

Fortunately the experienced factor smelled a rat. Never in his experience had Notices of Assignment been returned so quickly, especially seven in a row. Most take several hours, often days, to receive. Calls were made to the customers, none of whom of course had ever heard of this client, and the plot was thwarted.

Small factors are vulnerable to fraud as are larger factors. However, if we limit our client volumes and advances to quite small amounts, crooks will not go to the extremes with us this one did, because the money they'd be trying to steal from us isn't worth the effort. I can't imagine a crook going to the trouble of setting up seven phone lines and fax machines to rip me off for a few thousand dollars. Even if he did and then got away with it, that kind of loss is not going to put me out of business. It'll make me mad and fume, but at the end of the day the loss will not be catastrophic to the survival of my company.

After hearing a story like this, we may think that fraud is a factor's greatest danger. We may assume that avoiding large-scale fraud by factoring small receivables will protect us little guys from huge losses. Well…yes and no. True, we cannot be defrauded for hundreds of thousands of dollars – but we can still lose plenty of money, whether by fraud, client mismanagement, or a number of other causes.

The greatest risk factors of *any* size face is not fraud: it is over concentration. Factors with too much of their capital invested in any one client, customer, or even invoice run the risk of serious or even catastrophic loss.

Most of the factoring companies of any size who go out of business do so because they take a hit from a client or customer in whom they are over concentrated. If you intentionally limit the size of your client and customer credit limits, and the size of invoices you buy – and most important, *abide* by those limits – your chances of a catastrophic loss are diminished to nearly zero. Yet we often hear of

factors taking big hits and going out of business. It happens all the time. A large factor many of you have heard of, who had been in business for many years, recently took a $4 million dollar loss and went out of business. It happens to the best of them.

Whatever you do, no matter what size your operation is, avoid over concentrations. Don't invest more than you can afford to lose in any client, customer, or invoice. That simple procedure does not cost a penny, yet it can save you thousands upon thousands of dollars – and even save your company.

If you ever have the opportunity to hear Bob Zadek speak you should do so, regardless of the size of your factoring operation. And if you are thinking about graduating to larger clients and receivables at some time in the future, his seminars and legal documents are well worth every penny you pay for them.

Realize that in the bigger league of six and seven-figure transactions, risks are involved that go well beyond the scope of the material you'll find from Dash Point Publishing and Small-

Factor.com. This material is written for small factors who do not factor large volumes. If you intend to enter those deeper waters, you need the financial capability, you need adequate legal representation from someone like Bob Zadek – and you need the stomach for the risks involved with transactions involving a lot of zeros.

Personally, I like working with little guys. They suit me just fine. I also like the idea of never paying five figures in legal fees.

The following article was published in Issue #16 (February 17, 2003) of *FactorTips*.

+ + +

ACH and a
Story about Bankers

Not long ago a prospective client from another state asked if I could make ACH deposits into his account instead of sending a bank wire or an overnight check. At that point all I knew about ACH was that it stood for "Automated Clearing House" and that it was a common method for companies to directly deposit payday checks into employees' bank accounts, rather than handing out paychecks. It was an electronic transfer of funds from one bank account to another.

His request led to an education about bankers for me.

As I thought about this alternative means of transferring factoring funds, I saw its advantages. Up to that time I had been providing funds the traditional ways – using FedEx or Airborne Express, wiring funds, or depositing a distant client's advance or rebate check in a local branch if there was one near me. The first two were fairly expensive for the client (I charge $20 for either, plus the client pays to receive a bank wire on the other end). Depositing checks in local branches was time consuming: filling out checks, endorsing them, preparing deposit slips, driving to the various branches, waiting in line, and finally driving back home. The more clients I funded that used other banks, the longer this was taking.

Using ACH seemed like an excellent idea and a much better alternative to the time consuming process of check writing. In fact it seemed like a practically free bank wire. Certainly my large national bank, whom I'd been with for nearly 10 years, would have no problem allowing me – a *stellar* customer – to use this (I assumed simply alternative) means of transferring funds to my clients' accounts. It's just like writing a check, only done electronically. Right?

Wrong.

"Our local branches don't handle ACH account requests," I was sweetly (but ominously) told. "You need to apply for this through the online banking center." I didn't like sound of the words "apply for." I just wanted an easier way to get money to my clients. Why would I need to "apply for" that? What's more, going elsewhere within Big National Bank meant I lost the friendly and familiar smiles of all the tellers I knew so well. Undaunted in my ignorance, I moved forward.

I applied online for ACH as instructed, and after waiting several days received this reply: "Our Business Risk Management Center is unable to approve your request at this time." End of online message.

I couldn't believe it and called the cheerful young voice for online banking questions. She confirmed my rejection. "But..." I stammered, "I've been a customer here 10 years! I've had all my business accounts, personal accounts, my kids' accounts, and home mortgage with you all this time! I'm one of your best customers!" "I'm sorry," she said, "but there is risk involved for the bank with ACH transfers."

Risk? *I'm a risk* to this bank?! In all my accounts of 10 years' standing, when I've never bounced a single check or been a day late with any mortgage payments, *I'm a risk?* Do you know who you're talking to, sister?

No she didn't. And frankly, she didn't care.

"Ok," I reasoned. "I'm a reasonable guy. Maybe I asked for too large of a line." (When you apply for this, you request a daily limit, up to which you can transfer in and out of your account.) "I'll pare my request down considerably. Maybe this will make my account's 'risk' seem less...risky." After all, my application was being reviewed by Big National Bank's "Business Risk Management Center," wherever the heck that was. Certainly not in my local branch. These people would certainly have an eagle eye for risk.

So I reapplied, submitting more documents this time like I was directed. Then I waited *two weeks* this time. And didn't hear anything. And still didn't hear anything. So finally I called this young woman, who was the only contact I had with online banking which was the only means to this service I had come to believe would save me many hours of time each week. When she answered the phone, I asked if my account had been approved this time.

"Oh," she said. "That just came in today. I'm sorry to say your request was declined."

WHAT?!? Again?! *"Why?"* I choked. I couldn't believe what I was hearing. "I don't know, sir. I'm not the decision maker. I can only tell you what the decision is."

"Yeah, but does this decision maker know I've been a perfect customer for this bank for as long as I have?" ("...Probably since you were running around a grade school playground at recess." – I thought, but fortunately didn't say.)

"I don't know, sir," was her (mantra-like) answer. "But there is risk to the bank with this service." Being told yet again that I posed a risk scorched what little composure I had left. I lost my cool.

"This is bull*!!" I unfortunately blurted out. No answer. "I guess your bank wants a loyal customer of 10 years, who has brought many clients as new accounts, to take his business elsewhere."

Silence.

Finally she replied, "I guess that's your choice, sir."

Yeah, right. My choice. You little grade school Hatchet Girl. My youngest kid is older than you and you just told me I have to make major changes to my way of doing business, to my banking practices, that I'll have to change all my automatic and online and credit card payments, that this will affect most of my clients' bank accounts, and...I was getting really *mad* now. In fact I was mad enough to change banks right then and there. "This is bull*!" I repeated and slammed the phone down.

Now mind you, I'm usually a pretty calm, easy-going person. Most people who know me describe me as "a real nice guy." I've only lost my composure like this one other time in the last 12 years that I can remember. Even when I do get mad, I practically never swear at people. Especially young women who just 10 years ago were running around the grade school playground at recess. But this time, I was steamed.

"What's the matter with these morons at Big National Bank?" I wondered. Then I realized, "You know what? This is *exactly* the ringer banks put most people through when they apply for a small business loan. This is what they've been through when they reach the end of their rope and finally call a factor." Hmmmm. "Only I didn't go through this to *borrow* money," I reasoned to myself. "I don't want to *sell* my invoices. I *buy* invoices."

But that fact meant absolutely nothing to Hatchet Girl or Anonymous Loan Officer at the Business Risk Management Center, wherever that was.

I quickly took this insult to my self-respect as a bank customer, and affront to my dignity as a factor, as a challenge. "By God, I'm a *funding source*. People come to *me* for money. If these idiots who've banked my money for 10 years don't want my business any more, who does?"

Immediately I thought of the manager of a nearby regional bank whom I'd met at a networking group about a

year ago. She'd referred a couple factoring deals to me since then, and each time made it clear she'd love to have my banking business… but moving banks had always seemed more trouble than it was worth. Until this moment.

I picked up the phone and called. "Linda, does your bank offer ACH transfers?" "Yes we do." "Will I be approved for them if I apply?" I was learning the terminology. "Why don't you come in and we'll see," she answered.

So I went in a couple days later. Now that I had calmed down since my conversation with Hatchet Girl, I asked, "What is this big risk I pose to a bank by wanting to do this? I just want an alternative to writing checks."

She replied, "ACH is an electronic transfer using the bank's money. These transfers are made through the Federal Reserve Bank and go directly from our bank to your client's bank. That means you're transferring money with no float and the transfer of funds is immediate. You could transfer funds you don't have in your account, and disappear the next day. Therefore the bank looks upon this daily transfer as a loan for which you must qualify. You need to meet the requirements for a loan: business financials, tax returns, personal credit report, the whole bit."

Ok, that explained the reluctance of Big National Bank's Business Risk Management Center, wherever that was. Even though I saw this as just a different way of writing checks, the Anonymous Loan Officer at the Business Risk Management Center saw it as a loan for which I didn't qualify. That made me a risk despite my 10-year perfect multiple checking accounts history and 100% on-time mortgage payments. The Anonymous Loan Officer probably didn't even know about those. If he did, he certainly didn't care.

So I applied with Small Regional Bank not only for ACH transfers, but – what the heck – I'll throw in a request for a small line of credit while I'm at it. It's done on the same form, besides. Linda quietly took my information and submitted my request, then I waited a few days.

I was turned down again.

At least this time the loan officer from Small Regional Bank had the decency to call me. She told me her name was Janet, asked several questions about my business and experience – and even about the factoring books I've written – and then turned me down herself.

As this (sickening) conversation ended, I asked what would happen if I just requested the minimum daily ACH transfer possible, $10k per day – and dropped the line of credit request. She said she'd need to see more documentation. I agreed, prepared what she wanted (and threw in two of my books for good measure), and took them to the branch the next day.

Now…here comes the part you need to understand about banks and how they operate. A couple months earlier, Dave, my personal banker at Big National Bank, had left his position there. I was sorry to see him go as he had helped me several times in the past. In a remarkable coincidence, Dave had just started working for Small Regional Bank – right here at my neighborhood branch, no less. He knew my long history at Big National Bank, that I was a good customer, and even that I was a decent human being…which I was beginning to doubt, with all this rejection I'd just experienced.

I gave him the requested paperwork along with the books. He asked if I wanted Janet to give the books back when she finished them. "If she turns me down again, yes," I said with a chuckle (but was actually dead serious).

Then I asked him to put in a good word for me with Janet. "Dave, you know I'm not going to abuse this. You know what kind of a bank customer I am. I just want to save myself a lot of time by making electronic transfers from my computer, instead running all over town making deposits for clients." He nodded in understanding.

Then, curious about all these loan refusals which were taking their toll on my self-esteem, I asked Dave what the real problem was here. He said that banks typically look for a 3 to 1 ratio with these types of transactions. That is, for every dollar you want to "borrow" – in this case, that I want to send in daily ACH transfers – the loan officer wants to see 3 dollars in your account and/or as equity on your balance sheet. My company was too highly leveraged (translate: I didn't have enough cash on hand or equity on my balance sheet) to qualify.

Oh.

So that's it. *Now I understand.* My perfect 10 year history meant zilch.

I wondered if Hatchet Girl knew about needed ratios. Had Anonymous Loan Officer at the Business Risk Management Center, wherever that was, ever explained them to her? "No, I doubt it," I thought. "She probably doesn't even know what a ratio is."

I was steeling myself for what I was sure would be a final rejection from Janet. But a few days later she called to say my application was approved. I was both stunned and grateful. I felt like an unworthy yet incredibly fortunate serf who had been bestowed undeserved favor from the Queen Herself. I fought the urge to grovel on the ground and kiss the feet of my benevolent benefactor. And as I hung up the phone, I stepped back momentarily from this image and wondered, "My gosh, what's happening to me?"

The next time I was in the bank, I asked Dave if he had put in a good word for me with Janet. He quietly nodded. And though he didn't say so, the realization hit me: *"That's why I was approved."*

So now I can make electronic ACH bank transfers, at least up to my maximum daily amount, which will save me hours of time. I will no doubt have days when the total needed for transfers will exceed my approved limit; when that happens I'll have to delay some transfers a day or do them the old way. But at least I can make ACH direct deposits. Finally. I feel like a worthy human being again, though humbled by this experience of multiple rejections.

Why have I told this story? There are two lessons here.

First, as a factor needing regular cooperation from your bank, you must understand how banks work. Financial ratios can mean more than your history, especially with large banks in which decisions are made by people far removed from your friendly local branch. And even more, a good word from the right person can change a decision that might otherwise go against you.

Second, when clients come to you, remember that most arrive with their self-esteem bruised and battered by bank rejections, just like mine was. But unlike me, they don't have a Dave to put in a good word for them. Thus they come to you seeking the cash they sorely need but can't get from Big National Bank's Business Risk Management Center, wherever that is. And they've dealt with multiple frustrations from several Hatchet Girls of their own.

So be gentle with them. Do your best to help them. If you can factor their receivables, routinely provide excellent service. If you do, you will appear to be riding in on a white horse and will have their utter loyalty.

And if you decide you want to transfer funds with ACH – which *will* save a lot of time – come armed with a very strong balance sheet and a lot of liquidity. If you don't, be ready for a curt and impersonal rejection – probably from someone who not all that long ago was running around a grade school playground at recess.

Glossary

Terms in the Definition column that are capitalized and in bold print are included in this Glossary.

Term	*Definition*
Accounts Payable	Amounts owed to other companies for goods and services.
Accounts Receivable	Amounts owed by other companies for goods and services.
ACH	Abbreviation for "Automated Clearing House." A means of electronically transferring funds from one bank account to another.
Advance	A percentage of an invoice paid to a client by a factor upon sale of the invoice by the client.
Aging Report	A summary of a client's **Accounts Receivable**, broken down by customer and/or length of time the receivables have been outstanding.
Assets	Anything of commercial or exchange value a business, institution or individual owns. Assets include cash, property, and **Accounts Receivable**.
Assignment	Term used when **Accounts Receivable** are factored. The **Client**'s right to the accounts is sold, or assigned, to a Factor.
Bad Debt	Unpaid receivables which have been written off as uncollectable.
Balance Sheet	A financial report which lists a company's **Assets**, **Liabilities**, and the difference (shown as equity), on a given date.

Bank Wire	A means of electronically sending money from one bank account to another.
Break-Even Point	The level at which a business' total costs equal total revenue.
Broker	An individual or business who, for a fee, matches a company seeking factoring services with a **Factor** appropriate for that company's needs.
Cardinal Rule of Money	"Don't risk more than you can afford to lose" on a given transaction, **Client**, or **Customer**.
Cash Flow	The difference between cash received and cash paid out.
Client	A company who factors its **Accounts Receivable**.
Co-Factoring	A process by which two or more **Factors** combine their resources to provide funds and/or services, and share in **Fees** which result. Also called **Participation**.
Concentration	The portion of a **Factor**'s total factoring funds vested in a single **Client** or **Customer**.
Credit Report	A report obtained from a commercial credit agency which lists the payment history, debts, public records, and credit risk of a company or individual.
Customer	The company who has received products or services from a **Client** and will pay the resulting **Invoice**(s). Referred to by some factors as the **Debtor**.
DBA	Abbreviation of "Doing Business As."
Debtor	The company who has received products or services from a **Client** and will pay the resulting **Invoice**(s).

Referred to by some factors as the **Customer**.

Discount
The amount paid by the **Client** to the **Factor** for the factor's services; it is calculated by subtracting the total amount **Advance**d and **Rebate**d by the **Factor** from the face value of the **Invoice**. Also called the factoring fee.

Discount Schedule
A document that shows the **Discount** (or factoring fee) paid to the **Factor** based on the length of time a **Customer** takes to pay an **Invoice**.

Due Diligence
Information gathered by a **Factor** to determine whether or not to accept a **Client** and/or **Customer**. Also referred to as **Underwriting**.

Factor
A company or individual who purchases **Accounts Receivable** from a **Client** at a **Discount** from the face value of the **Receivables**.

Factoring
The sale of **Accounts Receivable** at a **Discount** to a **Factor**.

Fees
Amounts charged by a **Factor** for: a) the **Discount** b) **Application** and **Due Diligence** processing and/or c) funds transfer costs such as **Bank Wires** and overnight delivery.

Financial Statements
Reports, which may be requested or required as part of a **Factor**'s **Due Diligence**. The most commonly requested are a **Profit & Loss Statement** (P&L, also called **Income Statement**) , a **Balance Sheet** and a business owner's personal **Net Worth Statement**.

Fixed Costs
Expenses which do not vary with the volume of one's business.

Invoice	A document from a company to a **Customer** that states the amount owed by a **Customer** for goods or services rendered by the company.
Liabilities	Claims on the **Assets** of a company or individual, excluding the owner's equity. Liabilities include **Accounts Payable**, other debts, taxes owed, etc.
Limit	The maximum amount that will be **Advanced** by a **Factor** to a **Client** for all **Customers** or for a specific **Customer**.
Lien	A legal claim against property or other assets, submitted to state and/or county authorities. **Factors** commonly file a **Lien** (**UCC-1**) against a **Client's Assets** to secure against possible loss.
Loan	A sum of money provided to an individual or company that is to be repaid with interest. **Factoring** is not a Loan.
Net Worth Statement	The list of an individual's **Assets**, **Liabilities**, and the difference between them.
Non-notification	Term used when a **Customer** is intentionally not made aware that a **Client** is **Factoring** their **Invoices.**
Non-recourse Factoring	If a **Customer** does not pay the **Factor** within a specific period of time, the **Client** is not responsible for repaying the **Factor** the **Advance** and **Discount** (provided the invoice is not disputed).
Notice of Assignment	A document given to a **Customer** stating a **Client's** invoices have been factored and that payment should be made to the **Factor**.
Notification	The term used when a **Customer** is made aware that a **Client** is **Factoring**.

Operating Profit	The amount of **Fees** generated in excess of **Fixed Costs** plus **Variable Costs**.
Opt-In Email	The practice of sending commercial e-mail to recipients that have agreed to receive messages on a particular subject.
Overhead	The costs of a business that do not include cost of goods sold; sometimes called indirect costs and expenses.
Participation	A process by which two or more **Factors** combine their resources to provide funds and/or services, and share in **Fees** which result. Also called **Co-Factoring**.
Personal Guaranty	A contractual agreement between a **Factor** and business owner or corporation executive in which the owner or executive assumes personal responsibility and liability for the obligations of the business to the **Factor**.
Profit and Loss Statement	A **Financial Statement** that shows the income, expenses, and net profit or net loss for a given period of time (usually monthly, quarterly, and yearly).
Purchase Order	A document itemizing an order for goods or services from a **Customer** that includes items desired and prices.
Purchase Order Funding	A means of financing by which a **Factor** or other funding source **Advances** cash for a **Purchase Order**.
Quantity Discounts	A price reduction received by companies when they purchase larger amounts of a product.

Rebate	The balance of the amount paid for an **Invoice** minus the **Advance** plus **Fee**, which is paid by a **Factor** to a **Client** after receiving payment from a **Customer**. Its formula: Rebate = Invoice Amount Paid – (Advance + Fee).
Recourse Factoring	If a **Customer** does not pay the **Factor** within a specific period of time, the **Client** is responsible for repaying the **Factor** the **Advance** and **Fee**.
Reserve	The **Invoice** amount minus the **Advance** plus the **Fee**, which a **Factor** holds until a **Rebate** is due.
Schedule of Accounts	A document provided by a **Factor** that lists all **Invoices** factored at a given time by a **Client**. It includes at least the **Customer**, **Invoice** number, **Invoice** amount, **Invoice** date, and signature of the **Client** with a declaration of **Assignment** to the **Factor**.
Spam or Spamming	Email that is sent to a large number of recipients without their permission.
Spot Factoring	The process of **Factoring** one or very few invoices on a one-time or rare basis.
UCC-1	Abbreviated term for **Uniform Commercial Code**-1. A document filed with the Secretary of State and/or County Recording Clerk in which the Client's property being secured is located. With factoring, this filing evidences and perfects a factor's security interest in a **Client**'s personal property, especially **Accounts Receivable**.

UCC-3	Abbreviated term for **Uniform Commercial Code**-3. A document filed with the Secretary of State and/or County Recording Clerk to declare a change in a **UCC-1** previously filed, such as termination of security interest or another change.
Underwriting	Information gathered by a **Factor** to determine whether or not to accept a **Client** and/or **Customer**. Also referred to as **Due Diligence**.
Uniform Commercial Code	A law which regulates the transfer of personal property.
Usury	Laws (which vary from state to state) that regulate the amount of interest which can be charged to a borrower.
Variable Costs	Expenses which vary with the volume of business.
Venture Capital	Funds invested in a business usually considered high-risk. Investment is made by individuals, companies, or institutions, and commonly results in the investors owning a portion of the business.
Verification	The procedure by which a **Factor** confirms the validity of **Assigned Invoices** from a **Client**. Ordinarily, a **Factor** will determine the product has been rendered to the satisfaction of the **Customer**, the **Customer** intends to pay, and payment will be made to the Factor.
Volume, Monthly	The total amount of **Invoices** factored by a **Client** during a month's time.
WIIFM	Pronounced "Whiff-em," abbreviation of "What's In It For Me?"
Wire	See **Bank Wire**.

Index

business plan, 53, 140
Business Summary Report, 216
BusinessCreditUSA, 217, 218, 221, 223, 395

C

cable TV, 136
calculator, 78
California, 13
Callender, Jeff, 3, 4, 6, 13, 17
capital, 27, 29, 30, 53, 54, 55, 92, 99, 100, 140, 171
Capitol Resource Funding, 86
Capitol Services, Inc., 198
Cardinal Rule of Money, 73, 78, 86, 95, 144, 397, 418
careful, 31, 70, 71, 74, 77, 81, 84, 85, 133, 134, 152, 172, 226, 233, 317
Casano, Joseph, 23
cash flow, 401
Cash Flow Convention, 13, 384
cassette, 385
Certificate of Acceptance, 175
Certificate of Corporate Resolution, 12, 299
CFOL.com, 386, 387
Chaining Clients, 146
Chamber of Commerce, 123, 133
chargeback, 234, 326
Chart of Accounts, 348, 351
check-up calls, 235, 237, 280, 337
ChoicePoint, 203
Clark, Kari and Kevin, 14, 347, 367
classified ads, 130
client, 13, 401
client referrals, 128
co-factor, 48, 61, 62, 64, 74, 90, 95, 96, 97, 98, 101, 154, 393
cold calling, 119, 127, 128, 393
collateral, 187
collection calls, 235
comfortable, 60, 64, 95, 96, 99, 119, 144, 172, 185, 226
Commercial Finance Institute, The, 383
Commercial Finance Online, 386
common sense, 23, 68
competitive, 21, 45, 111

Composite Credit Appraisal, 208, 209, 225
Comprehensive Report, 196, 225
concentrations, 34, 147, 157, 158, 159, 226
confidence, 69, 79, 95, 133
ConsultBlu, 259, 260, 261
consulting, 13, 22, 257
contract, 65, 92, 99, 128, 144, 145, 163, 241, 278, 317, 318, 325, 326, 333
conventions, 13, 62, 126, 385
copy machine, 39
corporation, 80, 90, 100, 299, 421
creativity, 47
credit card, 28, 29, 85, 86, 218, 222, 353
credit insurance, 167, 168
Credit Insurance, 395
credit report, 38, 140, 141, 175, 180, 181, 182, 183, 192, 195, 196, 207, 214, 216, 217, 218, 219, 221, 223, 224, 225, 233, 394, 395
credit unions, 85
credit worthy, 33, 34
creditworthy, 125, 182, 394, 395
Customer Contact Sheet, 12, 279
customer support, 240

D

Dash Point Financial, 13
Dash Point Publishing, 4, 24, 374, 378
database, 129, 155, 195, 207, 214, 217, 239, 273, 377, 388, 392, 393
Days Behind Terms, 181
DBT, 181, 182
Diligenz, 199
direct deposit, 30, 63
direct mail, 118, 119, 135, 136, 393
discount, 27, 29, 32, 33, 35, 36, 38, 92, 146, 210, 278, 293
Discount Schedule, 12, 278, 279, 293, 419
discouragement, 40
dispute, 31, 63, 155, 163, 321, 331
Distinctive Solutions, 14, 239, 242, 378, 384, 385

DASH POINT PUBLISHING

Order Form

Fax Orders: (253) 719-8132
Include this completed form.

Telephone Orders: (866)-676-0966 – Toll Free!

Web Site Orders: www.DashPointPublishing.com

Email Orders: info@DashPointPublishing.com

Postal Orders: Dash Point Publishing, Inc.
PO Box 25591
Federal Way, WA 98093-2591

Please send the following resources: _____

_____

_____

_____

Please contact me regarding:

☐ Consulting   ☐ Factoring my company's invoices
☐ Seminars   ☐ Other: _____

Name _____

Address _____

City, State, Zip _____

Telephone _____

Email _____

Sales Tax: Please add 8.8% for products shipped to Washington state.

Payment:

☐ Visa   ☐ MasterCard   *Make checks to:*
☐ Discover   ☐ AmEx   ☐ Check   Dash Point Publishing

Card # _____

Name on card _____   Exp. date _____